Economic and Political Liberalization in the Middle East

ECONOMIC AND POLITICAL LIBERALIZATION IN THE MIDDLE EAST

Edited by

Tim Niblock and Emma Murphy

British Academic Press
London · New York

Published in 1993 by
British Academic Press
45 Bloomsbury Square
London
WC1A 2HY

An imprint of I.B. Tauris & Co Ltd

In the United States of America
and Canada distributed by
St Martin's Press
175 Fifth Avenue
New York
NY 10010

A CIP record for this book is available from the British Library

A full CIP record is available from the Library of Congress

ISBN 1–85043–600–2

Printed and bound by
WBC, Bridgend, Mid Glam.

CONTENTS

TABLES

PREFACE

This is the first full-scale book to emerge from the activities of the Research Unit for the International Study of Economic Liberalization and its Social and Political Effects, at the University of Exeter. Tim Niblock would like to thank the Canon Foundation in Europe for the generous support which it provided for his research on economic liberalization in the Middle East and for convening a symposium to discuss the ideas for the book. The assistance given by Richard Burke, chairman of the Foundation, and his staff was invaluable. The Canon Foundation's involvement was within the context of a collaborative relationship with the International University of Japan; Professor Kuroda and his colleagues at the IUJ provided great encouragement and support.

The transliteration system employed in most of the book has been modified from that used in the *International Journal of Middle East Studies*. In the chapter on Tunisia, however, the names of politicians have been left in the French-style transliteration through which they are generally known.

The Harvard system has been used for references to books in the text. The author's name and the date of publication are given in the text, while the full reference is given in the overall bibliography. A numbered footnoting system, however, has also been employed – where elaborations are made of points in the text, or where the reference is to material in a media source. The bibliography is divided into general works; liberalization theory/experience in general (books and reports); liberalization theory/experience in general (articles and chapters); developing countries generally (books and reports); developing countries generally (articles and papers); the Middle East (books and reports); and the Middle East (articles, papers and theses).

The editors are grateful to the Islamic Development Bank for having made available a grant to enable this book to be put onto a 'fast-track' arrangement for publication. This has been most valuable in ensuring that the highly topical material reaches a public audience as quickly as possible. The Islamic Development Bank is, however, in no way associated with any of the views expressed.

Tim Niblock
Emma Murphy
University of Exeter 1992

INTRODUCTION

Emma Murphy and Tim Niblock

'Economic liberalization' is taken in this book to cover any measure which strengthens the role of the market in the economy. The range of measures which are encompassed by the term is extensive: the privatization of formerly state-owned industry; the encouragement of private investment (whether domestic or foreign); the opening of stock markets, in which shares of public companies can be traded; the relaxation of state control over credit (whether as regards the level of interest rates or the purposes for which credit is made available); the cutting of state expenditure, with the consequent reduction of the overall burden which the state infrastructure imposes on the economy; the loosening of state controls over foreign and/or domestic trade; the re-ordering of labour laws such that wages and conditions reflect the value placed on labour by the market, rather than following governmental guidelines; and the re-structuring of the public sector so as to make public corporations able to respond directly to market conditions, as opposed to being continually subject to decisions taken from above in ministries.

One central perception runs through the chapters of this book. It is that in assessing the contribution which economic liberalization can make to a country's development, the purely economic aspects should not be taken in isolation. The social and political dimensions of the economic liberalization process are of critical importance. Not only do they affect the prospects which a liberalization programme has of actually delivering economic benefits; they may also impinge on the coherence, effectiveness and unity of the state itself. The sociopolitical dimension is particularly important in underdeveloped countries.

Economic liberalization generally widens the gap between rich and poor, at least in the short term, increases regional disparities, and deepens dependence on external powers and institutions. Whereas in developed countries the state may be strong enough to withstand the social pressures which ensue from economic liberalization, and may retain a panoply of instruments which enable it to continue shaping social interaction, the state in underdeveloped countries often has neither the inherent strength nor the needed instruments. The social discontent unleashed by economic liberalization may create political dynamics which undermine regimes, and perhaps even tear the state apart (for example, through engendering religious fundamentalism and regional separatism). To believe that the problems faced by formerly centrally planned economies in the Third World can be solved simply by privatizing state assets and taking off state controls is both facile and misguided.

The complex relationships between the economic, social and political dimensions of economic liberalization programmes are explored in this book. Part One is thematic; Part Two consists of case studies of individual Middle Eastern countries. In Chapter One, Edith Penrose questions the assumptions which underlie much of the existing work on economic liberalization, and in particular the approach which is taken by the international financial institutions. She argues that the liberalization measures which are imposed on poorer countries when they are impelled to seek financial support have little justification beyond bringing benefit to the donors.

A perspective from classical antiquity is used to set the context for considering the political aspects surrounding the process of economic liberalization. Patricia Springborg, in Chapter Two, shows how it was the ancient Middle East which pioneered the political institutions which are associated with economic liberalism in the West. She contends that these institutions stem from the phenomenon of urbanism, which developed in the Middle East long before it did in Western Europe. In Chapter Three, David Pool brings out the complexity of the linkages between economic and political liberalization in the contemporary Middle East. Economic liberalization has in some cases helped to establish a process of political liberalization, yet the economic reforms may also ultimately sustain or re-introduce authoritarian forms of rule. Political liberalization also has a backward linkage, in that it can act as a brake on economic liberalization.

In Chapter Four, Tim Niblock uses case studies of Egypt, Algeria and Iraq to indicate the significance of international factors in initiating and shaping economic liberalization policies. A paradox arises here.

The tendency to experiment with political liberalization has been greatest where external pressure for economic liberalization has been strongest. Yet when the state loses its ability to set its own policies, it loses the power to create the social conditions necessary for a stable democracy. The social problems which can be engendered by economic liberalization form the focus of Chapter Five, by David Seddon. The chapter traces the pattern of popular protest which has followed the introduction of economic liberalization policies in different parts of the Middle East. Seddon argues that as long as the states of the area continue to pursue reform programmes which fail to provide sufficient tangible benefits for the majority of the population and are seen to create unreasonable social and economic deprivation and inequality, popular protest remains likely.

Prospects for achieving economic benefits from one particular aspect of liberalization, that of privatization, are covered by Paul Stevens in Chapter 6. Stevens argues that privatization will only be beneficial to the economies if it leads to increased competition, reduces harmful interference from the state, develops capital markets and creates a new incentive system for labour. He contends that the character of politics in the Arab world renders it unlikely that these developments would actually follow. Political reform, therefore, may be a necessary condition if privatization is to bring any benefits. In Chapter Seven, George Joffé examines the role of foreign investment in the liberalization process, focusing on the gap between rhetoric and reality. Although most Middle Eastern states undertaking such programmes offer substantial incentives for direct foreign investment, little such investment has actually been forthcoming. The primary reason why Middle Eastern governments proclaim such enthusiasm for foreign investment, he contends, lies in their need to show some concurrence with the perceptions of the IMF and World Bank. The encouragement of foreign investment by Middle Eastern governments is more an affirmation of their acceptance of the new economic orthodoxies than a statement of their intent and expectations.

The first two chapters of Part Two cover the two most sustained experiments with economic liberalization in the Arab world: those of Egypt and Tunisia. In Chapter Eight, Robert Springborg shows how the economic liberalization process in Egypt began with an attempt to achieve rapid breakthrough on virtually all fronts. When this failed (in the late 1970s), the government resorted to a strategy of gradual reform, making as much haste as was permitted by a potentially volatile public. He contends that political conditions will determine whether the existing liberalization strategy proves successful: a sudden breakthrough towards dramatically increased economic liberalization could result from either greater authoritarianism or democratization. He sees Egypt's political and economic systems as now being poised between breakthrough and breakdown. In Chapter Nine, Jon Marks argues that Tunisia's economic liberalization programme, despite the plaudits which it has received in the West, has been severely constrained by political factors. The most critical of these factors is the reluctance of those in positions of power to relinquish any of their influence. He maintains that a new political environment is needed, where economic growth can be sustained by the emergence of genuine consensus politics, whatever the risks for the established order.

Chapters Ten and Eleven both cover Syria. This is justified by the writers' widely differing concerns. Raymond Hinnebusch focuses on the forces which promote and those which inhibit the process of economic liberalization. He shows how economic liberalization began in the early 1970s, advanced very slowly over the two decades which followed, and is currently accelerating. He contends that resistance to capitalist development comes from the combination of an autonomous authoritarian state and a fluid rent- and trade-based dependent economy with porous borders. Miyoko Kuroda is more concerned with the appropriateness to countries like Syria of currently accepted conceptions of economic liberalization. She maintains that there is no real possibility for Syria to develop through integration into the international capitalist system. A way out of the dilemma which this poses is to seek the development of the traditional economy. The strong social organization of the Syrian *suq* could form the basis for a type of economic liberalization which does not involve a close dependence on international capitalism.

In Chapter Twelve, Anoushiravan Ehteshami traces the full circle through which the policies of the Iranian state towards the private sector have travelled since the days of the Shah. He shows how the emergence of a united leadership around the Rafsanjani–Khamenei axis made possible the adoption of a concentrated policy of economic liberalization, privatization and deregulation, undoing the nationalization and intensified state control which had characterized the earlier part of the revolutionary period. The 'Islamic economy', Ehteshami suggests, is now little more than a mythical concept, advanced more as an alternative to revolutionary economic policy than as its result.

The case of the Israeli economy is taken up by Emma Murphy, in Chapter Thirteen. She argues that the nature of the economic liberalization policies pursued by Israeli governments has been shaped and limited by the character of the Israeli state. The pursuit of the Zionist aim to ingather Jews, and the resistance which the Israeli state has encountered within and outside Palestine, have made necessary an activist state role in the economy. Paradoxically, despite Israel's close links with the capitalist countries of the West, the likelihood of any substantial economic liberalization is small.

The book concludes with case studies on Yemen and Oman, in Chapter Fourteen. Gerd Nonneman suggests that conclusions about the linkages between economic and political liberalization can be drawn from a comparison between these cases. In Yemen, the economic liberalization measures created a potential for social unrest and political upheaval. The government needed to defuse or pre-empt this by liberalizing politically. In Oman, the state's resources allowed the government to liberalize without creating economic hardship, in turn obviating (at least in the short term) the need for more than small adjustments to the mechanisms of political participation.

Issues of economic liberalization and democratization seem likely to remain central to the politics and economics of Middle Eastern states through the decade of the 1990s and probably beyond. It is hoped that this book will help to clarify the options which face the states of the region, and provide a basis for further enquiry and analysis.

PART ONE

1· FROM ECONOMIC LIBERALIZATION TO INTERNATIONAL INTEGRATION:

The Role of the State

*Edith Penrose**

In view of the variety of historical, philosophical and socio-political interpretations of what is meant by liberalization, one must first state as briefly and clearly as possible what is meant by the term. For the purposes of this chapter, liberalization relates to any process of change in the organization of human society that is designed to produce greater freedom for individuals in that society, the freedom of each individual being constrained only by the need to sustain the freedom of others. It follows that the empirical content of liberalization, thus defined as a process, will depend on specific circumstances of time and place.[1]

'Economic liberalization' is not a free-floating concept, unconnected with a broader and very far-reaching set of political and economic ideas. It is a major strand in the seamless web of liberal thought. In European thought liberalism can be looked at as having three inter-locking strands: political, economic and social. The first is often summarized as liberty under the law, individual freedom to act subject to the freedom of others, with as few restraints as possible on individuals. As the name implies, economic liberalization is the extension of this to the right of each individual to engage in private economic activities subject only to restrictions considered absolutely necessary to protect the rights of others. A major issue, of course, will

* The author is indebted to Nancy Baster for comments which much improved the organization of this chapter.

always be the location of the boundary line between the permitted and the restricted.

The nature of what some have called social liberalization is much more controversial. It perhaps arose in its most explicit form in the early decades of the twentieth century in Germany followed by Great Britain and some other European countries, becoming of crucial importance during the great depression of the 1930s in the United States, with President Roosevelt's New Deal and its emphasis on Freedom from Want. In principle, it became clear that political and economic liberalization would be unacceptable and unworkable if its very operations precluded large sections of society from sharing in its benefits. The question is, does freedom, liberty under the law, and the right of individuals to engage in private economic activity, using their own resources, including their labour, require that the social, political and economic organization of society should be such as to make possible the exercise of this right, this 'human right', for all individuals? Can 'labour' be treated like any commodity in a free market where an excess supply has to be eliminated by price, if the effect is to eliminate, as it were, the very human beings whose labour can not be profitably employed?

Western thinkers tend to view liberalism as essentially of European origin, arising as mercantile elements began to replace feudal elements in European civilization in the thirteenth to fourteenth centuries and leading to fundamental social revolutions in the seventeenth and eighteenth centuries.[2] If we view liberalism as a coherent philosophy of social organization, this may be correct. But a great deal of what is often today called liberal thought appeared much earlier in the Middle East, notably in *The Muqaddimah* of Ibn Khaldun, the great Algerian historian, scholar, statesman and philosopher of the fourteenth century. His exposition of the rise of civilizations, the role and proper governance of cities, the essence of 'royal authority' and its relation to *asabiya* (a kind of legitimacy resting on group feeling, assent and support) written nearly six centuries ago is shot through with recognizably modern liberal approaches (Ibn Khaldun, 1958).

Similarly, many aspects of what we see as very modern development in liberal institutions existed in earlier advanced societies. In this volume Patricia Springborg's chapter on the origins of liberal institutions in the ancient Middle East is particularly valuable in reminding us of this. She shows that as early as 2500–2400BC in the great cities of Middle Eastern civilizations, powerful and wealthy mercantile trading classes could force the bureaucracies of palace and temple to accept what in many respects we now call liberal or 'reform' measures, some of which even had 'capitalist' characteristics. She sees individuals, using their own resources in trade, accumulating capital, protected to a considerable degree from government depredations, and she finds in this some aspects of an early form of capitalism. After all, in its simplest sense, capitalism can be defined as the use by owners of their own property to produce goods for sale, and the re-investment of some of the profit. This does not require the existence of a capital market and has been characteristic of much small-scale production for centuries.

Dr Springborg asks the question, why did these highly developed, technologically competent early economies not emerge as fully capitalist economies? Part of her answer lies in their failure to develop an appropriate form of business organization: 'Essentially it was because business generated a specific professional form, the partnership, neither based on a division between owners and non-owners, nor giving rise to the employer-employee relation.' Thus the seeds of capitalism, so to speak, could not produce very big plants.

In Europe, as capitalism displaced feudalism, a differentiation emerged between the political realm (rulership with responsibility for law and war, legal violence, authority and ceremony) and the realm of the production and distribution of goods and services. The realm of the 'economy', which extended beyond the borders of the state, became a 'semi-independent state within state', a sphere of activity with its own structure. As a result the relationship between the realms became a central question for debate and in the process 'the overarching unity and mutual dependency of the two realms' tended to be overlooked.[3]

In England joint-stock companies emerged in the sixteenth and seventeenth centuries but not until the end of the seventeenth century could they become fully private. As these private corporate forms developed, the nature of capitalism began to change, much larger economic units became possible, private enterprise was no longer synonymous with individual or family enterprise and capital markets in corporate securities became a dominant source of business finance.[4]

The third world, economic development and international politics

Central to the course of international political and economic history in the 70 years after the First World War was the ideological struggle between what are commonly thought of as 'communism' and 'capitalism'. After the Second World War the struggle intensified and seemed to extend to wider international arenas with the rise of the cold war in which the United States and the USSR were the chief protagonists.

At the same time rapid decolonization in Africa and Asia brought more and more independent countries into the United Nations. These began to claim a new role in the world and international interest in their economic and political development grew. What was considered by some to be a new branch of economics – development economics – gained prominence and had much influence on the formation of policies in governments in the developing countries as well as in a growing number of national and international agencies eager to help. There was little agreement on the best path to take but the early development economists, perhaps influenced by the Marshall Plan, optimistically hoped that it would not be too long before all but the most miserably endowed of third world countries could take off on a reasonably progressive path of development. All that was needed was very generous financial and technical assistance.

It seemed to be assumed, and was explicit in most of the development plans that governments were encouraged to produce, that the state would play a strong role and intervene to guide investment into the most effective channels. Few development economists opposed government economic planning, and even fewer supported minimal state intervention and maximum reliance on unguided market forces.

Progress was disappointing and it was not long before the optimism of the 1960s began to fade. Development was proving to be a more difficult and deep-seated problem than had been fully realized and increasing numbers of countries were in serious financial and economic difficulty, succumbing to both adverse external shocks and internal failures.

By the mid-1970s the far-reaching and hopeful theories of economists were coming to be replaced by a series of more pragmatic proposals to deal with specific problems that were threatening economic and political stability. But it was the oil crisis that brought the development crisis to a head; it also brought about a distinct change of emphasis in the policies proposed by the international aid-giving community.

The increases in oil prices in the 1970s produced very large increases in oil revenues for the oil-producing countries, which had very little choice other than to deposit their excess revenues with the international banking system. The banks in turn had of course to find profitable outlets for these funds, and it seemed both appropriate and profitable that they should be recycled in loans to developing countries, many of which thereby acquired enormous external deficits. The world went into recession and the economic difficulties of the developing countries were intensified. It soon became clear that the international banking system itself would be in serious trouble if the debts could not be collected or renegotiated satisfactorily.

It was in this period that a substantial change in the approach to development policies by the World Bank and the IMF in particular began to emerge. When the economic disorders in the developing countries worsened, the latter turned to these institutions for help. As conditions of financial assistance, the IMF demanded substantial reductions in government expenditure generally and the implementation of a series of policies designed to stabilize finances, adjust prices, exchange rates and interest rates (required for domestic and international balance), and the reform of other aspects of economic policy in the interest of economic efficiency. Included in the reform measures was an insistent demand for 'economic liberalization', by which was meant a reduction in the economic role of the state, accompanied by an increase in private, including foreign private, investment and an 'opening up' of the economy generally. Many, perhaps most, academic economists, including development economists, began to adapt their advice to the 'new realities'.[5]

The argument had shifted its base: no longer was there to be so much faith placed in development planning and active government investment policies, whether they be import-substitution or export-promotion policies. An expanding private sector, private foreign investment and a rolling back of the state became the fundamentals of policy. Although the World Bank would continue to finance its development projects, the failure of the earlier approaches that had disappointed the exaggerated expectations of the time was attributed not primarily to internal structural or sociological difficulties or to the external economic shocks of the 1970s and 1980s, but to the fact that they were based on the wrong ideological orientation.

Given the circumstances of the developing countries there could, of course, be no question that an urgent adaptation to the high level of debt, stabilization of both internal and external financial affairs, and adjustment to the adverse turn of events in the outside world were required. But sceptical critics of the new orthodoxy voiced some suspicion that the change in the direction of the newer policies, towards economic liberalization, was motivated more by the hidden agenda of the international banking system to collect debts and obtain free access to the economies of the third world than by a genuine concern to improve economic performance. The academic economists of the 'dependency school' warned of the dangers inherent in the opening up demanded.

To top it all, at the beginning of the 1990s came the collapse from within of the communist economies of the Soviet Union and Eastern Europe. The industrialized capitalist market-oriented camp, led by the United States, immediately raised the flag of victory, feeling justified in seeing in the event the final triumph of free enterprise capitalism and the failure, not only of communism, but of any strong role for the state in economic affairs with the exception of certain types of macroeconomic policy.

Thus arose a new emphasis on an old slogan, and economic liberalization in the third world quickly became the pressing immediate objective of international policy. Because of the heavy indebtedness to the banking system of most of these countries, this policy would have to be enforced largely by the IMF. It would have to be backed up by the World Bank, aid-giving official agencies, and many of the other relevant agencies of the United Nations. In all of these the United States has an overwhelming financial and political influence. Everything else had failed, most of the developing countries were in a serious economic condition, stabilization of their financial affairs was clearly urgent, but the role of the state in the new liberalization reforms was by no means clear.

The view of the world of which the importance of economic liberalization is an integral part both provides the basic purpose of and sets the constraints on the implementation of reforms designed to achieve its objectives. Broadly speaking, the expressed objective of the international agencies attempting to promote liberalization is to improve the efficiency of the relevant economies, when the perceived inefficiency is believed to be the result of inappropriate state intervention in the past or of continuing inappropriate policies in the present. It includes the recognition of the importance of flexibility of response to changing economic conditions and of the importance of private (which in a corporate economy is not the same as individual) initiative and action to this end. Although the World Bank does have some projects directed towards easing the social tensions consequent on some of the reforms, the serious difficulties of liberalization have not been adequately taken into account.

This section has tried to show that economic liberalization can not easily be detached from the broader framework of liberal thought; equally, it can not be entirely detached from the actual behaviour and practices adopted in the developed countries from which the pressure to liberalize comes. Nevertheless, it is clearly expected that some aspects of it can be successfully introduced as at least semi-detached, that is to say, as liberalization only in relation to those aspects of markets and government financial policy selected by outsiders as the most important. Whether this is a reasonable expectation will have to be looked at carefully as we consider the experience and prospects of economic liberalization in the Middle East.

Social liberalization and bureaucracy

With capitalism inevitably came involuntary unemployment and social protest, and many countries accepted that governments should extend their responsibilities and attempt to ensure the availability of employment. The inevitable result was an aggravation of the problem of bureaucracy and other forms of state job creation, which quickly increased government budget deficits, especially as recession took hold; also aggravated were the financial problems of developing countries with inadequate tax regimes and government resources. But to cut back on government expenditure, and especially unproductive bureaucracy is, as we shall see, one of the objectives of economic liberalization, and for governments one of the most difficult to achieve.

Thus in the discussion of economic liberalization today, especially with respect to developing countries with little-developed modern social security systems, an old but persistent question continues to be raised: does some form of social liberalization logically become a necessary condition of the new market-oriented liberal society? Does the development of political and economic rights have at some point to extend to encompass a greater degree of substantive support for the exercise of equality before the law for those unable to take part in the market system? Or does such a development undermine a truly liberal system and become inconsistent with economic liberalization as a process?

It remains true, however, that highly centralized governments maintaining their position through large state bureaucracies tend to create serious barriers to political and economic liberalization and to economic development itself. In the Middle East, as in many other developing countries, the state bureaucracies are busy with an enormous amount of unproductive paper work which retards the efficient management of government and private business. They are often heavily penetrated by seriously corrupt vested interests working for their own private purposes. The result is the maintenance of an economically and politically powerful organization which resists any change that reduces its power or membership.[6]

Of all the Egyptian institutions, for example, the state bureaucracy is believed to be among the strongest opponents of economic and political liberalization. The difficulty in reducing the state bureaucracy, however, is aggravated by a rapidly growing population and increasing unemployment. The expansion of public employment was one means of alleviating the political and social consequences of the latter: open unemployment 'was avoided or contained by creating a large mass of underemployed and necessarily frustrated and inefficient public employees and officials'. The number of government employees, excluding the army, 'are estimated to have increased from less than 310,000 in 1947 to nearly 770,000 in 1960 and 1,035,000 in 1966/7' (Mabro, 1974: 292–310; O'Brien, 1966: 62ff).

The adverse effects on an economy of such developments are serious, but the dilemmas facing governments often seemed to leave little choice, at least in the short run. As yet, neither the national nor international authorities have properly faced up to this social problem, the 'third strand of the seamless web' of liberalization. It should be given a prominent role in discussions of economic reform and seen as a crucial element in the appraisal of how far economic liberalization can be successfully implanted. To help contain, at least to some degree, the destabilizing effect of reform on popular attitudes, and the consequent 'street protests', is presumably one of the objectives of some of the World Bank projects, but these are very limited in relation to the seriousness of the problem.

In the Middle East, as elsewhere, for every country requiring IMF intervention in recent years, the intervention was made necessary by the acquisition of unmanageable external debt and the consequent economic strains which could not be ignored. We have already discussed the relation of national debts to the oil crisis and the desire of the international banks to lend, combined with the willingness of the governments to borrow. This, in addition to the effects of the subsequent recession and other adverse economic events, brought about continuing severe deficits in the current balance of payments of the debtor countries, unacceptable inflation, severe distortions in relative prices, and general stagnation of the economy. These difficulties required immediate and pragmatic action.

Pragmatic and ideological measures as proposed by the IMF
The attempts to deal with debt with the help of the IMF have been subject to the acceptance of measures variously labelled as stabilization, adjustment, and reform policies. One group of recommended measures relates primarily to external economic relations. It includes the liberalization of exchange rates, which in many cases requires devaluation and exchange rate unification, and measures to improve the current account balance through the promotion of exports. Another group of measures deals largely with internal 'structural adjustments' that are believed to be required for reasonably efficient and flexible economic performance. This group commonly includes, where appropriate, the reduction of subsidies and price controls on consumer goods, especially on energy and agricultural products, an increase in interest rates, and the reduction of budget deficits, especially reductions of expenditure on the civil bureaucracy and the military.

Depending on the severity of the economic crisis, which has varied among countries, most of the pragmatic and specific policies proposed by the IMF seem, with modification in some circumstances, to be both appropriate and necessary. Prices generally must be got reasonably right; a reasonable external balance must be obtained as well as an acceptable internal fiscal balance. Most of the specific measures to deal with particular problems would eventually have been necessary under almost any viable economic system, but many of them would in any circumstances have taken considerable time to become effective. However, one should assume that short-term progress would be very much slower than otherwise in the absence of adequate financial support for social measures that would make the transitions politically acceptable. Considerable help from the World Bank and other agencies would be a necessary, even if not a sufficient, condition for success. As noted above, such support was very limited, and public resistance often forced governments to abandon measures they had imposed.

Nevertheless, in the Middle East some progress has been made in most of the countries, although in general the several analyses conclude on an uncertain and rather down-beat and very cautious note. This is not surprising, in part because even relatively straight-forward and simple solutions to technical problems, in economic terms, often come up against deep-seated sociological and institutional obstacles which take time to overcome.

But there is another and wider issue underlying some of the internationally received economic and political proposals. Behind the overall liberalization approach lies an ideology, a view of the world, which goes further than reform of ill-adjusted prices and macro-economic variables. Because of this, many proposals seem to have been pushed much further than is necessary to readjust and invigorate the relevant economies, arousing considerable resistance. This springs from the vision of a new world integrated with and by free-enterprise capitalism.

A major difficulty, in the writer's view, is that the ideological inspiration of the vision has put out of focus the reality of the economic world we actually inhabit at the turn of the twenty-first century. Partly because of this, the liberalization package proposed will not only fail to deal adequately with the immediate and non-sustainable distortions at which it is aimed but, more seriously, may create even more difficulties for the economic co-operation of govern-ments in the modern world. Reference has already been made to the consequences of inadequate provisions for dealing with the social dimension. But the insistence on privatization and a little-controlled acceptance of foreign goods and capital seems to ignore the conse-quences for developing countries of important aspects of the operation of the modern capitalist economic system.

The ideology of 'free private enterprise' and foreign investment
As noted above, private ownership of companies, or private enterprise, is not identical with individual enterprise. There are, of course, many small businesses which in total play a dynamic and important role in any society. They are vulnerable to adverse events and may at times require considerable support. But, although dominant in numbers, they often account for a smaller proportion of the national product (excluding peasant agriculture and personal services) than do large companies, which in small markets may have strong monopolistic positions. These may be natural monopolies like railroads and public utilities, or manufacturing companies where economies of scale are important, or industries producing, say, armaments. For these and

perhaps some others, private ownership is not necessarily in the public interest. The broad argument that if a company is state-owned it must be inefficient is insufficient to convince everybody that such industries should be privatized or that public monopolies should be turned into private monopolies. A strong case could be made to support the view that the British public's experience with this policy has not been entirely happy.

As Paul Stevens shows in his chapter, prospects for successful privatization in the Middle East appear to be poor for a number of reasons, including those mentioned above. The political as well as the economic infrastructure necessary to support profitable privatization does not widely exist. Reduced government interference with private enterprise is not enough to produce increased private investment. Even greater resistance may be provoked if privatization, combined with free access to foreign investment, simply results in the absorption of domestic industry by multinational operations, as soon as conditions appear favourable.

Partly because of the Israeli problem, an openness to private foreign investment has had especially unacceptable political implications for many countries in the Middle East. Raymond Hinnebusch, in his chapter in this book, reminds us firmly of this when he notes that uncontrolled 'liberalization in the third world means internationalization of the economy', and so long as the external environment, including the West, appears hostile to national aspirations it will be unacceptable.

In opening up to foreign investment, it seems likely that the choice for existing business interests would largely be either one of selling out to, or making 'alliances' of various kinds with, large multinationals. Excluding the extraction of natural resources and banking, especially off-shore banking, it seems that tourism and textiles are among the industries that appear to be most attractive to foreign investors. As an extension to the worldwide activities of international companies in tourism, much new direct investment in hotels, beach and other leisure activities and transport facilities has occurred. The receiving countries may gain economically from this in spite of the large import content of such activities and the way in which package tours are financed. The social benefit is highly controversial.

Foreign investment in textiles and some other light manufactures and in assembly processes is often closely related to export markets provided by foreign companies attracted by lower labour costs, and various forms of contractual arrangements are entered into. There is little doubt that this kind of investment is valuable for the receiving country. Whether or not it uses domestic raw materials, it does provide employment, making productive use of the country's most abundant factor of production, as well as markets and opportunities for further expansion in the industrial sector.

As these chapters show, except in the larger oil-producing countries, neither privatization nor direct foreign investment has been of great consequence in the Middle East, with foreign companies reluctant to invest. This reluctance is not seen in general to have been due to any rejection by the governments but rather because economic and political conditions do not appear to have offered attractive investment opportunities.[7] Dictatorial regimes, wars and revolutions, economic crises in oil and debt, the rise of radical religious movements, conflict with Israel – all produce high uncertainty which hardly induces much confidence in potential foreign investors. This raises the question of how much it really matters whether or not governments try actively to encourage foreign investment.

Characteristics of the economic world we live in

The IMF presses for openness to, and integration with, the world economy. But a question which is virtually ignored is whether the economic system which characterizes both the international economy and the economies of the developed industrial states is properly classed as 'liberal', in the sense in which economic liberalization is applied to the countries where reform is demanded. It is not difficult to point out that many of the measures that are demanded of developing countries by way of reform are not obviously reflected in the behaviour, policies and attitudes either of the countries demanding them or of the international community generally.[8] Governments are urged to reduce substantially their role in the economy and to rely increasingly on market forces. Carefully interpreted, there is much to be said for this. But at the same time both the nature of the market forces in today's world, and the appropriate role of the state in relation to such forces need to be appraised impartially. This has not been done. The obstacles to a significant reduction in the role of the state, and with it the role and size of the state bureaucracy and therefore of the vested interests profiting from association with and influence on it, are well documented in these papers. 'To roll back the state' is a common slogan used to identify the objective of liberalization policy.

This, in turn, is sometimes interpreted as a policy of weakening the state as a means of strengthening the market, and with this the prospects of democratic capitalism, in the belief that here is the way to promote development, as well as international integration.

Let us consider for a moment the nature of industrial competition in the world economy. A very large and apparently growing proportion of exports as well as imports of industrial goods is in the hands of large bureaucratic organizations, whose headquarters and control reside in the developed countries where the world's economic power is found.[9] These companies are usually heavily diversified, often research-based, integrated vertically, horizontally, functionally, and geographically across national frontiers, with enormous resources at their disposal. The dynamic, highly innovative, high technology industries of the world (automobiles, petrochemicals, most developments in electronics and communications technology, pharmaceuticals, not to speak of international finance, and even mass tourism on which so many countries or regions depend heavily) have, in effect, been created by such large organizations. Most of them began as national entities but have become almost universally and increasingly transnational in nature. Production, sales, marketing, and distribution functions are carried out in many different independent countries. Increasingly even national management of local operations is the rule, although important aspects of finance, research and overall strategy are necessarily centrally determined by centrally convened committees on which, however, managers of several nationalities coming from different countries may sit. Some of them have become primarily holding companies and are no longer properly classed as industrial.

These are increasingly the characteristics of modern international capitalism. These are the mighty oaks that have grown from the little seed of the private joint-stock corporation planted in fertile soil a century or more ago.[10] But they are not oaks, they are intelligent, fallible, human competitors. From their rivalry, called competition, both destructive of the old and creative of the new, has come the power and glory of capitalism. This capitalism is not liberal, nor particularly democratic (although in some areas it is perhaps becoming more so). It is very powerful, not very stable but subject to great fluctuations, and not to be despised.

The question as to how small developing countries can or should manage their external economic affairs in such a world, and what is the most appropriate role of government, is not easy to answer. It arises in its starkest form for those less-developed countries that have got themselves into serious economic trouble with foreign debt, budgetary imbalances, inflation, prolonged and disruptive trade deficits and stagnating economies, and must turn for financial assistance to the international financial authorities, including the IMF, commercial banks and the World Bank. In addition to specific adjustment measures, they are advised to open their economies to imports, privatize their domestic companies and encourage foreign investment.

Such encouragement may require inducements, such as protection against imports, as in Turkey when an import substitution development strategy had been adopted. MNCs are not noted for their support for free trade or genuine liberal competitive practices; one need only examine the attitudes of United States-based companies when it come to Japanese competition from equally powerful Japanese multinational companies. The former allege, of course, that Japanese competition is unfair, just as it used to be alleged that low-wage competition was unfair, and they acuse the Japanese multinationals of dumping and other offences.[11]

How do the rules of classical liberal competition apply to this framework? Not very well. The players in the arena are large organizations with large bureaucracies, each operating within its own planning framework. Their activities are constrained by the market to the extent that they can not themselves create, manipulate or control the demand for their products, and by competition from rivals, actual or anticipated, to the extent that they can not make agreements with them or take them over. Competition among such organizations is not just a question of efficiency in production or competitive pricing in free markets in which demand is independent of the supplier, etc. Their activities are of course subject to the law, but the bureaucracies are often associated with the making of laws and are not infrequently in a position to evade them.[12]

It is this system, still in the process of evolution, that the developing countries may find not only necessary but indeed desirable to join as active participants. The question, again, is what is likely to be the best route to membership? Simply to open the door to take over? Perhaps. But what this writer suggests, without space to argue the issue fully, is that what some call liberal capitalism is in the process of metamorphosis and that a creature with different and as yet unknown characteristics will emerge. The desirability of such change will not be appraised here; the intention, rather, is to argue that those countries that are not as yet fully assimilated into the capitalist industrial economy, as it exists in the industrial world today, are justified in adopting a cautious, selective, and perhaps even defensive response. To liberalize all aspects of their economic policy in the belief that, with such policies, they are thereby joining the system with which the future lies, could be to give unnecessary hostages to fortune.

The implication is not that opportunities for productive association with the international companies should not be accepted, whether within their structures or outside, as is now often the case for example in distribution and as intermediate suppliers; nor is it implied that such association necessarily means undesirable absorption from the national point of view. Both are questions for the countries concerned. But surely the terms of any large-scale association should be decided by negotiated agreements, not imposed as a condition of financial succour from the IMF and commercial banks. If a genuinely international IMF/World Bank existed, free of ideological preconceptions that favoured the already economically powerful, there might usefully be an advisory place for it at any negotiating table.[13]

Even the most cursory glance at economic history impresses one with the widely different paths to industrial development taken by the now developed countries: England in the industrial revolution, with its early start, technological innovations, changes in land tenure and the supply of industrial labour, and its policy of promoting exports in the context of the expansion of military influence and commercial empire;[14] the United States with a continent at its disposal and abundant imports of people and capital, government land policies and strong protection against imports; Japan with its own home-grown-and-managed industrial genius; the newer NICs (newly industrialised countries) of Southeast Asia. All of these relied heavily on government involvement in economic affairs.

Even if we could find empirical generalizations that would serve to create models for developing countries, one of them would certainly not be indiscriminate openness to the world economy. Most successful countries were, and are, open to imports of capital, goods or services only to the extent that these advanced their purposes. In practice, of course, the degree to which the principle of free access has been applied to its own international transactions by any country has always depended on how far the pressures of groups gaining or losing from such freedom of movement have been in a position to determine the political decisions made by government. This has varied among countries, from industry to industry and from time to time. But neither the principle of free trade in its traditional theoretical setting nor violations of the principles in practice are the key issues. After all, violation of an applicable principle is, in theory, no good reason for abandoning the principle. But it is highly questionable whether the principle is applicable. Economists of liberal persuasion may argue, and demonstrate with unexceptionable logic, that the countries imposing any restrictions on international movement of goods and capital were mistaken and would have been better off had they followed a more open path, but their counterfactual propositions are hardly convincing.

Trade relates to the movement of goods and services. Foreign investment also gives rise to trade as the liability incurred by the receiving country is offset by credits gained in other directions. It is not so much negative effects, if any, on the balance of payments that often disturb the receiving countries, as the fact that private foreign investment gives the foreign investor direct access to, and control over, domestic productive assets of the receiving country. The foreign investor may buy a local going concern or may construct new productive enterprises; either way, domestic means of production come under foreign control. For a variety of reasons, including the effects on national taxation, environmental degradation, trade union policies, participation (or lack of it) in domestic politics, and many others, it can not be assumed that foreign investors naturally act in the national economic interest. If this statement is accepted, then it follows that national governments are entitled at the very least to monitor and control free access to their economies.[15]

Thus, the extent to which direct foreign investment should be encouraged can not be decided simply on grounds of principle; it is essentially a question of practical efficacy. The general advantages of such investment are well-known, as are the disadvantages. New concerns have become more prevalent in recent years – in particular, the danger of long-run depletion of natural resources and damage to the environment. Especial caution should be exercised in selling off rights to exploit natural resources without appropriate examination and monitoring.[16]

In integrating the Southeast Asian countries into the world economy, the state seems to have played a dominant role in an alliance with the domestic 'grand bourgeoisie' and the capitalist international companies. In the Middle East, such a development obviously requires the co-operation of the state and external official and commercial bodies, but it is unlikely that the liberal 'roll-back-the-state' model provides the relevant framework of analysis.

In this respect, Ruth McVey writes in a study of Southeast Asia, where 'capitalist transformation has . . . been taking place for well over a century' that:

> Until very recently it was taken as axiomatic by most Western analysts that for entrepreneurship to flourish in Southeast Asia it must have autonomy from the State . . . This ideologically comfortable assumption was reversed by 'developmental authoritarianism' and the general rediscovery of the State. A new model emerged to describe the kind of state appropriate to third-world modernisation. (McVey, 1992)

Even if Dr McVey is facing up to reality, for many, given their preconceptions, so uncomfortable is the ideological position suggested with its overtones of political authoritarianism invoking fears of the despotic state, that they reject it without investigation. There is, admittedly, much that is authoritarian whenever fundamental changes in an economy need to be brought about by authority. How much, depends on the circumstances. Authoritarianism was particularly manifest in Singapore and South Korea as the discipline of industrialism and integration was imposed; there seems to have been less elsewhere. But the truth is that Singapore and Korea were able successfully to attract private foreign investors, who, incidentally, often feel more comfortable with a strong state than with a weaker one buffeted by the winds of 'democracy'. There may have been some protest from the liberal world, but it did not come from the international banks and financial institutions.

In other words, the theory and practice of free competition, whether textbook, workable, monopolistic, or oligopolistic, does explain many aspects of the capitalist market enterprise economy. But it can not be used to justify the assumption (and this, too, the textbooks recognize if carefully studied) that 'liberalization' – the removal of government interference in the market and/or the privatization of enterprises – will, in the contemporary world of modern capitalist competition, enable the less-developed countries to join the club on anything like equal terms. But if they are in the club on unequal terms and, under the rules imposed on them, are supposed to open their economies, not only to the exports that their competitors want to sell them but also to the capital investment their rivals want them to receive, including investment in the form of takeovers, what can they expect?[17]

Much of the criticism of this recommended policy has come from those fearing the results of dependency and a return to neocolonialism. Dr McVey herself asks the question of how long it may be before these countries are not just victims of the new integration but will obtain a genuine capitalist base of their own; she is by no means defeatist but makes no attempt to speculate about the political effect of the form their economic integration might take in the future.

Transition to politics

The approach of the international financial community to countries in economic trouble has progressively moved from emphasis on stabilization, which implied a direct concern for the financial instability threatening a number of the developing countries. It necessarily soon extended to the problems of internal economic adjustment required if these countries were to establish more than ephemeral stability. Finally the central concern seemed to shift to the question of liberal policy reforms that were thought to be required to establish a long-run base for economic development. These categories overlap and merge into each other, but it is clear that the emphasis on reform is now moving to another stage, one that goes beyond the economic sphere to the political. Admittedly, again, economic and political considerations can not be entirely separated, but just as, in the meaning of words there is a clear difference between the proximate objectives of stabilization, then adjustment, and then reform, so there is between economic and political reform. The cliché of the slippery slope becomes dangerously applicable.

Many of the chapters in this volume refer to socio-political concerns, which are concerns for the survival of cultures, national values and degrees of sovereignty.[18] These are major issues not to be dismissed lightly; after all, throughout history stronger countries have politically, economically and culturally dominated or absorbed whole peoples. It should not be assumed, as is too often the case, that all of this necessarily comes from a deliberate and conscious attempt to subjugate the weaker to the interests of the strong. That the players are many and the motives always mixed provides no excuse, however, for a failure to examine carefully both players and motives as well as likely effects of actions. The history of the integration of developing countries has passed through periods in which weaker peoples have been forcibly annexed and brutally treated, sometimes virtually exterminated. These attitudes are no longer acceptable (unless, of course, the national interest/security demands it), but one should not be surprised that some doubts exist, not least in the Middle East.

Even as this book goes to press, the news media are reporting instances which illustrate both the complexity of the issues and the ambiguity of the players, and raise the question as to how far demands by one country on others are acceptable. It is reported that the president of the United States has demanded that China must adopt 'democracy', and that the prime minister of the United Kingdom has suggested that 'good governance' should be a condition of economic aid. The Group of Seven are postponing aid to Kenya, pending social and political reform.

A great deal of financial assistance has been given to many countries by the West, assistance which was largely determined by international political considerations and with little regard for the nature of the regimes receiving and disbursing funds. As some of the old rivalries and fears have diminished, so also has the attractiveness of some of the erstwhile clients. Moreover, as the excessive optimism about prospects of rapid economic development faded in the face of the intractability of the deep resistance residing in the sociological and political inheritance of countries, it seemed necessary to place more emphasis on slower-acting but fundamental efforts to re-form both social attitudes and political structures.

It would not have been difficult to predict this sequence of events with some confidence, and there is no escaping the fact that the process inevitably involves increasingly pointed external interference in the internal affairs of countries. In consequence, it becomes of major importance that there be a large measure of international consensus with respect to the legitimacy of the reforms demanded of receiving countries as a condition of eligibility for financial assistance. This consensus can not be expressed *only* by donor countries expecting to gain economically from international economic aid and insisting on their own, perhaps not widely shared, view of the world, nor by the international organizations that are dependent on only a few countries and are seen by many to be run for the benefit of their own vested interests, be they bankers, private investors or exporters. The only existing forum more or less approaching universality is, of course, the United Nations.

In the writer's view there probably is a very great deal of agreement on issues of human rights, on some as yet ill-defined form of participatory democracy, and perhaps on other moral, social and political matters, even though the agreement is usually more in word than deed. How far a consensus could be achieved on the current interpretations of economic liberalization involving openness to all types of foreign investment, to the acceptance of a minimal role for the state, elimination of subsidies, all trade protection, and other matters which figure largely in IMF and World Bank programmes is doubtful, to say the least. It has yet to be demonstrated.

This, of course, is putting a complex problem far too simply, but it does highlight a major question as a society develops/re-forms: why should it be assumed that the right direction of such development can be found in the past experience of very different societies and, in particular, in all of the deeply embedded political, sociological and economic preconceptions to which Western liberals have been conditioned.[19]

This raises the further and deeper question of how far the sovereignty-centred nation-state is acceptable today. It has been argued here that in economic matters the stronger states are not justified in attempting to impose on those weaker countries that need their help economic conditions which have little justification other than that they benefit the donors. The imposition of political conditions in return for help is in a different category. Perhaps, although it is by no means certain, the time is right to consider whether it is not possible to find a consensus, not necessarily a uniformly observed practice, regarding the appropriate conditions. Such a consensus could perhaps take the form of international conventions, dealing with, for example, certain types of human rights and restraints on state brutality, and even on aspects of the relations between the state and its people.

Notes

1 Dahrendorf, R. 'We are living in a world of uncertainty. Since no one can know all answers, let alone what the right answers are, it is of cardinal importance to make sure that different answers can be given at any one time, and especially over time. The path of politics, like that of knowledge, must be one of trial and error.' (Dahrendorf 1987) This article is a first rate non-dogmatic exposition of the changes in liberal thinking as circumstances and problems have changed.

2 For example, Professor Dahrendorf holds that liberalism 'grew out of the English Revolutions of the 17th century, spread to many countries in the

wake of the American and French Revolutions in the 18th century, and dominated the better part of the 19th century' (*ibid.*).

3 See the excellent essay by Robert L. Heilbroner, 'Capitalism' in Heilbroner (1987).

4 Even in eighteenth-century Britain there was considerable hostility to 'commercial dealings in paper assets'. In 1733 the British Parliament outlawed 'jobbing in stocks and shares', thus sustaining 'a tradition of family-based business organisation in Victorian Britain that proved itself to be ill-adapted to meet competitive challenges from American and German corporations during the second industrial revolution of the late nineteenth and twentieth centuries' (O'Brien, P. K., *Power with Profit: The State and the British Economy, 1685–1815*, Institute of Historical Research, University of London, 1992).

5 So rapidly has academic opinion been changing its direction everywhere along with the times that one political economist wondered whether academics are generally willing to give 'Vicar of Bray explanations – ready to serve any principle in power'. Ruth McVey, 'The materialization of the southeast Asian entrepreneur', in McVey (1992).

6 With respect to the different objectives of liberalization processes at different times, Dahrendorf notes that 'in the face of the "cage of bondage" (Max Weber) of modern bureaucratic government', the 'prevailing theme' may be the 'optimal, if not the minimal state', in Dahrendorf (1987).

7 See Joffé's chapter. It would be useful to encourage more research into the kinds of association developed between foreign and local entrepreneurs in either the formal or informal sectors in developing countries. It would also be useful to explore in some detail the relationships between those who hold political power and the leaders of business. Studies of the rise of the Southeast Asian NICs indicate that although the linkages between domestic business élites, international sources of finance and investment, and domestic government were the prime movers in industrial development, their activities often opened opportunities for smaller enterprises. See McVey (1992).

8 To give only four examples:
a) The subsidization of agriculture in Europe. The United States, for which agricultural exports are of great importance, no longer has as much of the earlier politically irresistible need to subsidize or protect its own farmers, except in some areas, e.g. sugar, and can afford to put pressure on Europe, which in turn opposes many of the US measures to encourage American high technology industries.

b) Heavy restrictions on immigration. This is certainly a severe and illiberal restriction on the free movement of a major factor of production, contrasting strangely with the demand for the free movement of foreign capital into those countries from whom the export of workers is restricted. As in the less-developed world, whether or not imports of either commodities or factors of production are permitted depends very much on what they compete with in the importing country, or the felt need for them.

c) Deliberate government manipulation of interest and exchange rates as an instrument of macro-economic policy.

d) Very close alliance between governments and companies deemed of special importance in the national interest, e.g. the major defence industries. Other instances could be noted, and there should be little surprise if it is sometimes found difficult to convince the prospective converts of the good intentions of those offering carrots and wielding sticks. Such policies are most effective when the carrots, or at least their smell, are sweeter than the sticks are hard.

9 We hear a great deal about the abuses of state bureaucracies, but consider the areas in which business bureaucracy is a problem, anxiously studied in business schools and creating a lucrative market for consultants. Where is the market in which one of the most powerful motivations of large business corporations is to devote its efforts solely to maximizing profits from production and sale of goods and which refrains from trying to establish monopolistic positions in order to capture maximum rents? Where does one find that the primary and an obvious motivation of the leaders of such corporations is to avoid using their positions to obtain a large slice of such rents in the form of golden handshakes, golden handcuffs, executive salaries, bonuses of many kinds, or sheer fraud, with a degree of success that is surely not to be underestimated? In any organization where there are people in a position to obtain salaries or incomes greater than free market forces would have produced, there is rent-seeking. State bureaucracies provide only one of many types. The social cost of rent-seeking is essentially the social cost of creating the protection. See the excellent article by Gordon Tullock 'Rent-seeking', in Eatwell, Milgate and Newman (1987).

10 Joseph Schumpeter wrote a perceptive book some half century ago in which he analysed the evolution of capitalism and its relation to society. He insisted that it was important to distinguish capitalism as a market system from capitalism as the thriving, creative, innovating force of the economy, the chief function of which was what he termed 'creative destruction', a continual destruction of the old and introduction of the new in all aspects of the economy, that is, in products, technology, markets and marketing. To this aspect of capitalism he attributed the extraordinary increase in productivity and standards of living in most countries of the world. See Schumpeter (1942), esp. chapter VII.

11 In general such charges are only successful because GATT provisions regarding dumping rest, once again, on ideological and outdated considerations, and are, to say the least, fashioned largely in the interest of the US-based MNCs. See Penrose (1990), pp. 181–7.

12 It is well known by those who work in this area that many large companies can afford more and better lawyers than can most governments, including that of the United States!

13 It has been suggested that a reformed GATT might be a useful instrument in this connection.

14 The importance of the role of the state and, in particular, of the military in promoting the industrial expansion of the British economy from the late seventeenth to early nineteenth century is brilliantly discussed by Professor P. K. O'Brien, *Power and Profit*.

15 This is, of course, in no way intended as an objection to a country ceding aspects of its sovereignty to any economic or political group that it may decide to join.

16 Some governments have long been committed to a closed communist-type of economic development policy and in deciding to abandon their old ways can move too rapidly and too rashly in the opposite direction, with disappointing results. In attempting to make a U-turn, so to speak, they are liable to accept the new ideology without carefully scrutinizing specific decisions. For example, it was reported in *The Guardian* (1/11/91) that Guyana's government, allegedly following the general policy advice of important British politicians to privatize, sold a timber concession on nearly half a million hectares of forest land to Lord Beaverbrook who, in a complicated arrangement with a Dutch timber company, sold his interest and gained some £50 million on the transaction as a 'success fee'.

17 The modern economic theory of contestable markets is a much more appropriate way of looking at the nature of competition in today's world than is the classical liberal free competition model. But what chances will the new countries have in the contest for markets if they enter on their own? 'If you can't beat 'em, join 'em' may be the new approach, but on what terms?

18 Apparently Japan, the latest of the undoubtedly successful established industrial countries, although virtually closed to foreign capital and only carefully open to foreign trade, was nevertheless very wide open to foreign ideas, intellectuals, exports, publications, teachers, and to the adoption of foreign technology. Many Middle Eastern countries are much less open in these respects, not in the interest of their economic development but for ideological reasons of their own, some of which are also advanced as grounds for resisting foreign investment.

19 Myoko Kuroda's chapter in this book directly questions the fundamental preconceptions of Western economic liberalism and the desirability of embracing economic integration. Kuroda points out that the liberalization ideology in its modern capitalist context leaves little room for traditional values and many aspects of the culture of other societies. She discusses the traditional elements in the evolution of the successful Japanese economy and finds some comparable developments in Syrian economic history. She is concerned that too much that is valuable in culture and tradition will be lost with integration under the all-pervasive umbrella of multinational companies; in the competitive arena she notes, 'the weaker might have almost no chance to win' and proceeds to discuss, largely in relation to Syria, an approach to 'liberalisation' in Islamic terms.

2· THE ORIGINS OF LIBERAL INSTITUTIONS IN THE ANCIENT MIDDLE EAST

Patricia Springborg*

This chapter advances two main themes: that the ancient Middle East probably pioneered those political institutions that we associate with economic liberalism in the West; and that in the taxonomy of social forms, political institutions (understood in the more restricted sense as derived from the *polis*) may be generally correlated with economic liberalism. Both belong to the wider phenomenon of urbanism. Ancient Near Eastern society, as one of the earliest recorded forms of urban, densely settled, entrepreneurial and highly transactional societies, exhibited certain structural affinities with modern industrialized society. This is due in part to historical contingency and the transmission of institutions. More generally it is due to the problems which urbanism poses and the restricted range of viable solutions to those problems.

It is my purpose to explore these theses by contrasting city-state formations, to which the Greek *polis* and earlier Mesopotamian and Egyptian cities belonged, with agrarian-based monarchies, to which the early European nation states belonged for most of their histories. Marx and Weber tried to capture the differences between these social forms, making the distinction between *homo politicus* and *homo oeconomicus*. They emphasized the difficulties encountered in grafting city-republican *political* institutions on to monarchies characterized by the economies of collective housekeeping (Springborg, 1986, 1992). It is the greatest of ironies that, a more-or-less successful graft having

*The author wishes to acknowledge her indebtedness to her publishers for permission to reprint some material from Patricia Springborg, *Royal Persons: Patriarchal-Monarchy and the Feminine Principle*, London: Unwin Hyman, 1990; also Patricia Springborg, *Western Republicanism and the Oriental Prince*, Cambridge: Polity Press, 1992.

taken place, the old landed monarchies of Western Europe, and their schismatic republican colonies in the New World, should now be in the position of exporting liberalism, political and economic, back to the Middle East. This essay attempts the beginning of an account of how this could be so.

The relation suggested here between economic liberalization and political institutions is that liberal political institutions are correlated with a very specific kind of economy: urban. The needs of urban society can only be serviced if a number of characteristics are present: relatively decentralized power-sharing arrangements with a high level of citizen-participation; representation of class interests as well as of individual interests; and highly articulated and specialized branches of government divided into legislative, executive and judicial functions.

Urbanism and the political/economic order in the ancient Middle East

Across several disciplines scholars have observed certain shortcomings in the received historical canon which posits an evolutionary schema from primitivism to *polis* to modern (Western) nation state, the states of the East constituting a residual category. Studies in Assyriology, Iranology and Egyptology disclose highly developed ancient civilizations, which exhibited considerable technological competence. More disquieting still is the fact that economic and technical competencies were accompanied by the full array of social and cultural traits that we associate with development as it is currently conceived. The capacity of the irrigation societies, so called, of ancient Sumeria, Mesopotamia more generally, Egypt and China to make the transition from city-state to empire, a transition that the Greek *polis*, for instance, never made (Anderson, 1974a; Mann, 1986), was a function precisely of the following developmental competencies:

- impersonal government administered by a bureaucracy;
- the conception of man as citizen;
- forms of political representation;
- the creation of an economic surplus;
- a monetarized economy, accompanied by institutions of credit, commercial law, trade treaties and international laws of contract;
- a standing army, equipped with advanced military technologies;
- social stratification along functional lines, comprising classes of

farmers, artisans, merchants, an administrative élite and priestly caste;
- the concept of nature as governed by rational laws;
- instititutions for the acquisition, organization and dissemination of knowledge;
- the development of writing and basic sciences of mathematics, geometry, astronomy, navigation, architecture, engineering and highly developed skills in construction, metal-working, pottery, textiles, sculpture and painting (Drucker, 1979; Mann, 1986).

To take the case of Sumeria, one of the earliest examples, scholars (Diakonoff, 1956, 1974; Jacobsen, 1970, 1976; Kramer, 1963; Oppenheim, 1969) now suggest that city-states like those of Lagash were administered by parallel temple and palace bureaucracies, agents of each required to countersign shipments in and out of the state granaries, for instance (Oppenheim, 1969; 7ff). The considerable lands of the city comprised palace and temple complexes and their holdings, noble estates and the lands of commoners, organized in 'patriarchal clans and town communities', whose property could be bought and sold by chosen family representatives in transactions for which, around 2400 BC, we already have documentary evidence (Kramer, 1963: 75–7).

Corresponding to these, now classic, property divisions was a surprisingly conventional division of political power. Early evidence for representative councils in Sumer is to be found in the Gilgamesh Epic, as it also exists for Egypt in the Great Corporation of Heliopolis, recorded in the mythological 'Contendings of Horus and Seth' (Anthes, 1954; Griffiths, 1960). By 2300 BC evidence exists for a bicameral assembly in Lagash, the upper house of which was controlled by the nobility, the lower house confined to commoners, access being granted on property qualifications. Magistracies, appointed on an annual basis, were rotated among an isonomous élite constituted by the judicial, administrative and merchant classes (Oppenheim, 1969). Lagash has the honour of recording in its annals the first known use of the word freedom (Kramer, 1963: 79), celebrated in the Urukagina Reform Document of around 2350 BC in terms strikingly reminiscent of Solon's *seisachtheia* nearly 1800 years later. Freedom meant precisely protection against the predations of the palace tax collector, as well as redress of administrative abuses by the 'ubiquitous and obnoxious bureaucracy' of the temple. Urukagina, like Solon later, promised release of those imprisoned for debt bondage.

The corporate structure of Mesopotamian *poleis*, the roster of magistracies and legal and financial institutions, anticipate to a significant degree the institutions of classical Greece. Citizenship in Mesopotamian cities, like that of Athens, depended on twin criteria of birth to free parents and ownership of municipal land. Citizenship brought with it rights and duties: economic, social, legal and religious privileges, but the duties of taxation and military service. Corporate action on the part of the city suceeded in some cases in reducing those personal liabilities which ran counter to its economic interests. Thus citizens of Nippur, in central Babylon, were officially exempted around 1900 BC from corvée duties to the king of Isin. The cities of Babylon and Sippar claimed divine protection of their municipal rights, placing a religious symbol at the city gate to proclaim their special legal status. A mark of the self-consciousness of their freedom is registered by the citizens of Babylon in a letter to King Ashurbannipal, in which they proclaim that 'even a dog becomes free and privileged when he enters their city' (Oppenheim, 1969: 7).

Distribution of power in the cities is documented in innumerable tablets of contract which were customarily witnessed by municipal and royal officials, priests, professionals, family and neighbours, enumerated according to rank. Public administration in Sippar, for instance, fell into two classes. Local government was administered by royal appointees. But at the level of municipal administration of the city (*alum*), or city-and-aldermen (*alum u sibutum*) as a corporate entity, executive power was placed in the hands of one official: the 'overseer of the merchants' (*akil tamkare*). He is reminiscent in name and function of the *wakil tujar* of Islamic times, who served variously as representative of foreign merchants (like the consul in the Italian cities of the Levant), superintendent of the port, tax-farmer of customs and other excises; and as a notary, his warehouse or agency house (*dar al wakala*) serving as a neutral meeting ground for the transaction of business, and even as a bourse (Goitein, 1967: 186–92). The similarity of function, and even an etymological kinship in the terms *akil, wakil*, for 'overseer of the merchants' in Mesopotamia in the Old Babylonial period, and Egypt under the Fatimids and Ayyubids, would seem to refer to a continuity of social forms with all the relevant social and religious underpinnings.

The relationship between the city as a corporate entity (*alum u sibutum*), or city and aldermen, and the overseer of the merchants (*akil tamkare*) in Babylonian times, is not completely known. The designation of the community, *alum u sibutum*, seems to refer in Sippar to all free males within the city who met and acted as a body for certain purposes. Throughout the period that the documents record (*c.* 1894–1595 BC) the overseers were all natives of Sippar, drawn from an oligarchic élite. We know that they were elected for one year only and it seems likely that they were, according to established Babylonian practice, elected by lot, but from a very circumscribed list of eligible candidates. The lot, later characterized by the Greeks of the classical period as the most democratic of electoral procedures, since it took choice entirely out of human hands on the supposition that all candidates were in principle equal, had been used in Southern Mesopotamia in the Old Babylonial period to decide the order of inheritance to the paternal estate. Common law of the region for the city-states, which unlike pastoral Israel did not follow the principle of primogeniture, stipulated that sons inherited in full shares, daughters in half shares, but who was to get what in circumstances where many of the assets were indivisible, in the form of oil presses, abattoirs, agricultural land or urban real estate, had to be decided with minimum conflict.

In Assyria the lot was used to elect the eponymous official (*limmu*) after whom the year of his term was named. Oppenheim (1969: 10) has to say of the system of election by lot among notables: 'power was wielded not on the basis of personal status (based on charisma, wealth, genealogy) but in rotation among peers, who enjoyed what the Greeks called *isonomia*'. *Isonomia*, literally equality, we know had an elastic sense in classical Greece, being used in the famous song about the tyrannicides, Harmodius and Hipparchus, to describe the outcome of their action as nobles who established an oligarchy: 'they made Athens *isonomous*'. Like all political terms, *isonomia* was relative, but the aspiration to equality, if only equality among peers, was consistently intimated by what Herodotus referred to as 'the fairest name of all'.[1] One of the most interesting aspects of the election by lot of the chief municipal officer of Sippar, designated 'overseer of the merchants', is the possibility that the brevity of his term, for one year only, may have been due to his performing the equivalent of the Greek liturgies. As 'mayor', the *akil* received the revenue from royal land, but in return he had to guarantee to the king the payment of taxes levied on the city; the privilege of office and its accompanying financial liability was thus shifted annually to spread the burden among the class of notables (Oppenheim, 1969: 9–10). The liturgies, by which costly public works were levied on wealthy citizens in exchange for social prestige and public honours, lay at the very foundation of the economic systems of the ancient world.

Some of the best evidence we have for government by an impersonal bureaucracy is yielded by the third millennium Mesopotamian site of Ebla, in the form of some 20,000 clay tablets. A prosperous city of some 260,000 people, Ebla was ruled by a king (*malik*, cf. Hebrew and Arabic *malik*), a council of elders (*abbu*, see Arabic *abu*, 'father' and cf. Roman *patres*, senators) and some 11,700 bureaucrats whose ledgers, daybooks and inventories account for some 13,000 clay tablets (Bermant and Weitzman, 1979; Matthiae, 1980). Further evidence for bureaucratically administered rule of law is to be found in the provisions of a series of codifications of the common law of the area, from the Ur-Nammu Code of 2050 BC up to and including the famous Hammurabi Code. The code of Ur-Nammu upheld the rights of orphans, widows and small-holders against powerful 'grabbers of property'. It undertook regulation of the marketplace by the introduction of standard weights and measures, instituting a schedule of fines for infringement against the laws of fair trade, in line with other codes for the areas, including the Hittite. Court proceedings for the period record litigation regarding 'marriage contracts, divorces, inheritance, slaves, hiring of boats, claims of all sorts, pledges and such miscellaneous items as pre-trial investigations, subpoenas, theft, damage to property, and malfeasance in office' (Kramer, 1963: 84–5).

In ancient Egypt too, although perhaps a less litigious society, property transactions were a document-ridden affair, asset dossiers comprising every piece of paper associated with a given piece of property (Lloyd, 1983: 314; Pestman, 1983). Contrary to modern assumptions, ancient Egypt was a society also characterized by independent city-development in its early history (Bietak, 1979; Trigger, 1983: 40, 48), private and noble patronage systems (Kemp, 1983: 83–5), and a high level of individualism as attested by the personal signatures of artists to works as early as the Pyramids of Giza (Drucker, 1979: 44). As late as 1960 a well-known Egyptologist could claim that 'Egypt through the New Kingdom' was 'a civilisation without cities' (Wilson, 1960). But this judgement has been rejected by recent archaeologists whose work concentrates on town sites previously neglected for the monumental and better-preserved temple structures. In their recent authoritative social history of ancient Egypt, Trigger and Kemp (Trigger *et al.*, 1983) argue that in the predynastic period Egypt had probably seen a pattern of urban settlement similar to that of Mesopotamia. The development of sacred cities rather evenly spaced along the Nile from Upper to Lower Egypt, which were retained and constantly rebuilt after the unification of the Two Kingdoms right through to the Graeco-Roman period, would suggest that this was the case.

Situated in a self-draining flood plain, Egypt in the predynastic period saw the development of town sites in the islands or turtlebacks (*gezirat*) which rose above the general flood level of the Nile, or on levees which controlled it (Bietak, 1979: 100–102). Ideograms for urban settlements, of which there are two in hieroglyphics, one indicating a round fortified settlement, the other a rectangular, fail to distinguish towns by size or to discriminate between village, town and city. The distinction which they emphasize seems to relate not only to the shape, but also to the function, of the settlement. The rectangular settlements, it is argued, developed out of the royal stronghold as centres of royal administration; the settlements represented by the round ideogram being controlled by the former and subject to their taxing authority (Bietak, 1979: 98–9). Already these distinctions relate to developments well down the track since they are predicated on the existance of the monarchy. Early town development which displaced the nomadic tribes had grown up around the gold trade and access routes to the Red Sea that allowed the development of settlements from Aswan to Abydos; the future nucleus of Upper Egypt as a territorial kingdom (Trigger, 1983: 40) dates to the unification of the two kingdoms around 3100 BC.

The reasons for the pattern to diverge from that of the city-republics of Mesopotamia (Trigger, 1983: 50–1) are social, regional (avoiding the word political) and geophysical. The city-republics of Mesopotamia, faced by hostile neighbours on all fronts, retained their fiercely guarded independence as warrior states. But Egypt, whose unique geophysical isolation by desert and sea promised the absence of such threats, saw economic and political advantage in the incorporation of the Nilotic settlements into a continuous realm. Unification of the Two Kingdoms produced peace, but not at the cost of provincial apathy: the pharaohs of the Two Kingdoms continued to rebuild and refurbish provincial temples, with whose fortunes those of the provincial notability were inextricably linked. Threats of unrest and economic disruption were sufficient to maintain the unity of the realm for three thousand years, although the strength of provincial centres *vis-à-vis* the crown waxed and waned throughout the period, producing predictable, but not uncontrollable tensions.

That urban autonomy developed to a considerable degree in Egypt is suggested by the fact that specific legal procedures and practices under the monarchy were never systematized in any documents that have survived, and were probably supplied by the persistence of customary law that predated the unified state. As counterevidence, it is worth pointing out that Polybius and Diodorus Siculus record books of Egyptian law, which the Greek legislator Solon came himself to consult, being tabled in the courts. Whatever the case in the matter of legal codification, the monarchy was both founded upon, and subsequently embellished, provincial settlements, and it is speculated that 'whatever nominal claim the king may have had to pre-eminent domain, older patterns of land-holding at the village level, and possibly among the upper classes also, were not unduly interfered with by the king' (Trigger, 1983: 57–8).

At what point Egyptian towns developed the full array of characteristics we associate with urbanism – concentrated settlement; internal differentiation into quarters corresponding to occupational divisions; specialized division of labour; functions as industrial and market centres; defence and religious functions (Bietak, 1979: 103) – we cannot be sure. The creation of artificial settlements associated with the pyramid temples of the third millennium BC produced an unusual phenomenon: monuments to central power that took on a provincial life of their own. When these huge mortuary complexes, with their endless retainers and administrators, no longer served as monuments to reigning dynasties, they served instead as cult-centres and power bases for provincial notables.

The political economy of pyramid-building has been admirably analysed by Barry Kemp (1983: 86–9), who shows that as well as creating a demonstration of royal power, these gigantic public works produced technological spin-offs and 'an economic stimulus broadly equivalent to "built-in obsolescence" in modern technological societies' in the 'constant search for more economic means of achieving a given result' (Kemp, 1983: 87, 89). Their construction required a highly disciplined work force and attracted surplus labour from neighbouring states. A variety of evidence suggests a considerable influx of Mesopotamian skilled craftsmen, who came as metal workers and civil servants, from the Gerzean period (*c.* 3500–3000 BC) on, but disappeared just as suddenly in the early Dynastic period (Trigger, 1983: 50–1).

Trigger speculates that this craft specialization and use of immigrant labour attracted by the outreach of Egypt's long-distance trade, while serving initially to break down tribal structures and encourage the growth of complex hierarchical provincial settlements, subsequently worked to undermine their autonomy as the royal patronage on which it was based extended to control all labour. Up to a certain point, however, the development of provincial cult centres based on towns 'as nodal points in the economic organisation' (Trigger, 1983: 48) and as political centres, did not differ markedly from developments in Mesopotamia.

Gradually the extension of centralized government administration in Egypt brought all major officials, bureaucrats, soldiers and retainers under government control, and the government became the major employer of labour, skilled and unskilled, and even the source of foreign goods through its monopoly of import/export (Trigger, 1983: 50, 59). A large bureaucracy comprising three principle divisions, 'the department of the head of the South', the 'office of government labour' and 'the treasury' (Kemp, 1983: 82–3), organized the collection of taxes in kind, the storing of these goods in government warehouses, and their redistribution to those entitled to receive royal largesse (Trigger, 1983: 58).

Methods of computation based on the measurement of the Nile, by means of the famous Nilometer, and the biennial census, a royal tour of inspection of all taxable resources known as the 'following of Horus', allowed officials to calculate crop yields as a basis for tax assessments. The birth of geometry has long been attributed to the related need to recalculate property boundaries after the annual inundation (Baillet, 1913: 650, citing Herodotus 2.109, and Diodorus, 1.81). The census and other administrative devices were incorporated into royal ceremonial, and the king himself took part in these tours of inspection, the biennial census of cattle being sufficiently important to lend its name to the term for the regnal year (Kemp, 1983: 82). The development of book-keeping and even writing are traced to the administrative needs of the state in this early period, and one cannot but be impressed by the detailed efficiency with which, for instance, records of all labour contracts, the location and residence of all labourers, were kept for the purposes of corvée duty and to permit the general right of the king to call on private labour at will (Baillet, 1913: 600–01).

The comparison with Western societies

It is not necessary to list in detail the technological accomplishments of ancient Mesopotamia and Egypt. It is worth pointing out, however, that each of the instances Max Weber gives in his 'Preface' to *The Protestant Ethic and the Spirit of Capitalism* (Weber, 1958: 15ff) for the administrative, scientific and technical superiority of the West over the East is erroneous. So ubiquitous are the assumptions of Western development and Eastern underdevelopment that a thinker who spent a good deal of his life writing about Eastern systems felt no need to check his facts. He claims that Babylonian astronomy lacked a mathematical basis, neglecting to mention also the invention of geometry as Egyptian (King, 1978, 1980); that Eastern legal traditions lacked the systematic quality of Roman and canonical law, whereas, in fact Roman Law is derived from the law-codes of the Eastern provinces, codified by those Easterners, Papinian and Ulpian from the Beirut school of law (Cumont, 1956 edn; Rostovtzeff, 1932; Driver and Miles, 1952, 1955). Weber (1958: 15) further claims that 'though the technical basis of our architecture came from the Orient . . . the Orient lacked the solution to the problems of the dome'. Quite the contrary. The Orient provided the solution not only to the problem of the dome, but also of the arch.

On the subject of the compilation and dissemination of knowledge, Weber claims that Western universities are superior to those of China and Islam, 'superficially similar', but lacking 'the rational, systematic and specialised pursuit of sciences with trained and specialised personnel' (Weber, 1958: 15–16). He neglects to point out that Islamic universities like al-Azhar were older than those of the West, which did not begin life as scientific institutes either. Evidence for the early existence of medical and law schools, to which women were also admitted, dates in fact to the third millennium Ebla site, which also furnishes lists of precious metals, minerals and other scientific information (Bermant and Weitzman, 1979: 153–5). Weber goes on to claim, rather surprisingly since this is his special subject, that it is an accomplishment of the West to staff its bureaucracies with a specially trained *organization* of officials. More startling still is his claim that the organization of labour based on freedom to contract is a triumph of the West. But stipulations regarding freedom to contract are to be found in the earliest-known Mesopotamian law codes, the Hammurabi Code for instance, including extensive treatment of both agricultural and commercial labour contracts regarding rates of hire, offences and liabilities involving oxen, husbandmen, agricultural implements, graziers, shepherds, wagons and seasonal workers; and wages and rates of hire for craftsmen (Driver and Miles, 1952, 1955).

Islamic society, like the Mesopotamian societies which governed its sedentary forms, was surpremely contractual (Springborg, 1987), a characteristic which underlay much of its success. By the standards of economic development, the Islamic cities achieved a size, based on the division and specialization of labour, unparalleled in Europe until the nineteenth and twentieth centuries. Charles Issawi, the economic historian, reports the population of tenth-century Baghdad at around a million, while Cairo in the fourteenth century is reported by a French traveller to have been twice the size of Paris, with four times the population. By 1800 AD Istanbul had a population of a million, while Baghdad and Cairo's populations had declined, compared with the population of London of 400,000 (Issawi, 1969: 102–5). The Jewish historian of Islam, Solomon Goitein (1967: 99), observes that in the Geniza documents of medieval Cairo, 'The terms for about 265 manual occupations have been identified thus far, as against 90 types of person engaged in commerce and banking and approximately the same number of professionals, officials, religious functionaries and educators'. Goitein compares this total of some 450 recognized occupations 'with the 150 or so professional corporations traced in ancient Rome by J. T. Walzing in his monumental *Corporations Professionelles* on the one hand, and the 278 *corporations de metiers* listed by André Raymond (1957) for Cairo in 1801', on the other, as well as the 435 recognized occupations compiled by Qasimis, father and son, for Damascus at the turn of this century (Goitein, 1967: 99).

The question arises, why, with such a finely gradated division of labour, capitalism did not emerge in the East. Essentially it was because business generated a specific professional form, the partnership, neither based on a division between owners and non-owners, nor giving rise to the employer–employee relation (Goitein, 1967: 154–5, 203, 263). There were important social reasons for this, not least of which is the fact that the employer–employee distinction approximated too uncomfortably the relation between master and slave, in what were originally slave-owning societies (Goitein, 1967: 77) – the slaves incidentally being either black, or that other inferior class of persons, Europeans, captured on the corsair route! Centuries of small business organized in partnerships, in which some partners contributed capital, others labour, but all were happily 'owners', shut out the large-scale industrialist as a dominant type. Based on the family, the neighbourhood or the confession, these business partnerships cemented primary social ties; even women were frequently partners, whose economic independence has often been misrepresented. What can one think of the subjugation of women in a society in which mothers gave their daughters names like 'Female Ruler', 'Mistress of the Turbans', 'Mistress of the Clerks', 'Mistress of Byzantium', 'Mistress of Baghdad', 'Mistress of the Muslim West', 'She Who Rules Over Everyone', 'Fame', 'Victory', 'General', even 'King' (Goitein, 1978: 314–19)?

The conception of the city-republic as constituted out of a series of voluntarily contracted partnerships has a great ancestry, for all that the 'right to contract' is conceived as a peculiarly modern form (Maine, 1861; Morgan, 1877; Marx, 1973 edn, 1974 edn;). Not only did the ancient *poleis* of Mesopotamia and Greece draw together a mixed collection of small associations contractually construed, based on kinship, friendship, cultic, economic and commercial functions, but they were understood by their members to be so constituted. This is quite clear from the account of the foundations of the *polis* given by Aristotle,[2] who for centuries was read as lending support to an organic theory of society in response to Plato's theoretical attempts at social engineering. In the case of the city-republics of Sumeria, Assyria and Babylonia, the evidence is quite explicit, but articulated in a documentary rather than a theoretical mode. It lies in the innumerable records of contract preserved on clay tablets and unearthed over the last century. It can also be inferred from the rare interventions of the city as a corporate governing body to adjust the alignment of economic and social forces, where the balance of interests had broken down.

Eclipse of classical municipal institutions in the Middle East

It is true that even if the classic municipal institutions of the *polis* – assembly (*ecclesia*), council of elders (*gerousia* or *areopagus*) and the magistracies – can be shown to have had their ancestry in the second and third millennium city-states of Mesopotamia, they did not pass on their legacy to the Islamic cities as such. In the Hellenistic period, the age in which the municipality flourished most, cities of the Eastern provinces were endowed with democratic constitutions by successive emperors, recreated if not created for the first time in Egypt for instance (Bowman, 1971). But the general decline of municipal institutions in the later Roman Empire, a product of the imperial bureaucracy and its omnivorous appetite for taxes, had its repercussions in the Islamic period. While Roman emperors of the later period tried to arrest this decline and revive the cities, if only to curb the central bureaucracy while improving the tax base, political office carried with it such financial liability that few candidates were willing to man the municipal magistracies. Thus the *curia*, that 'class of leading citizens represented on the council, was degraded to a group whose main function was to serve as hostages for the taxes imposed on the city, obliged to make good any deficit from their own pockets' (Stern, 1970: 27). The situation in Ptolemaic Egypt was particularly noteworthy. There the principal municipal office of *gymnasiarch*, at first voluntary and held for a year, became, as more functions and public works were attached to it, and as the Graeco-Egyptian ruling class became increasingly impoverished, a liturgy that fewer and fewer were willing to fill, so that eventually children were named to the office on the assumption that their parents would pay.

So ended a system of autonomous municipal government that had lasted some three millennia. It was only in Europe, when city life revived from the eleventh century on, that governmental institutions of the classical period, magistracies, assembly and courts, were deliberately recreated. Whatever in the way of a genuine restoration this may have constituted – for 'from the very beginning urban life in the western Roman provinces north of the Alps [had been] much weaker than [that] in the eastern provinces' (Stern, 1970: 32) – it also represented the impetus of Western indigenous élites to further their cause by the imitation of classical forms of political representation. In this respect the newly constituted nation states of Western Europe mounted a challenge to the Eastern cities for their own legacy, while in the East developments followed the trajectory of the later Roman Empire. This is not to say that the East ceased to have representative institutions. In the *majlis* and *masjid* (Morony, 1984), it certainly had institutions for petitioning the ruler, the redress of grievances and bottom-up as well as top-down communication between ruler and ruled. However, these forms are not 'liberal' institutions as we usually understand them. They correspond much more closely to the monarchical forms of clan or aristocratic council by which northern Europe for most of its history was ruled.

Notes

1 Herodotus, *Histories*, 3.84.
2 Aristotle, *Politics*, 1.1.

3· THE LINKS BETWEEN ECONOMIC AND POLITICAL LIBERALIZATION

David Pool

Over the past decade many states have been promoting economic liberalization with varying degrees of enthusiasm and intensity. Some have also initiated a process of political liberalization around the same time as, or subsequent to, these economic changes. It is too early to assert, as some politicians have, that we are entering a new era of democratization and that proceeding parallel with it is the retreat of the state in the face of the advance of the market. It may be that from a longer historical perspective both processes will prove to be short lived; that economic change will follow its own course independent of political change; or that combinations of economic and political liberalization will introduce new and uncontrollable sociopolitical dynamics. To suggest discernible patterns or to state in a precise way what the linkages and connections might be are no easy tasks.

In different parts of the world, the sequencing of economic and political change has varied. In some Latin American states, economic liberalization under authoritarian military regimes unleashed political forces which have ushered in a 'transition to democracy'. Most accounts have emphasized the desertion of the 'middle sectors' and the bourgeoisie as the crucial factor (O'Donnell *et al.*, 1986). In Eastern Europe, popular uprisings have led to the disintegration of authoritarian regimes and a process of political liberalization. In the Soviet Union too, gradual economic liberalization appears to have been a significant factor in the demise of economic and political centralization and the ideology associated with it. Different patterns of sequencing notwithstanding, economic and political reform appear to go together and provide a fascinating subject for comparative enquiry, no less in the Middle East than elsewhere.

There are states in the region, such as Jordan and Algeria, so different in their social and political formations, that introduced sweeping political changes involving relatively free national and local elections respectively. Both have also acceded to solutions proposed by external financial institutions to their economic crises and introduced measures of economic liberalization. There are also states where these processes can be viewed from a longer historical perspective. Turkey has undergone alternating periods of authoritarianism and competitive multi-partyism since 1950, and varying combinations of liberal and authoritarian forms of government have been associated mainly with statist strategies, but also on occasions with market-orientated economic policies. There are also examples which indicate that the progress of political liberalization is not unilinear. Since the mid-1970s the Egyptian and Tunisian governments have promoted economic liberalization, inaugurated degrees of political reform and then shifted back to repressive political practices.

Regimes of different ideological persuasions have introduced economic liberalization measures. In Turkey, it was an authoritarian-military government which paved the way for IMF/World Bank stabilization measures, in Algeria and Tunisia ideologically different but structurally similar party-states, and in Jordan a monarchy operating through a semi-authoritarian, clientelistic 'politics of notables'. There are also states like Iraq, Syria and Libya where some degree of economic liberalization has taken place but no political reform (Vandewalle, 1991; Lawson, 1990). The experience of Lebanon is also instructive: a *laissez-faire* economy, a minimal state and the provision of welfare goods through the private and voluntary sector (under the auspices of a narrow coalition of bankers and merchants) were the economic basis which underpinned the only democracy in the Arab Middle East. Although free of the authoritarianism to which neighbouring states were subject, the political and economic penetrability of the system and the inequalities of wealth and power associated with it resulted in its disintegration. The political history of Lebanon raises in stark form the political evils of the absent non-interventionist state.

Before presenting some observations about contempoary linkages between economic and political liberalization, two prior issues must be covered: first, connections between economic and political change rest on general theoretical positions and assumptions; second, policies of economic and political liberalization in the Middle East have particular and specific roots in prior patterns of state, society and economy relations, and an understanding of these is crucial in examining the process of liberalization. For the former we shall leave aside grand historical analyses and concentrate on two approaches to the interconnection of economy, society and politics: modernization, and state and class. For the second we shall present an overview of the legacy of the previous political economy.

Modernization, pluralism and democracy

Writers within the modernization school link the absence of democracy to the absence of modernity, the major characteristics of which are processes akin to Western social, economic and political development. Industralization, urbanization, the growth of communications, and the expansion of education and literacy are thought likely to create a differentiated, pluralist society which will sustain democracy. Criticized earlier for naively transferring processes drawn from Western historical development, interest in this approach has recently revived (Diamond *et al.*, 1989). Pluralist ideas have reappeared in academic analyses, and references to pluralism are even scattered through the Tunisian and Jordanian National Pacts. The only Middle Eastern state to which this model has been applied with any consistency, however, is Turkey. It is evident even there that the modernization approach has failed to explain the recurrent breakdowns of democracy. The intellectual difficulties of modernization assumptions are evident in the conclusions of Ozbudun, who writes, without a trace of irony: 'Turkey is one of the few countries that are more democratic politically than they ought to have been according to their level of socio-economic development' (Ozbudun, 1989). Even if one accepts the assumptions linking together level of socioeconomic development and form of regime, the Turkish case illustrates that social pluralism can produce unmanageable conflict.

State and class

Another approach which has been used to account for economic and political change is the state-centred one. Arguments cluster around the issue of the autonomy and relative autonomy of the state from class interests and class pressures. Originating from the dependency school and French neo-Marxism, the focus has been on the nature of, and links between, dependent capitalism, the state and the bourgeoisie. There is an extensive general literature on these topics and a growing number of case studies treating aspects of Middle Eastern political economy, the richest of which deal with Egypt (Cooper, 1983; Waterbury, 1983; Moore, 1986). We shall make brief reference to these and note a particular problem for the analysis of political liberalization. Cooper has grounded his arguments about Egypt on the nature of state capitalism, and concluded that there is a tendency towards cyclical moves between state and private capital, and shifts between authoritarianism and liberalization. John Waterbury has argued that the Egyptian state remains autonomous of classes and mediates and balances between them. Without stating it explicitly, Moore sees a relative autonomy with some potential for class power independent of the state. He has concluded that although economic liberalization in its early stages was a tactic to maintain state authoritarianism, the process has decreased the autonomy of the state to the extent that there could possibly be a transition to political pluralism.

Although these kinds of explanations are more fruitful than those deriving from modernization theories, there is a problem in proving the relative power of the state and classes. Changing patterns of the distribution of class and state benefits provide some evidence, but whether they are indicative of changing state strategies and coalition support-building rather than class power remains unclear. Springborg has provided an excellent analysis of class power through a case study of decision-making (Springborg, 1989), but while case studies do provide insights they are somewhat episodic.

The kinds of studies mentioned above are particularly relevant for understanding the extent to which political liberalization is linked to or has originated from the state, particular classes or some combination of segments of both. As we shall see below, the evidence is episodic and possibly too impressionistic to provide a full answer. There is a certain advantage, however, to be gained from a comparative analysis.

The legacy of the past: from quasi-democracy to state-led development

The contemporary connections between economic and political liberalization must be placed in their historical context because the social and political consequences of the statist period determine the capacity and will of regimes to introduce economic liberalization measures and also shape political responses to their implementation. The constellation of interests and beneficiaries which emerged or were promoted in this period will be affected by economic policies which are detrimental to them.[1] As Waterbury has pointed out bluntly: 'One must be clear that the process of economic adjustment and reform entails social pain' (Roe et al., 1989: 55).

The package of policies associated with economic liberalization, if fully implemented, will produce advantage and disadvantage for groups within society and within the state, changing class balances and the social bases of regimes. Cutting state expenditure, removing subsidies from consumer items and public-sector industry, shifting from protectionism to more liberal trade regimes, introducing market mechanisms for wages and interest rates, privatizing state-owned concerns and encouraging foreign investment have been and will continue to be risky ventures for Middle Eastern governments. Introducing such measures at a time of world economic recession compounds the problems.

The process of political liberalization is as fraught with difficulty as the economic. While economic liberalization affects vested interests built up in the statist period and challenges ideologies associated with it, political reform re-introduces two political issues which were central to the demise of the post-colonial order and the transition to authoritarian-statism. First, the revival of parties and assemblies re-introduces institutions which, in the past, were operated by and for narrow ruling groups and were linked with the retention of Western influence and a Western form of government. Second, the enhanced external presence following from economic liberalization (through the roles played by the IMF, World Bank, bilateral aid agencies and direct foreign investment) cuts against strong nationalist ideological currents. Although the nationalism which was associated with authoritarian-statism never broke ties to international capitalism and capitalist states, nationalism, in its different forms, is still a powerful mobilizing force in the Middle East and North Africa. Even in Turkey, where Ataturkism fused Westernization with nationalism, there remain powerful sentiments against external influence.

It is important to stress this past inter-relationship between nationalism, parliamentary institutions and the authoritarian-statist period for three reasons:

- the kinds of institutions which are currently being introduced as part of political liberalization have been discredited in the past;
- the ruling groups which operated them were overthrown by social forces which had no ideological commitment to political liberalism or democratization, and there is no evidence to believe that those currently re-introducing parties and assemblies have undergone some ideological transformation;
- although the authoritarian-statist period has ended in severe economic crisis, the core of the nationalisms associated with that period has not been totally eroded.

In the following brief review the focus will be on the Fertile Crescent, but authoritarian-statists in North Africa took a similarly dim view of parties, elections and assemblies.

The assemblies originally established in the Middle Eastern-mandated territories continued after independence, as did the Egyptian parliament after formal independence in 1936. Although kings, presidents and prime ministers followed the colonial precedent of rigging elections and banning radical parties, and there were occasional military interventions, parliaments played a significant political role between 1946–58 and 1961–3 in Syria, 1932–58 in Iraq, 1936–52 in Egypt and 1946–75 in Lebanon. In most Middle Eastern states, the dominant political groups were landowners, many of whom were also tribal leaders and merchants. The concentration of land-holding was marked, such that several hundred families owned the bulk of the land: in Egypt in 1952 the top 1 per cent owned around 72 per cent of the land, in Syria 2.5 per cent owned 75 per cent and in Iraq 2.8 per cent owned 70 per cent. The great majority of the assembly members were from these families, their power deriving from control over their tenants and sharecroppers. They had no interest in abandoning the institutions which buttressed their power, enabled them to block land reform and to which they were elected and re-elected by a captive peasantry.

Although radical and reformist parties emerged in the parliamentary period and some of their members won elections in urban constituencies, politics was dominated by shifting blocs and coalitions of landowners. Governments were formed from the more enlightened urban-based landlords, former officials or co-opted technocrats, and rose and fell without disturbing landlord control or the power of the landlords over their peasants. The inability of new groups to break this stranglehold brought an end to the first phase of quasi-democracy. The expansion of education brought forth new strata, made up of teachers, bureaucrats, technicians and engineers. Patronage and co-optation ceased to be a viable means of including opposition and potential opposition, and industrial development was insufficient to provide adequate employment.

The new middle strata provided the social base for reformist and radical parties, which were nationalist and developmentalist. The exclusionary nature of the parliaments was an important factor in discrediting liberal, representative institutions in the eyes of these new groups. Furthermore, governments and parliaments were associated with nationalist failures or betrayals of nationalism: they had agreed to unequal treaties with the former colonial power, had permitted the establishment of foreign military bases, had been unable to achieve Arab unity (and at times had actively opposed it), and had been responsible for the establishment of Israel and for defeat in the 1948 Arab–Israeli war. Arab unity, full national independence, reform and industrialization were viewed as having been blocked by a representative system which had perpetuated the rule of landlords (through governments drawn from or linked to them).

Change came through the seizure of state power by reformist officers, after prolonged periods of nationalist and reformist agitation. Relations between officers and civilian political movements varied. In the case of Egypt in 1952 and Iraq in 1958, it was an indirect one. In the case of Syria, the Ba'th party purposely pursued a policy of recruiting officer members or sending civilian party members to the military academy. Whatever the civil-military relationship, expanding the scope of democratic institutions had little or no priority. In Jordan and Iran, where pro-Western regimes survived, the nationalist-reformist threat inaugurated a more centralized repressive authoritarianism, but under monarchs rather than officer-presidents.

Although history does not necessarily repeat itself, some general conclusions can be drawn from the preceding review which are relevant for the contemporary process of liberalization. In the early period of quasi-democracy a specific ruling group sustained the operation of faction-based parties and assemblies (in a controlled and circumscribed fashion), but only as long as these institutions sustained the political and economic power of the ruling group. As a result, the institutions were discredited. In the subsequent period neither military officers nor the 'state salariat' nor the 'middle sectors' had any interest in expanding participation or in ensuring the greater accountability of governments through such institutions. The operation of post-colonial quasi-parliamentarianism had the effect of marginalizing those of a liberal, democratic or social-democratic persuasion.

Yet the current phase of political liberalization is based partly on these earlier discredited institutional forms, the maintenance of which served the interests of coherent ruling groups. Whether Middle Eastern social formations have been sufficiently transformed to sustain such institutions is questionable. The absence of ideological support or a social base for the new system raises further questions about its sustainability. Liberalization or democratization would seem to have little future without liberals or democrats and there is little evidence that those who promoted this process were of either persuasion. To the contrary, King Husain of Jordan, Zine el-Abidine Ben Ali of Tunisia and Chadhli Ben Jadid of Algeria were directly associated with the earlier authoritarian period. Continuing with this ideological theme, it is worth emphasizing that one success of the authoritarian-statist regimes was popular mobilization through nationalism, and it is ironic that many aspects of economic liberalization policies have impinged, and will impinge in the future, on nationalist sentiment, whether based on secular or Islamist ideas.

Contemporary economic and political liberalization

If economic liberalization entails political risks for governments, and the credentials of those introducing political liberalization are suspect, any analysis must deal with the question of why such changes have been initiated. In brief, severe domestic economic crises involving high levels of debt paved the way for international financial institutions to secure the compliance of indebted states for economic reform policies. Since the chapter by Niblock deals at some length with the origins of economic liberalization, and the continuing external press-ures sustaining it, we shall focus here on the links between economic liberalization and the introduction of political liberalization. Whether there will be a transition to democracy or a breakthrough to pluralism is a matter of speculative debate. What is clear is that both economic and political liberalization have been partial.

There is a range of explanations as to why the extent and intensity of economic liberalization have been limited, despite the declared commitment of governments to implement liberalization policies as a way out of economic predicaments. Some responsibility can be placed on bureaucratic inefficiencies and inertia. Much more significant in slowing down the liberalization process, however, have been the political risks which accompany the process. The early stages of economic liberalization have given rise to popular protest. The reduction of public expenditure, particularly for consumer subsidies, has resulted in riots and demonstrations in Egypt, Jordan and Tunisia. Depressed wage levels have been factors in increasing labour militancy. The crisis of urban housing and employment in Algeria has produced a violent and volatile mass politics. Limited and partial liberalization is a rational political strategy for governments and bureaucrats, and it accounts for much of what World Bank economists call slippage. Although regimes have attempted to balance differential social advantage and disadvantage, inequalities have and will inevitably go along with the process. Even though the statist period produced inequalities of its own and left as many in poverty at the end as at the beginning, the introduction of economic reform contemporaneous with austerity has inaugurated new patterns of inequality.

Outside powers, moreover, may have an interest in supporting a limited and partial pattern of liberalization. States like Turkey and Egypt can count, and have counted, on their strategic significance to reduce pressures from international financial institutions. Even in the period of Soviet decline, the importance to the West of maintaining the social and political stability of such states has remained great. The ties between France and her former North African colonies, and North Africa's proximity to Europe, give EC states a considerable interest in a stable Algeria, for example. Another factor which impinges on Algeria concerns oil: oil-producing states like Algeria count on oil and gas prices rising in the future, and may decide to stall any extensive implementation of liberalization policies.

There are also internal imperatives influencing the behaviour of the external financial institutions directly associated with the implentation of liberalization measures. The World Bank, for example, provides funds to compensate for social disruption and these go some way to boost government spending (Kirkpatrick and Onis, 1991). This, however, may not be sufficient to avoid unrest. Social protest provides Middle Eastern regimes with valid and valuable arguments against agencies which are seeking to accelerate policies of structural adjustment and stabilization. Although there is some debate about whether political instability is a consequence of structural adjustment, or whether it is a consequence of inflation which can be prevented by

structural adjustment, the evidence provided by analysts is not sufficiently strong for the agencies to be able to assert that they were not
the authors of chaos (Haggard and Kaufman, 1989). One further
factor which can facilitate intentional slippage is the bureaucratic
politics of agency rivalry, which, as Springborg has pointed out,
allowed the Egyptian government, for a time, some bargaining power
(Springborg, 1989).

The implementation of economic liberalization, then, has remained
partial. Middle Eastern states are at a variety of different stages within
the process. Even in Turkey, a decade after the establishment of a
structural adjustment and stabilization programme, 55 state enterprises still account for 33 per cent of output and absorb 60 per cent
of public investment, and the government, through its Public Participation Fund, is purchasing shares of the privatized PETKIM petro-
chemical complex.[2] The two states with longer experience of economic
and political reform, Turkey and Egypt, are indicative of a general
pattern which later liberalizers appear to be following: *Economic
liberalization sets constraints on political liberalization, and although a
degree of political liberalization can facilitate the introduction of economic
reform measures, the social and political consequences of such measures put
limits on the extent of political reform. As a result of this symbiosis and
dialectical tension between the two processes, economic liberalization is
marked by progress and regress and political liberalization is authoritarian,
cautious and controlled.*

As pointed out earlier, in Turkey economic liberalization was
introduced under authoritarian auspices. The return to parliamentary
democracy in November 1983 did not mark a return to the *status quo
ante*. Although there was a resumption of multi-party politics, there
were restrictions on political activities. The freedoms of trade unionists and trade union organizations, and the autonomy of universities
were curtailed. Furthermore, the re-introduction of elections and the
pursuit of electoral victory by the Motherland party affected the
extension of economic liberalization in a way that 'increased the state's
discretionary power and control over the distribution of economic
resources' (Kirkpatrick and Onis, 1991: 32). In other words, political
re-liberalization expanded the role of the state and had a negative
effect on economic reform.

This dynamic interplay between the two processes is not simply a
function of competitive elections and electoral coalition-building. In
Egypt over the last fifteen years, there have been some advances in

economic reform and a degree of stalling, while political liberalization has oscillated between rigorous governmental control and relatively free elections. It is not that these inter-related processes induce paralysis in policy, but that they influence each other in both positive and negative ways, to some of which we shall now turn.

The two majors factors influencing the introduction, form and nature of political liberalization are the economic liberalization process, and the tactics and strategy of regime survival. Both have resulted in greater political freedoms, accompanied by attendant political controls. Although there have been both organized and spontaneous pressures from below, the process has been one of controlled authoritarian liberalization. Freedom to organize and register political parties, to participate in local and national elections and to publish more freely have been promoted, along with some legal guarantees. Governments have, however, retained control through legal and administrative means. In Tunisia, Algeria and Egypt, restrictive voting thresholds have been placed on party representation in national assemblies. There are government restrictions on the content of political programmes and party policies. Ministries of the Interior vet party finance and are in control of party registration. Provincial and local administrations have the power to ban election meetings and rallies. In Tunisia, there are limits to the criticisms that can be made of government officials. Electoral laws have been designed, and where they have not worked re-designed, and constituencies drawn to ensure that rulers and their parties and factions are not edged aside. The example of Turkey's first multi-party election in 1950, when President Inonu inaugurated free elections and lost, has not been replicated. Presidents Sadat and Mubarak of Egypt, Ben Ali of Tunisia, Ben Jadid of Algeria and King Husain of Jordan have not lost their positions as a direct result of elections and retained their power to form governments and shape government policy. Symbolic of government caution was Algeria's introduction of free elections at the local level only. The attempt to hold national elections undermined the power of the FLN, the ruling party.

Similar in consequence to legal and administrative controls has been the process of liberalization by élite consensus. In Tunisia and Jordan, the president and king (respectively) organized discussions with key figures and organizations to ensure agreement on the rules of procedure and opposition behaviour.[3] The first agreed principle of the Jordanian National Pact asserts, unsurprisingly, that the form of government is a 'parliamentary monarchy' based on respect for the constitution. Much is made of the 'democratic revolution' of 'political, party and thought pluralism', but the origins of Jordanian political liberalization lie with the riots in the south which resulted from the reduction in government subsidies on a range of items. Another section of the pact binds the participants to the maintenance of 'social peace' and, in effect, depoliticizes the very sensitive issues growing out of economic liberalization. A similar set of assumptions is apparent in the Tunisian National Pact (Anderson, 1991). The stress on pluralism is paralleled by one on national unity and the legitimacy of the existing political structure. So far, this has not led to any real power-sharing and, to the seeming consternation of the president, did not even produce a single seat for the new parties in the elections.

Consensualism from above has gone along with more traditional co-optative practices. Key opposition figures have been brought into positions in the Jordanian National Assembly and into the Tunisian cabinet. This consensual and co-optative process establishes constraints on politicians, parties, movements and individuals. It creates a means whereby they can be legitimately excluded from politics if they do not follow the new rules of the game so voluntarily agreed on.

A further, and somewhat contradictory, facet of the introduction of political reform is that it has in some respects strengthened the position of rulers. This has occurred in different ways. In Jordan, given the difficult economic decisions which have to be made, the king has benefited from being able to place greater responsibility on government and parliament for domestic policy-making. In states where party and state had been fused, the unravelling of this connection, in the early stages at least, has increased the powers of presidents and the factions around them. Such a process can be noted in Sadat's Egypt, and in Algeria and Tunisia. Furthermore, where new rulers have succeeded long-established nationalist figures, for example, Nasser, Boumedienne and Bourguiba, the introduction of an apparently more liberal political process has enhanced the standing of the new ruler without involving any derogation from their effective power.

It is also the case that political reform has at times facilitated the introduction of economic liberalization. In Egypt, Anwar Sadat's opening of the political system to *manabir* from within the Arab Socialist Union furnished him with allies against political and bureaucratic forces resistant to economic liberalization. In Algeria, after consolidating his power within a military faction (Zartman, 1984), Ben

Jadid utilized political liberalization to counter opposition from FLN apparatchiks, state economic managers and high bureaucrats accustomed to economic privilege, high status and a great deal of power and influence. It has even been suggested that the Algerian president would not have been unfavourable to the Islamic Salvation Front (FIS) attaining around 30 per cent of the vote in the 1990 local elections, with this objective in mind (Burgat and Leca, 1990). Co-operating with a FIS majority in the national assembly after their electoral victory in the December 1991–January 1992 elections turned out to be another matter.

The privileges which accrued to the anti-reformist, state and state-party based groups during the statist period have limited the ability of the latter to forge alliances with those groupings which have been hurt by cuts in public spending and by other austerity measures. Economic liberalization erodes the position of statist élites, and political liberalization undermines their ability to organize support. While economic liberalization hits the pockets of the poor, political liberalization has had the effect of fragmenting the political mobilization of their discontent as austerity measures bite. Counting on a fragmented opposition, however, has only been partially successful. In Jordan, Algeria and Tunisia a great range of parties and movements has surfaced: parties of left, right and centre, Islamist movements and, in Algeria, Berber parties. Despite earlier prohibitions against parties which were based on religion and ethnicity governments proceeded to register them, possibly on the basis of divide and rule tactics. In some cases, these latter have simply not worked. The electoral success of FIS in Algeria and the activism of the Nahda party in Tunisia produce the prospect of 'rule' gaining ascendancy over 'divide'. Nevertheless, the tactic of fragmenting the Islamist movement in Egypt has not been without achievement, and this seems the likely route for the Algerian regime.

It should also be emphasized that, given the partial nature of the progress of economic liberalization, governments still have considerable patronage at their disposal. The public sectors in the states we have mentioned are still large, a great deal of employment is governmental and many of the resources which flow into the rural sectors come from the state. As has been pointed out in the case of Turkey, governments can still utilize resource distribution as a vehicle of coalition building, whether or not there are elections.

Conclusions

In general, presidents and kings remain in charge of a state-controlled process of partial liberalization, which has its origins in strategies of economic reform and regime survival. The assertion of a civil society, autonomous of the state and organized through political parties, is not yet part of the picture, although continuing economic reforms and an electoral process might bring that about. It is more likely, however, that the more full-blooded and intense economic liberalization becomes (and privatization of state-owned concerns could be a pivotal issue here), the stronger the tendency will be for a retreat to a stricter authoritarianism. It is certainly possible that the partial incorporation of new parties into politics will create an impossible tension between the parties' accountability to government (for their good behaviour) and their accountability to their constituencies. At the present time, the newly emergent political institutions are accountable to government rather than vice versa. If, however, there are many years of austerity ahead, and if privatization increases unemployment substantially and the economic reforms generate neither growth nor employment, the differences of interest between opposition movements and reformist governments are likely to become greater. Such differences could predominate over a common commitment to political liberalization.

We would conclude that at the present conjuncture there is an uncertain and unpredictable balance between the two processes. Economic crises have brought about some degree of economic liberalization, and the latter has been a factor in establishing a process of political liberalization. Yet the introduction of political liberalization under conditions of economic reform can sustain or re-introduce authoritarian forms of rule. Political liberalization also has a backward linkage, in that it can act as a brake on economic liberalization.

Underpinning the balance and tension between the two processes, and playing a determinant role in the longer term, is the relationship between state and class. Even though there have been societal pressures for reducing authoritarian controls, the process of political liberalization has been state-induced, and the state retains a considerable degree of management over the process. In its turn, economic liberalization has changed and is likely further to change the political balance between classes, shape new social inequalities and create different patterns of access to the state. It is the volatility of these latter processes which is likely to determine whether political liberalization is maintained in its current partial form, extended into a process of democratization, or ushers in a new period of authoritarianism.

Notes

1 See Waterbury's advice to princes introducing structural adjustment, in Roe, Roy and Sengupta (1989).
2 'Turkey', *Financial Times Survey*, 20/5/91.
3 al-Mithaq al-Watani al-Urduni, Min. of Information Amman, nd.

4· INTERNATIONAL AND DOMESTIC FACTORS IN THE ECONOMIC LIBERALIZATION PROCESS IN ARAB COUNTRIES

Tim Niblock

Structural adjustment and economic liberalization

Much of this chapter is concerned with the role which the International Monetary Fund (IMF) has played in promoting structural adjustment. Some clarification, therefore, is required of the relationship between structural adjustment and economic liberalization. Structural adjustment stemmed from international economic developments occurring in the mid- to late-1970s: the major changes in international prices, interest rates, financial markets and trading conditions which took place at that time. Economies which were affected adversely by these changes needed assistance in adjusting to the new conditions. At first, the IMF's main emphasis was on stabilization. In the 1980s (especially in the later part of the decade) however, the IMF began to press for more fundamental reforms: reshaping the public sector, providing a framework within which the private enterprise could thrive, liberalizing trade and banking, and undertaking a strategy of privatization. More recently, IMF concern seems to have spread to some political spheres: institutional reform, capacity-building and governance (Cassen, 1991: 1–2). World Bank policy has, of course, complemented that of the IMF. By the end of the 1980s, nearly one-third of new World Bank lending was devoted to programme loans which contained specific policy reform conditions.

Although the IMF's main interest in economic liberalization relates to the later roles, the stabilization policy also carried with it aspects of economic liberalization. Some of the stabilization measures were intended to encourage incentives, especially in promoting exports. Moreover, the insistence on bringing the economy into balance involved reducing budget deficits, and this in turn usually meant cutting state expenditure and depending more on private investment, domestic and foreign, and private enterprise. In the words of Richards and Waterbury:

> Successful structural adjustment will require at a minimum reduced government spending, a shift of investment resources from the urban to the rural sector and from the public to the private sector; a move away from a planned economy to one in which the market plays a major role in allocating resources; and, in the most general sense, a move to an economy in which equity concerns may be 'temporarily' sacrificed to those of efficiency. (Richards and Waterbury, 1990: 230)

Economic liberalization, class and the international economy

It is evident that the initiation of programmes of economic liberalization is in part the response of the state to the economic difficulties engendered by existing economic policies. This, however, does not tell us why the state chooses this particular strategy, that of economic liberalization, for the resolution of its economic problems. Other strategies might have been 'adopted. Nor does it account for the specific characteristics of the economic liberalization programme which the state adopts.

In the field of political economy, two main kinds of explanation have been put forward to account for the trend towards economic liberalization in underdeveloped countries. The first emphasizes the international dimension. The integrative tendencies in contemporary international capitalism, it is contended, make it increasingly difficult for states to pursue an autonomous form of economic development. If production is to expand effectively, it needs to make use of the technology, resources and expertise which are available internationally. This can only be acquired through trade or through foreign investment. The economy therefore needs to be either attractive to foreign investors or capable of exporting competitively, or both. Either process involves structuring the economy in ways which are cost-effective in capitalist terms. The economic arguments, in this interpretation, link in closely with political pressures. International financial bodies, such as the IMF and the World Bank, and great power policies play an active role in bringing about the political and economic changes which enable national economies to be integrated into the international economy.[1]

The second line of analysis focuses on the social structure of underdeveloped countries. The reformist/revolutionary state-form established in many third world countries after the colonial era has, it is contended, in-built tendencies which make it transitional. On the one hand, the top-heavy nature of the political institutions which are set up weakens spontaneous political organisation – such that even those social groupings whose interests are served by radical policies lack any strong organisation, and thus any ability to prevent policies from changing. On the other hand, the reformist/revolutionary state breeds a state bureaucracy, whose interests ultimately run counter to a further strengthening of egalitarian tendencies. The state bureaucrats, moreover, accumulate funds and begin to seek investment opportunities, thereby developing strong links with the commercial bourgeoisie. The reformist/revolutionary state, therefore, is gradually transformed into a bourgeois-bureaucratic state – built on the linked interests of the state bureaucrats and the commercial bourgeoisie, and having a strong interest in opening up the economy and providing opportunities for investment.[2]

The two lines of analysis are, of course, not mutually exclusive. Each set of factors may provide some of the impetus towards the introduction of reform programmes. Nevertheless, it is important to try to assess the relative importance of each, for this can clarify the dynamics which surround economic liberalization programmes.

The theme pursued in this chapter is that while domestic developments may have laid the basis for governments in the Arab world to undertake economic liberalization, the liberalization which has stemmed from this basis has been limited. Rather than reflecting the rise of a bourgeoisie which is strong enough to control the state apparatus, forcing the state apparatus to withdraw from large areas of economic activity and hand these over to private invetsment and enterprise, the economic liberalization process has been constricted by the dependence of the commercial bourgeoisie on the state. The bourgeois-bureaucratic state, in short, does not have a strong interest in the structural transformation of the economy; only in a limited opening up of trade and investment opportunities. The gains which the private sector make depend heavily on the privileged relations which businesses have with state institutions (or, perhaps, with particular

Table 4.1: *Total External Public and Private Debt of Main Arab Debtor Countries, 1970–88*

Country	Total long-term debt (outstanding and disbursed) Millions of dollars		Total long-term debt (outstanding and disbursed) As a percentage of GNP		Total interest payments on long-term debt (millions of dollars)		Total long-term debt service as a percentage of: GNP		Total long-term debt service as a percentage of: Export of goods and services	
	1970	1988	1970	1988	1970	1988	1970	1988	1970	1988
Sudan	298	8,418	14.8	74.6	12	19	1.7	0.6	10.6	9.5
Yemen AR	–	2,378	–	41.7	–	56	–	3.4	–	16.0
Egypt	1,714	43,259	22.5	126.7	56	729	4.8	4.4	38.0	16.6
Morocco	727	18,767	18.6	89.8	25	814	1.7	6.5	9.7	25.1
Tunisia	541	6,121	38.6	64.2	18	380	4.7	11.5	19.7	25.5
Jordan	119	3,955	22.9	94.0	2	239	.9	19.6	3.6	31.9
Syria	233	3,685	10.8	25.0	6	119	1.7	2.6	11.3	21.1
Algeria	945	23.229	19.8	46.6	10	1,809	.9	12.7	4.0	77.0
Yemen PDR	1	1,970	–	199.4	0	31	–	10.8	0.0	46.5

Source: *Word Development Report 1990*. (World Bank, Washington, 1990).

individuals in the latter). The common view that the commercial bourgeoisie and the bureaucratic bourgeoisie have conflicting interests (with the former favouring the dismantlement of the public sector, and the latter opposing such moves) is, it is contended, incorrect.

The trend towards intensified economic liberalization in the late 1980s, this chapter argues, has been brought about largely by international factors. In a number of Arab states, this period has seen the dismantlement of significant parts of the public sectors, moving well beyond simply allowing the private sector more leeway. The channel through which the international dimension has impinged on Arab governments is that of indebtedness. The scale and characteristics of the foreign debt owed by the main Arab debtor countries in 1988 are presented in Table 4.1. A comparison is given of the debt which these countries owed in 1970, so as to show how the burden has risen. The International Monetary Fund has acted as the instrument through which the integration of the Arab economies into the international capitalist system has been forwarded.

Three cases of economic liberalization in the Arab world will be examined below, those of Algeria, Egypt and Iraq.

The case of Egypt

As can be said of so many aspects of political and economic life in the Arab world, more information related to economic liberalization is available on the case of Egypt (and more insight can be gained from this case) than for any other Arab state. Hence the space devoted in this chapter to Egypt. It will be shown below that the pursuit and shaping of economic liberalization programmes in Egypt over the 1987–91 period has depended greatly on pressures exerted from outside (largely the IMF). The Egyptian state emerges as a rather reluctant partner in the process.

The background: economic liberalization, 1972–87

The record of economic liberalization in Egypt prior to 1987 has been written about extensively (see the bibliography for some references), so it will not be covered in detail here. As is well known, the framework for that liberalization was provided by Law 43 of 1974, and its amendment through Law 32 of 1977. These laws provided for the opening up of the Egyptian economy to foreign investment; protection of investment against nationalization and confiscation; tax exemption for new investment, covering varying periods depending on the field of activity; and the recognition that private companies would not be subject to legislation or regulations covering public sector enterprises and their employees. Galal Amin has described this period, accurately, with the phrase 'from premature to half-hearted liberalisation' (El-Naggar, 1987: 98). The country was opened up to investment, but very little was done to dismantle or weaken state control over the economy.

Towards dismantling state controls: the basis of Egypt's dependence on the IMF after 1987

It is probably easier to bring out the international dimension in Egypt's recent trajectory towards economic liberalization than it is in the case of any other Arab country. Although economic liberalization has, in some way, been an aspect of Egyptian government policy since the early 1970s, the particular role of the IMF in guiding, and indeed forcing, the current increased pace of economic reform can be easily documented.

The leverage which the IMF has had over Egypt, and conversely the weakness of the Egyptian government's position, stems from the size of the Egyptian national debt. By the middle of 1988, total external debt came to about $45 billion (of which the military debt composed about $10 billion). The ratio of debt service to current account receipts was 45 per cent, and the ratio of total debt to Gross

Domestic Output was 115 per cent. The current account deficit for 1986/7 was $1.3 billion, and that for 1987/8 was $1 billion.[3] Much of the debt had been acquired in the late 1970s or early 1980s, when credit was easy to obtain. Many of the loans were contracted at high fixed interest rates, repayable after an eight-year grace period over 30 years. The burden of repayment, therefore, only began to be felt fully at the end of the decade.

The 1987 IMF standby credit: the agreement and its demise
The phase of intensified pressure by the IMF to bring about structural economic reform in Egypt began early in 1988. The context, however, was set by the standby credit which the IMF had agreed to make available to Egypt in May 1987, and by the IMF's perception that the reforms which the Egyptian government had promised were not being pursued in earnest.

Discussions between the IMF and the Egyptian government over the granting of a standby credit, which would be followed by the re-scheduling of Egyptian debt by the Club of Paris, had begun in 1985. Initially the IMF had sought wide-ranging reforms, involving the phasing out of consumer subsidies and the raising of energy and agricultural prices, but in the face of concerted resistance from the Egyptian government (which succeeded in mobilizing some support from the US government) a more modest package was agreed.

The letter of intent which underlay the standby credit envisaged a 2 per cent rise in the domestic lending rate (leaving this rate still well below the rate of inflation), a gradual shift to a floating exchange rate (whereas an immediate and complete float had originally been sought), and a reduction of the budget deficit from 15 per cent for the 1986/7 fiscal year to 13 per cent for 1987/8. The longer-term goals of liberalizing the public sector and raising energy and agricultural prices were acknowledged in the standby credit agreement, but no timetable for their implementation was stipulated.[4]

The value of the credit was SDR250 million ($325 million), to be drawn over 18 months. Egypt's main benefit from the credit, however, came through the subsequent re-scheduling of part of the country's $40,000 million (approx.) external debt. In June 1987, a Paris Club deal was concluded, covering all of Egypt's payments falling due between January and June 1987 on government and officially-backed civilian and military loans. The total amount re-scheduled by OECD countries and their banks came to about $7 billion, with an additional

$4 billion owed to Arab creditors.[5] All of the accords with creditors were signed by July 1988, except for one with Japanese creditors which was signed in December of that year.

The Egyptian government had good reason to feel pleased with what it had achieved. In a speech to the Egyptian people's assembly on 29 December, when the main lines of the understanding with the IMF were becoming apparent, prime minister Atif Sidqi said: 'In the talks which the government is conducting with the IMF and World Bank . . . the government's actions are dictated first and foremost by Egypt's interests. The goverment will not accept any conditions which contradict these interests'.[6] Such statements were to be repeated in future years, often to counter the impression of weakness when concessions were made. But on this occasion the sentiments were probably genuine: the government had effectively resisted the imposition of reforms by the IMF. A senior IMF official resigned in protest at the pressure which the United States government had exerted in securing the standby credit for Egypt (and one for Zaire agreed at the same time).[7]

Satisfaction with the conclusion of the agreement, however, was only short-lived. By the beginning of 1988, it was clear that the programme of reforms was inoperative. From the IMF's perspective, the adjustment of the domestic interest rates and the minor changes in the currency exchange system were inadequate measures of economic reform. The budget deficit appeared to be growing, and no action seemed to be envisaged on cutting consumer subsidies or on raising agricultural and energy prices.[8] The Egyptian government's response to this was that the reform process had been pressed as far as was politically and economically feasible at that time; any further pressure on the poor would lead to political unrest.

IMF pressure and Egyptian governmental resistance,
January–December 1988

The first six months of 1988 saw the IMF laying out in detail the reforms which now needed to be undertaken. The IMF called for 'shock treatment' to open up the Egyptian economy, insisting that this should be carried out before any new standby arrangement could be agreed (the May 1987 arrangement was due to run out in November 1988). The exchange rate system should be fully liberalized; energy (especially electricity) prices should rise by 30 per cent by 1 July, and further thereafter until they reached international levels; interest rates should rise from about 13 per cent to at least the rate of inflation (20–25 per cent); the informal sector (especially the Islamic investment companies) should be regularized; subsidies should be reduced; and the budget deficit should be reduced to within 10 per cent of GDP (from the intended level of 13 per cent for 1987).[9]

The Egyptian government responded by making some of the changes requested, but not all; and not the most substantial ones. In March 1988, some further liberalization of the exchange rate system was introduced: all remaining commercial bank foreign exchange transactions were moved to the free market bank rate of $1 = £E2.25. The central bank rate of $1 = £E0.70, however, continued to apply for oil exports, Suez Canal revenues, and Ministry of Trade imports of basic commodities.[10] If the exchange rate for the latter were changed, commodity prices would immediately be affected, and that was deemed politically unacceptable. In May, nonetheless, the prices of some subsidized basic commodities (petrol, cigarettes and building materials) were raised, and at the same time a law was introduced to regularize the activities of Islamic investment companies.[11]

With regard to the other reforms proposed by the IMF, the Egyptian government's position was that they would impinge seriously on the standard of living of the mass of the population and could not be implemented. The determination not to cut significantly the level of state subsidies and overall state expenditure was indicated by the government's budget projection for 1988/9, which was made public in June 1988. The projected budget deficit was almost 50 per cent higher than that for the previous year, coming to 16 per cent of GDP.[12] The government strongly opposed raising interest rates to the 20–25 per cent requested by the IMF, and described the proposed energy price rises as excessive. The transition to a free market exchange rate, the government maintained, would take several years.[13]

Talks between the two sides continued through the second half of 1988, particularly during the visit of an IMF delegation early in September. The IMF refused to envisage any further credit unless a fuller set of reforms were implemented, while the Egyptian government maintained that reforms of this nature were only feasible in the longer term, preferably with the support of an IMF Extended Fund Facility (EFF), made available over a period of 3–4 years.[14] The political problems which faced the Egyptian government in pursuing an intensified liberalization programme had become apparent in June when the people's assembly blocked the sell-off of a public sector hotel to private investors. The scheme had been put forward by the minister of tourism, Fu'ad Sultan, and involved the sale of the San Stefano Hotel in Alexandria. Government and opposition members of the assembly came together to oppose the sale, forcing the government to retain a stake in the hotel.[15]

Having failed to induce visiting IMF delegations to accept a more flexible approach, President Mubarak sought to strengthen his government's position against further IMF pressure. Describing the IMF's prescriptions as being 'quack medicine', which involved measures which were 'too many and too quick', he encouraged domestic opinion to support the government's stand.[16] More significantly, he attempted to appeal over the heads of the IMF board to Western statesmen (just as he had done, successfully, in December 1986). On a tour of European capitals in September, he warned of the instability which would be unleashed if Egypt was pushed too far and too fast.[17]

Neither tactic proved of value: when talks resumed in January 1989, the IMF had not significantly changed its position.[18] The determination of the IMF to bring about change was evident in comments made by 'Abd al-Shakur Sha'alan, the director of the IMF's Middle East department, in November 1988. He compared Egypt to 'an employee who earns 100 pounds a month, but spends 122', saying that it was absurd that only government employees, small farmers and low-income groups paid tax in Egypt, while rentiers and traders drew all the benefit.[19] In the round of IMF-Egyptian government talks which opened in January 1989 (and which had stalled before the end of the month), the IMF was proposing a tight programme of unifying the exchange rate, cutting the number of jobs in the civil service, and reducing military expenditure.[20]

Egyptian governmental concessions and further IMF demands,
January–December 1989
In the spring of 1989 the Egyptian government made a further set of concessions to the IMF, or at least introduced some changes in policy which were in line with IMF requests. The urgency of reaching an agreement with the IMF was increased by Egypt's commitment to resume payments on its military debt to the United States in July (the debt totalled about $4,550 million, and the interest and repayments due came to about $600 million annually). Failure to make these payments would be followed by the automatic penalties which the US Congress (under the Brooke amendment) had stipulated for non-

payment of military debt. All US aid to Egypt would be suspended once the arrears had been outstanding for a twelve-month period. The overall size of arrears on all official and government-guaranteed debt, moreover, had reached about $2,000 million in July 1989 (since the last re-scheduling period had ended).[21]

In April, electricity prices were raised by 30 per cent, and it was announced that domestic interest rates would rise, albeit only by 2 per cent on deposits and 1 per cent on loans.[22] In May, the actual rise in interest rates occurred, now set at 3 per cent for deposits and 2 per cent for loans, reflecting renewed representations from the IMF.[23] In June, the government released its budget estimates for 1989/90, showing a budget deficit which had been reduced to stay within the IMF proposed limit (10 per cent of GDP). Further moves were made on the exchange rate, with the devaluation of the fixed exchange rate to $1 = £E1.10.[24]

In mid-1989, legislation was completed for the reduction of inheritance tax and for the introduction of a unified investment law, two measures which the IMF had favoured.[25] The investment law, which eventually entered into effect at the end of 1989, involved a considerable loosening of restrictions on investment: easier arrangements for profit remittance, and the removal of some (but not all) price controls. Procedures were laid down for the Investment Authority to deal expeditiously with requests to establish projects.[26]

Perhaps even more indicative of President Mubarak's acceptance that the IMF would have to be accommodated, was the removal of Muhammad 'Abd al-Halim Abu Ghazala from his post as minister of defence and military production at the end of April 1989. Although the factors which brought about Abu Ghazala's removal may be complex, it was widely interpreted as being caused by the minister's refusal to cut the defence budget – a necessity if the IMF-proposed budget targets were to be met. Significantly, the new minister (Yusif Sabri Abu Talib) announced that his first objective would be to lessen the burden of the defence sector on the state and to rationalize the use of resources.[27]

Initially it seemed that the IMF would accept the reforms as an adequate basis on which to arrange a new standby credit. After a series of meeting in late March between IMF and Egyptian government officials in Washington, the IMF indicated that it was broadly satisfied with the policies which the government said it intended to carry out.[28] Prospects for an early agreement appeared to remain bright during the visit of an IMF delegation, headed by 'Abd al-Shakur Sha'alan, to Egypt in June.[29] Shortly after the latter visit, however, the board of the IMF appears to have decided that intentions alone would not be sufficient: a full range of economic reforms would have to be implemented before a further credit was agreed.[30] Talks between the two sides at the end of September failed to break the deadlock.[31]

The main concern on the IMF side seems to have been that the estimates for the budget deficit were unrealistic, and that a more thorough-going pruning of public expenditure would be necessary. It was noted that the budget envisaged subsidies still continuing to grow (by some 6 per cent), and that salaries in the public sector were to grow by 13 per cent.[32] The expectation was that the budget deficit for 1988/9 would equal about 18 per cent of GDP.[33] The IMF was also pressing for a significant devaluation of the central bank exchange rate and for further rises in interest rates. The former had already been devalued to $1 = £E1.10, but was still deemed overvalued in comparison with the commercial bank rate of $1 = £E2.58. The IMF proposed that the central bank rate be devalued immediately to $1 = £E1.40, and that a programme for the elimination of the fixed rate should be adopted. The top interest rates (on deposits) stood at 16.25 per cent, which was still well below the rate of inflation.[34]

The IMF's consideration of the position of Egypt was given an extra dimension by the initiation of a World Bank study of the government's economic reform programme, with a view to the bank subsequently providing funds to support the programme. The World Bank made it clear that no support could be given until the Egyptian government had reached agreement with the IMF. A team to undertake the study was despatched to Cairo in October.[35] One of the proposals which emerged at an early stage in discussions between the team and Egyptian government ministers concerned the reorganization of the Egyptian public sector, involving a reduction of the direct role of government in managing state-owned enterprises, and the possible sale of some 'non-strategic' assets.[36]

President Mubarak again sought the support of Western statesmen in the autumn of 1989, despatching a delegation led by Abu Ghazala (now a presidential adviser) to Paris and Bonn in September.[37] When talks between the IMF and the Egyptian government resumed in the spring of 1990, however, the IMF's requests were much the same as they had been before.

New governmental concessions, continuing IMF demands,
January–June 1990
Over this period the sparring between the two sides continued, with the Egyptian government gradually implementing reforms required by the IMF, but not adopting the full range of reforms which the IMF was seeking. It was clear that the IMF standby credit would not be granted until these reforms were in place. The pressures impelling the Egyptian government to satisfy the IMF had increased further since January 1989: the effective moratorium on servicing the US military debt had now ended; problems had arisen in securing imported food on credit, making it necessary for the government to pay for these in cash; the need for food imports was steadily rising, with imports expected to reach a record value of $4 billion in 1990; Egypt's overall debt had risen to $50 billion; and annual debt servicing charges came to about $2 billion, with arrears estimated at $4–5 billion.[38]

Delegations from both the IMF and the World Bank visited Egypt in February–March 1990. The talks with the latter appear to have had some positive results: a considerable measure of agreement was achieved on a programme for the liberalization of the management and pricing of the Egyptian public sector, which was the World Bank's primary concern. There was also a provisional understanding that the World Bank would provide support for the establishment of a social fund, geared towards mitigating the impact of the government's economic reforms. Approval for a World Bank structural adjustment loan to help finance these measures, however, was made conditional on the Egyptian government reaching agreement with the IMF.

The talks with the IMF revealed the continuing differences between the two sides. The major issues in dispute concerned interest rates, the exchange rate and energy subsidies. With regard to interest rates, the Egyptian government was proposing a further small rise in the top deposit rate (above the existing 16 per cent), together with an understanding that banks would be given greater flexibility in setting rates within a broad framework decided on by the central bank. On the exchange rate, the government suggested a further devaluation of the fixed exchange rate for the central bank pool of foreign currency (from the existing $1 = £E1.10). The IMF was seeking quicker and more far-reaching measures in both of these fields, and included a reduction of 10–20 per cent devaluation in the commercial bank exchange rate. It was also seeking a proper timetable for eliminating all energy subsidies, rather than looking to periodic price increases as had previously been done. Without such a timetable, IMF officials contended, there could be no realistic expectation that the budget deficit could be reduced.[39]

In April–May 1990, the Egyptian government intensified its moves towards economic reform. Further delegations from the IMF were due to visit the country in April and June, and Egyptian officials were also to participate in interim committee meetings held by the IMF in Washington from 6 to 8 May. The government was evidently intent on implementing reforms which would overcome the fund's reluctance to proceed with the standby credit.

At the beginning of April, President Mubarak announced the adoption of a privatization programme, which was to be overseen by the presidential adviser, Abu Ghazala. The framework for the programme had been developed in consultation with the World Bank team which had visited Cairo. The president announced that the 'present phase' involved compiling a list of companies owned by regional authorities, and of mixed-sector firms, which were suitable for sale to the private sector, wholly or partly. The companies considered suitable for transfer to private ownership would include hotels, small-scale state-owned industries, and firms in sectors where the state 'should not have a role', such as food processing, beverages and confectionery. It was made clear that there was no intention of privatizing large industrial units (such as the textile plants at Kafr al-Dawar and Mahalla al-Kubra, the Helwan iron and steel complex, or the Kima fertilizer plant). These were deemed to be of strategic importance.[40]

Also important was a series of price increases for energy and basic commodities which the government announced early in May. These increases, affecting the prices of butane gas, fuel oil, petrol, gas-oil, kerosene, natural gas, flour, rice, pasta and cigarettes, were substantial. The price of butane gas, for example, rose by about 130 per cent (although the new price still only covered about one-quarter of production costs). Other petroleum product prices rose by 30–40 per cent. The price of cigarettes rose by 20 per cent; and the prices of subsidized flour, rice and pasta rose by 35 per cent, 50 per cent and 100 per cent respectively. In addition, it was announced that the price of electricity would rise by 35 per cent in July. The government estimated that the measures affecting energy prices would reduce the annual energy subsidies bill by about £E5 billion ($1,938,000); approximately 25 per cent.[41]

As well as taking the above-mentioned measures, the government indicated that it was prepared to move further towards accepting IMF prescriptions. The government informed the IMF that it was considering devaluing the commercial bank rate by 5 per cent to $1 = £E2.80, and raising interest rates on deposits by two or three percentage points and those on lending rates by one percentage point.[42] The central bank exchange rate was devalued at the beginning of June to $1 = £E2.00.[43]

Following the visit of the IMF team to Cairo in June, the IMF made it clear that the progress towards reform was still insufficient. The areas of disagreement remained centred on the same issues as before: interest rates, the commercial exchange rate and energy prices. The budget deficit was seen as being too high, and the IMF expressed a wish to see the planned deficit for 1990/91 cut by 30 per cent.[44]

Towards an agreement with the IMF, July 1990 to May 1991

New economic reforms brought in by the Egyptian government over this period, largely in keeping with IMF prescriptions, led slowly to the conclusion of an agreement for an IMF standby credit. Although the Gulf crisis occurred at this time, there is little evidence that it affected IMF policy towards Egypt (despite suggestions that the United States was exerting pressure on the IMF to adopt a more understanding posture). The central IMF demands were unchanged, and the reluctance to achieve an agreement before reforms had actually been implemented remained.

An IMF 'technical team' visited Egypt in the later part of August, to monitor the progress which the government was making in implementing the policies which the IMF favoured. An indication of the continuing differences of approach between the two sides can be found in statements made by key participants in late September. Rafiq Suwailim, first undersecretary of the Egyptian ministry of economy and foreign trade, insisted in an interview with *Middle East Economic Digest (MEED)* that economic reforms had to be carried out in stages, and that the clamour for swift action to make the Egyptian pound convertible was not justified. An IMF official, speaking to the same journal, stressed that the IMF would not soften its terms and that 'the focus will be on what Egypt is doing to address its underlying difficulties rather than the short-term problems'.[45]

Following an exchange of letters between the Egyptian government and the IMF in early October,[46] and in the shadow of further IMF visits (in early December, early January and late March), the government introduced some more changes to economic policy. A set of measures to liberalize banking operations was enacted in November. These gave commercial banks greater freedom in setting interest rates, and protected bank accounts from being scrutinized by state organizations.[47] In January the government announced that the only fixed rate for commercial bank lending would be for three-month deposits, and this would be set at 12 per cent.[48] Interest rates in general rose by several percentage points. In February, long-awaited changes to the foreign exchange system were introduced, leaving licensed money-changers free to buy and sell hard currency, setting their own rates for this, subject to some general guidelines. The central bank rate of exchange fell from $1 = £E2.00 to about $1 = £E3,[49] and the commercial bank rate from £E2.70 to £E3.35.[50] It was announced that the rates would be unified within one year.

Attracting more public attention than the measures in the financial sphere was President Mubarak's announcement, at the inauguration of the parliamentary session in mid-December 1990, that the government had adopted a '1,000 days plan' to liberalize the economy and free it from state control. Details of the plan were not made public, but the measures to be taken over a three-year period were said to involve 'boosting the private sector, reducing red tape, and turning Egypt into a Korean-style economic powerhouse'.[51] They included, it seems, the complete removal of all government subsidies on basic foodstuffs; annual energy price rises to bring these prices into alignment with international prices by 1994; the abolition of the system of compulsory sale of particular agricultural products (e.g. wheat, cotton, sugar cane, rice and maize) to the state at set prices; the abolition of the central bank exchange rate, leading to the convertibility of the Egyptian pound; and the undertaking that there would be no fresh government investment in economic ventures.[52] The programme was conveyed to the people's assembly as an exciting governmental initiative, but the dynamics which brought it into being lay elsewhere: the measures composed part of the letter of intent which Mubarak despatched to the IMF early in 1991.

In April, with indications that a deal with the IMF was now possible, new measures were taken to fit in with proposals which the Egyptian government had submitted to the IMF. On 16 April, price rises on subsidized goods and services were announced (35 per cent on electricity, 30 per cent on petrol, and 20 per cent on railway tickets),[53] and on 20 April a bill to introduce a new sales tax of 10 per cent was put before the people's assembly.[54] The government was aiming to reduce the budget deficit to $9\frac{1}{2}$ per cent of GDP in 1991/2, to $6\frac{1}{2}$ per cent in 1992/3, and to $3\frac{1}{2}$ per cent in 1993/4. The intention was, furthermore, to move forward to phasing out most of the subsidies.

On 17 May, the standby agreement with the IMF was finally signed. The strategy of the IMF had now been achieved: Egypt had been made to hold to commitments on reform by means of the IMF insisting that a large part of the agreed reform programme be carried out before a standby credit was approved. The dividends which Egypt drew from the IMF deal were the following:

i An IMF standby credit of $372 million.
ii The restructuring of official debts through the Paris Club. The framework of understanding on this had been worked out in the early months of 1991; its acceptance rested on the IMF deal being concluded. The Paris Club agreement was signed on 25 May.

About $20,000 million in official debts were restructured under this agreement. 30 per cent of the debt was to be written off over 18 months, a further 20 per cent written off after 3 years, and the remaining 50 per cent re-scheduled.

Taken together with the cancellation of Egypt's military debts to the US, and of its debts to Gulf countries, which had been agreed during the Gulf crisis, this meant that Egypt's overall foreign debt would be reduced to about $20 billion.

iii A $300 million World Bank structural adjustment loan, which would be complemented by loans from the European Community and the African Development Bank totalling $250 million.
iv Some $400 millions in loan support from the World Bank, the USAID, Arab financing agencies and European governments for the establishment of a social fund, aimed at offsetting some of the negative social effects of the economic reforms. Particular attention would be paid to providing jobs for young people and promoting local development initiatives.

Conclusion
In short, despite the inclination towards economic liberalization which one would expect in Egypt's bourgeois-bureaucratic state, it has in fact been the external pressure which has played the leading role in the economic liberalization which has occurred in the last few years. Much of the opposition to the reform programmes which was expressed in the Egyptian people's assembly came from within the government party, the National Democratic Party. The government, under pressure from the IMF, had come to pursue an economic liberalization policy which ran counter to interests which were deeply embedded at the centre of the Egyptian state.

The case of Algeria
As with Egypt, external factors have been prominent in promoting economic liberalization in Algeria. In this case, however, the primary external factor has not been that of direct pressure exerted by the IMF, but rather the simple need to manage the large external debt. The government was determined not to lose control of economic policy. It sought, therefore, to find its own solutions to the debt problem, avoiding dependence on the IMF, especially in terms of rescheduling agreements. Paradoxically, however, the solutions which the Algerian government found it necessary to adopt were ones which the IMF might itself have chosen. In order to retain the confidence of the international banking system, to which most of the debt was owed, the government pressed ahead with policies which curbed state intervention in the economy and gave greater scope for the operation of market forces.

State control and changes in economic policy in the early 1980s
The policies which led to the construction of Algeria's state sector were laid down in the immediate aftermath of independence, with further reinforcement and extension after 1965 when Boumedienne took over the national leadership. Both in industry and in agriculture, economic production was brought under close state control. The Charter of the Agrarian Revolution (1972) formalized the division of the country's agricultural land into three sectors: the *autogestion* sector, formed out of the former colonial estates; the agrarian reform sector, organized into production cooperatives; and the residual private sector, 'ranging from micro-holdings to large grazier interests'.[55]

After Chadhli became president in 1978, some changes were made to established policies. These, however, mostly took the form of administrative adaptations, rather than of structural reform. In the industrial, commercial and financial sectors, the 35 or so large *sociétés nationales* which had dominated economic activity in each of these sectors were broken up. In their place there emerged the smaller *entreprises nationales*, which specialized in 'clearly defined production activities, usually separating the functions of production, distribution and marketing' (Sutton, 1990: 7). The numbers of these *entreprises* have been variously estimated at between 322 and 500.[56]

The changes which were instituted in the agricultural sector exhibited, paradoxically, a contrary trend to that found in the industrial/commercial/financial sectors. The 2,099 autogestion estates, and the 5,130 production cooperatives were consolidated into 3,415 *domaines agricoles socialistes* (Sutton, 1990: 26).

In addition to the adaptations to economic policy in the state sector, rather more scope than before was given to private investment. The 1982 *code des investissements* sought to encourage private investment in light manufacturing, craft industry and hotel infrastructure through providing a (rather cautious) range of guarantees, tax advantages and credit facilities.[57] Moreover, the creation of the *domaines agricoles socialistes* was accompanied by a very limited privatization of some agrarian reform land.

The growth of indebtedness in the mid-1980s
Despite being customarily classified as a 'capital rich' country, Algeria had accumulated substantial debts by the mid-1980s. In mid-1986, this debt was believed to stand at about $20 billion, although a subsequent re-assessment suggests that it was in fact slightly larger. With the fall in oil prices and oil exports in 1986 (and the continuing depressed levels of these prices and exports through the late 1980s) the revenues from which this debt could be serviced decreased sharply. Revenues from oil and gas exports, in fact, fell from some $13 billion in 1985 to about $8.3 in 1986. Hydrocarbon exports at this time made up about 97 per cent of the country's total exports. Debt servicing cost the country some $3.5 billion in 1986 (rising to $5.4 billion in 1988), which came to about 40 per cent of export revenues (47.6 per cent in 1988).[58]

Almost the whole of the Algerian debt was acquired at commercial rates and through commercial channels: either loans from international banks or trade-related credits under official insurance or guarantee. Bank for International Settlements estimates in January 1987 placed Algeria's debt to commercial banks alone at $12,590 million, which was substantially more than the commercial debt of any other Middle Eastern state (Egypt's debt to commercial banks, for example, stood at $8,837 million).[59]

In the latter part of 1986, the Algerian central bank sought to raise new loans on the commercial market to cover the country's balance of payments deficit. Despite the bank offering more generous terms than before, however, great difficulty was encountered in securing the funds. The sum raised was substantially less than that which had been sought, and even that was only acquired after some further improvement of the terms offered.[60] Algeria was no longer viewed by international bankers as a good risk.

The problem which the Algerian government faced at the end of 1986 and in early 1987 could have been resolved by the government seeking IMF support and/or arranging for the rescheduling of the country's debts. The government was, however, determined to keep policy-making firmly in Algerian hands. Options which gave external bodies a lever with which they could influence the country's economic policy, therefore, were rejected. The only real choice left to the government now was whether to limit itself to a strategy of austerity, or to seek more wide-ranging reforms aimed at making the economy more productive in the long term (hence reducing the likelihood of the problem of indebtedness arising again). The latter policy was adopted.

Economic liberalization without decreasing the size of the public sector, 1986–88

The economic liberalization programme which the Algerian government pursued between 1986 and 1988 was distinctive (within the Arab world). Its central concern was with the character and functioning of the public sector: the programme sought to retain a strong and dominant public sector, while ensuring that the sector's operation was governed by market principles.

Three main policies were pursued to achieve this objective. The first concerned the banking sector, where the reforms were set in train by the law on banking and credit, passed by the national assembly in August 1986. The law was complemented by the issue of specific regulations, ratified as presidential decrees, over the years which followed (the whole reform was expected to take about five years to implement). The move towards market principles in the banking sector took the form of giving the Banque Centrale d'Algerie greater freedom from bureaucratic control by the ministry of finance, with defined responsibilities (managing the money supply, the dinar exchange rate and the foreign exchange reserves), and giving commercial banks greater autonomy of both the central bank and the ministry. The five commercial banks, all of which were state-owned, were to be left free to choose their local customers and to make their own decisions on loans, within limits set down by an annual *plan national du credit*.[61]

The second field of public sector reform involved giving state-owned companies more freedom in determining their sales and investment programmes, through reducing the role played by supervising ministries. The first public commitment to this policy came in President Chadhli's address to the FLN central committee on 29 December 1986.[62] Exactly one year later, the national assembly approved legislation which laid down a new framework for the operation of the public sector. For the first time, a clear distinction was drawn between the role of annual shareholders' meetings (in which the agents of a state fund, responsible for the management of state shares, would have the predominant voice), boards of directors (which would be left free to determine medium-term strategy), and company managements (which would have the right to run companies on a day-to-day basis).[63]

Companies would now be able to make instant decisions on investments and on dinar or foreign currency financing, compete against each other, and advertise their products. Pricing, employment and salary levels would all be left largely to company managements. Documents resulting from tenders would no longer need to be submitted to ministries.[64]

The expanded independence of state-owned companies was also evident from the modifications made to the economic planning process. The new framework distinguished between long-term planning (still the government's prerogative), the five-year plans (prepared by the ministries after receiving information and projections from companies and departments), and the *plan d'entreprise* (decided by the public companies themselves).

The third area of public sector reform was in agriculture. Law 87–19, passed by the national assembly in December 1987, broke up the *domaines agricoles socialistes*. Ownership of the land which had been held by the *domaines* remained (mostly) in the hands of the state, but the land was divided into smaller units. Usufruct rights were given to smaller agricultural co-operatives (*exploitations agricoles cooperatives* [EAC]). Each EAC had to 'have a minimum of three members, who freely chose their new colleagues . . . Individually or collectively the members of the EAC can after five years sell or pass on their usufruct rights'.[65] By May 1989 there were some 22,028 EACs in existence, with an average of 7 or 8 members each (Sutton, 1990: 16). While the state had retained ownership of the land, then, it had created a system which operated largely by market principles, with more than 22,000 farms competing for the sale of produce.

The significance of the reform programme was emphasized in February 1988, when the Algerian cabinet was re-shuffled, bringing younger and more technocratic ministers into the government. In the same month, the first commercial bank loans to public companies were announced.[66] It was clear that, although economic policy was still being dictated from above, stress was now being put on market mechanisms. Hitherto, ideological commitment to state socialism had outweighed practical considerations such as maintaining food production; now success was being measured in terms of output.

The programme of reform of the public sector was accompanied by some tough austerity measures, the most far-going being introduced in July 1988. The measures were regarded as necessary if the confidence of creditors was to be retained, and if Algeria was to avoid becoming dependent on IMF support. Paradoxically, the overall policy was not dissimilar to that which the IMF itself might have prescribed. The level of imports for the year was cut to $6,042 million (from $10,160 million in 1987), leading to severe shortages of consumer goods, and at the beginning of October a wide range of price rises was announced.

The years 1986–88 saw negative or zero growth in GDP, and by 1988 more than 20 per cent of the work force was unemployed, with 110,000 job seekers joining the labour market every year.[67]

Domestic unrest weakens the government's financial credibility and forces further reforms, 1989–91
The harsh economic conditions facing the Algerian population as a result of the government's policies led to the extensive and violent rioting which occurred in Algeria in the middle of October 1988.[68]

In the wake of the domestic upheaval, the government renewed its assertions that it would not re-schedule its debts, nor seek IMF help. The impact of the upheaval, however, had rendered this line difficult to uphold. Under pressure from international quarters to regularise its external situation, the government turned to the IMF. In November 1988, Algeria drew from its reserves with the IMF, and in March 1989 from the IMF compensatory and country financing facility.[69] In May it negotiated a standby credit with the IMF.[70]

The extent of the IMF's support for Algeria in 1989 (totalling about $1 billion, if one includes World Bank loans which were made possible through the IMF's mediation) put the IMF in a position where it could press for significant policy changes. The reform programme agreed between the two sides in June 1989 envisaged a significant relaxation in the control of prices, salaries and interest rates; a 'shift in the overall economic management to the use of macro-economic instruments from the reliance on administrative targets'; and the placing of the private sector on a more equal setting with the public sector.[71] Some aspects of economic reform had, moreover, been introduced by the Algerian government shortly before the IMF agreement was made, apparently with a view to avoiding difficulties with the IMF. These included a credit programme limiting central bank advances to the economy; changes in exchange and interest rate policies (which fed into price reforms); and a stated intention to pursue a 'prudent' fiscal policy which involved the effective removal of subsidies.[72]

The pace of economic change advanced further following the emergence of Mouloud Hamrouche as prime minister in September 1989. A new reform programme introduced in February 1990 was designed to remove constraints on the flow of capital and on foreign participation in the economy.[73] Also in February, the Algerian government announced that it would be seeking the re-structuring of its external debt.[74] The further unrest in June 1991, with the subsequent appointment of Sid Ahmad Ghozali as prime minister, added a new dynamic to the economic reform process, not because the popular demonstrations demanded it (they did not), but because the danger of falling credibility (in the eyes of creditors) required it.

Conclusion
The Algerian case also, therefore, brings out the important role played by international economic institutions in the most recent progression towards economic liberalization.

The case of Iraq

A recent article by Kiren Chaudhry has described the privatization programme which was initiated in Iraq in 1987 as being 'the most wide-ranging privatization programme in the developing world' (Chaudhry, 1991: 14). Chaudhry sees the programme as having created economic and social problems which brought about the Iraqi attack on Kuwait in August 1990. While the writer of this chapter finds Chaudhry's article highly perceptive and well-argued, he does not share Chaudhry's views.

It will be contended here that the economic liberalization which has occurred in Iraq since 1987 has been limited. Although a large number of formerly state-controlled businesses were transferred to the private sector, the state's involvement in the economy was not weakened. Indeed, the Iraqi state could be seen to be freeing itself from the need to run concerns of peripheral significance to the country's economic development, so as to concentrate on initiating new and more important undertakings. The economy-based incentive to attack Kuwait came from the determination to maintain heavy state expenditure (on both economic and defence projects), and the lack of sufficient funds to meet this expenditure. The social problems which were spawned by such liberalization as did occur were no doubt significant; yet they could easily have been solved if the government's attention and resources had not been directed elsewhere.

The background: the growth of the public sector, and the agricultural reforms, 1979–86

Iraq's substantial oil revenues provided a strong basis for the expansion of public sector activity through the 1950s, 1960s and 1970s. 'Abd al-Karim Qasim's regime (1958–63) expanded the involvement of the state in the economy through land expropriation and redistribution, development planning and trade management; the 'Arif regime in 1964 nationalized all of the banks and insurance companies, together with 30 large industrial companies; and the Ba'thist regime which gained power in 1968 carried out some further land expropriation, nationalized the oil industry, and increased greatly public investment in all fields of the economy.

Some relaxation of state control of the economy began to be apparent from the end of the 1970s, particularly in the agricultural sector. Springborg (1986) has documented clearly the changes which this sector underwent in the five years after 1979: the number of collective farms fell from 77 in 1979 to 10 in 1983; and local co-operatives fell from 1,923 in 1979 to 811 in 1983. Under Law 35 of 1983, Iraqis and other Arab nationals were permitted to rent land from the Ministry of Agriculture and Agrarian Reform for between 5 and 20 years; no upper limit was placed on the extent of the lands which could be rented. There was a general lessening of controls over agricultural activities, and the policies on agricultural inputs (such as credit) became steadily more favourable to landowners.

These moves stemmed from a pragmatic acceptance that the state's command-control of agriculture had proved ineffective and damaging. State control of the overall economy was not significantly weakened or diluted.

Liberalization measures, 1987–91

A broader programme of liberalization was adopted at the beginning of 1987. In a speech to senior officials in the ministries of industry and heavy industry on 11 February 1987, President Saddam Husain told the officials that economic reform was needed so as to increase output. Wider differentials in earnings were required: 'A worker who works one hour more than his colleague should get more, and the worker who is more clever should also get more than others.' Managers of state-owned companies, moreover, should have more freedom of action: the ministerial authorities should supervise and plan, rather than intervene in, the detailed functions of affiliated companies. Heads of industrial enterprises should be able to make decisions about, and to implement, technical reorganization to improve efficiency, and to keep costs below returns. The private sector should be encouraged to invest more and improve the quality of its products.[75]

The rationale which Saddam put forward for his economic reform policy was that increased output would conserve foreign exchange, and the money saved could be used to 'buy weapons and other equipment needed on the battle front'.[76] The explanation is realistic. In February 1987 saving hard currency for the purchase of weapons appeared highly necessary: Iranian forces had advanced to the suburbs of Basra, and Iraq's economic situation was desperate. The price of oil had fallen from $28 per barrel in December 1985 to $9 per barrel in July 1986, thereby undercutting Iraq's strategy of building new oil export pipelines to bring in more hard currency revenues. Iraq's external debt in 1987 was estimated at some $50 billion, although this included loans from Gulf states which might not need to be repaid.

Over the months following Saddam's February 1987 speech, a number of measures were introduced which broadened the scope of the liberalization. The full range, which had been brought into being by the end of that year, involved deregulation of the labour markets; selling state land, farms and factories to the private sector; introducing incentives for state workers (such as the establishment of profit-sharing schemes for employees of state companies); shaking up the bureaucracy (and reducing the numbers of government officials); providing general encouragement to the private sector; and encouraging exports.

The deregulation of the labour market was implemented by simply abolishing the labour law which had previously been in force. The labour law had covered all those doing physical labour for the state, providing them with a degree of protection and the right to membership in a trade union. The abolition was announced by the president on 11 March.[77] Henceforward, there was only to be an 'officials law', applicable to all who worked for the state in any capacity. This meant that, on the one hand, the workers lost any special protection, and on the other employees could easily be shifted from over-staffed government offices to factories. The General Federation of Trade Unions was abolished, as also was the guarantee of employment which all Iraqi adults had previously enjoyed. Several thousand civil servants were given the option of resigning without penalty or of accepting new posts, usually as factory or workshop employees (previously administrative and service staff had on average accounted for one-third to one-half of all personnel in state enterprises). Two thousand employees were laid off by the Ministry of Heavy Industry alone.[78]

Economic production was to be encouraged by providing greater incentives in many different fields. State enterprise directors and factory managers were permitted to reward their workers with up to 30 per cent of the value of any increase in production. Private sector industries were permitted to export freely, provided 60 per cent of the value of the goods was remitted. Manufacturing industries were to be allowed to import raw materials and machinery needed for expansion and modernization, under arrangements which were not subject to foreign exchange restrictions. Arab investors seeking to import machinery, spare parts, furniture and equipment for new projects would also not be subject to foreign exchange restrictions applying to imports.[79]

Attracting most attention, however, was the sale of state assets.

Department stores, state farms, apiaries, animal husbandry schemes, dairies, petrol stations, poultry farms, hotels, bakeries, food-processing companies and some other factories were put up for sale, or else were made available to the private sector on long leases. Banks provided credit, on easy terms, for up to 50 per cent of the price or lease cost. It was intended that the private sector would also acquire a stake in Iraqi Airways, but the lack of investor interest in this resulted in the proposal being withdrawn in September 1988.[80]

The sale of agricultural undertakings went ahead during 1987, but that of industrial projects and of hotels occurred mostly during 1988 and 1989. In the spring of 1988, the sale of a soft drinks factory and a brewery was announced. In August, 15 'medium and large' factories were offered for sale, including 5 fruit and vegetable canning factories (in Diyala, Salah al-Din, Dohuk and Karbala governorates), 3 brick factories (in Baghdad and Misan), and two gypsum quarries (in Anbar and Irbil).[81]

A further significant measure of liberalization, introduced in August 1988, was the removal of price controls over a large number of consumer goods produced by the private sector, including eggs, chicken and meat. The government explained that the measure was intended to raise output, discourage over-consumption and waste, and save hard currency by cutting imports. The removal of controls was followed by an immediate rise in the price of all decontrolled products, mostly to two or three times the original prices.[82] Prices charged for public services also rose in the course of 1988–9: the cost for the installation of a telephone, for example, rose about 50-fold, and there was a general rise in charges for medical treatment (some of which had previously been free).[83]

Some liberalization of the financial sector was initiated at the end of 1988. The effective monopoly on commercial banking operations which had been enjoyed by the Rafidain Bank was terminated from 1 November of that year, through the opening of another state-owned commercial bank: the Rashid Bank. Arrangements were instituted for private shareholding banks to be able to obtain licences during 1989.[84] Also significant was the repeal of legislation banning commercial agents and intermediaries from having contact with Iraqi government ministries and departments. The changes to the Iraqi Commercial Agency and Intermediation Law, announced by the Revolution Command Council on 20 April 1989, gave commercial agents much wider scope for activity than they had before.[85]

A further measure of financial liberalization was the move to establish the country's first stock exchange. In May 1990 it was announced that a draft bill for the establishment of the exchange would soon be approved, prior to becoming law. A proper market place for the trading of stocks and shares was to be set up, superceding the informal trading system which local banks and government institutions had previously operated. The main objective of the exchange, government officials said, was to finance businesses by attracting both local savings and expatriate earnings.[86]

The limits of Iraq's liberalization

Although the measures just discussed may seem extensive, they in fact represent only a very limited liberalization of the Iraqi economy. This judgement rests on a number of considerations. First, most of the businesses sold to the private sector were loss-making. This, indeed, constituted the critical factor in determining which businesses would be privatized. In a speech on 7 June 1987, President Saddam told an audience of provincial mayors that

> From now on, the state should not embark on uneconomic activity. Any activity, in any field, which is supposed to have an economic return and does not make such a return, must be ignored . . . It is a more sound economic view to lose the factory and ignore it, than to continue with a loss-making economic activity if it remains in action.[87]

The theme that economically-profitable enterprises should remain under state control, and those incurring losses be sold, runs through the whole programme of privatization in Iraq. It is not surprising that the sale of these state assets proved difficult, despite the easy availability of credit to prospective buyers. In many cases, undertakings were leased rather than sold, once it had become apparent that an outright sale was not feasible. In short, the state was not divesting itself of properties from which it had benefited; only of those which had constituted a burden on state finances.

Second, the measures did not stem from any desire on the part of the Iraqi government to limit state involvement in the economy. On the contrary, the years which followed 1987 saw the Iraqi government embark on a wide array of new projects, geared towards building up a stronger industrial and military infrastructure. At the beginning of

1988, for example, the government announced plans to create a second petrochemicals complex, a second iron and steel works (to produce 1 million tons a year), an aluminium smelter (to produce 200,000 t/y), a nitrogen fertilizer plant (to produce 1 million t/y), a phosphate fertilizer plant (to produce 1 million t/y), a special steels plant, a factory to produce 1 million tyres a year, a saltworks to produce 400,000 t/y, two new power stations, and a plant to produce industrial gases.[88] As we know now, the Iraqi government was at the same time investing considerable sums in military infrastructure, such as the construction of the supergun. While divesting itself of some small-scale undertakings, therefore, the Iraqi government was investing (or preparing to invest) huge sums in heavy and military industry. Overall, the government was involving itself more deeply in the economy than ever before.

Third, some of the moves towards liberalization were countermanded, once their implications and effects became apparent. Of greatest significance here was the re-imposition of price controls, some eight months after they were first lifted. On 12 April 1989, the government announced that a committee was being set up to fix the prices of the goods which had been de-controlled.[89] In June, the government announced a price freeze and obliged retailers to put price tags on all goods, with a warning that all prices would be checked.[90] Subsidies on food prices were expected to cost the government more than $1,613 million in 1989/90.[91]

Even before the formal re-imposition of controls, however, the government had retained a strong influence over the newly-created free market. On the one hand, threats were used to keep prices down. A special meeting of the Revolution Command Council and the Ba'th Party Regional Command, convened on 15 October 1988 and chaired by Saddam, discussed recent price rises and determined that:

> The rise was not due to acceptable economic reasons, such as the rise of production costs and so forth, but was due to exploitation by some exploiting and harmful producers, or by those who play a parasitical role in production and marketing.[92]

Merchants, not surprisingly, felt impelled to lower their prices. The government's whole relationship with the private sector, indeed, appeared to be characterised by implicit threats. On 11 April 1989, a statement from the president's office said that the government would continue to support the sector, 'but we remind those greedy people that this policy does not mean leaving their hands free to exploit the consumers'.[93] On the other hand, the government retained control of the supply of, and prices for, feedstuffs etc. needed by private sector producers. It thus retained a lever with which to influence these producers.

Finally, a large number of the undertakings which were privatised went into the hands of individuals who were close to the regime. Reliable information on this is, not surprisingly, difficult to obtain, but it was widely remarked that Tikritis were prominent among those acquiring hotels, factories and agricultural projects.[94] Moreover, despite an RCC decree in March 1989 laying down that no one person, family or company could acquire more than one organization, it seems that some families did (directly or indirectly) gain control of a number of different undertakings.[95] Influence within the regime was the critical factor making this possible. The sale of state assets, therefore, appears not to have fostered the development of an entrepreneurial class independent of state institutions.

Conclusion

The process of economic liberalization in Iraq since 1987 has remained strictly within the limits that the government has seen fit to tolerate. Despite Iraq's large debts, the satisfaction of creditors played no part in either motivating or guiding the process of economic liberalization. State involvement in, and control of, the economy has not been significantly weakened. Although pronouncements on political liberalization accompanied the economic opening, these had little import. They were not made necessary by the economic changes, nor did they affect the actual operation of the political system.

Conclusion

The process of dismantling the economic power of the state in the Arab world only began properly at the end of the 1980s. Earlier moves towards economic liberalization, involving a more relaxed attitude being taken towards private investment, did not significantly diminish the state's role in the economy.

The substantial restructuring which has occurred in some Arab economies in the last few years has stemmed primarily from the articulation of these economies with the international economy. The large foreign debt which these countries have accumulated has impelled governments (whether through direct pressure from the IMF or through the general need to inspire confidence among creditors) to change policies. Domestic social groupings, such as the commercial bourgeoisie, have not played a significant role in achieving 'intensive' economic liberalization. The bourgeois-bureaucratic state emerged in Jordan in the early 1960s, in Tunisia in the late 1960s, and in Egypt in the early 1970s, yet it was only at the end of the 1980s that the withdrawal of the state became significant.

In the states where the process of economic liberalization has been shaped directly or indirectly by external pressures (Algeria and Egypt, but not Iraq), economic liberalization has been accompanied by some attempt at political liberalization. There are both tactical and structural reasons why externally-motivated economic liberalization is likely to have a political counterpart. Tactically, governments are driven to seek new sources of political support. They recognize that the stringent new policies which they are forced to adopt create the danger of political isolation; widening political participation broadens the base of responsibility.

Structurally, the governing institutions gain a greater autonomy of domestic social forces (especially the commercial bourgeoisie), albeit at the expense of losing some autonomy at the international level. The core relationship around which economic policy is formulated comes to be that between the governing institutions and the international financial institutions; not that between the governing institutions and the commercial bourgeoisie. State bureaucrats lose the ability to favour particular merchants or particular social groupings, because the relevant decisions no longer lie within their prerogative. Governments are no longer able to stay in power by buying support, providing favourable conditions for those who might otherwise engender unrest. A new basis for legitimacy has to be created: the government will need to demonstrate to the population that its authority rests on the popular will.

The prospects for economic liberalization actually laying the basis for stable democracies, however, are not at all bright. The powers which the state loses are ones which may be needed if a stable democracy is to emerge in an underdeveloped country: the ability to provide a 'safety-net' for the poorest elements in society, the power to direct investment to those areas of the country which are most disadvantaged, the prevention of too-wide divergences between rich and poor, among others. In short, unless the state is active in allocating investment priorities, controlling and directing imports, and in redistributing income, social tensions may make it impossible to operate a democratic system.

Of central importance in determining whether economic and political liberalization prove compatible is the state's retention of an ability to shape the social and economic conditions of the population, to create a framework within which the different class and social groupings can interact to their mutual advantage. If the state is to divest itself of its command-control of the economy, it needs to find new instruments to attain the social objectives which its command–control had formerly served. A more effective state machinery needs to develop, capable of regulating social conditions in new ways – through effective tax policies, social reforms and welfare programmes, for instance. In short, the state will need to strengthen its ability to shape society, even while occupying a less central role in the economy.

Notes

1 For an account which links together closely the economic and political factors, see Amin (1982).
2 The writer put across this view in Niblock (1989). It will be noted that the analysis in this paper runs counter to the viewpoint which the writer previously upheld. Also see Trimberger (1978).
3 *Middle East Economic Digest*, (henceforward *MEED*), 14/10/88.
4 *MEED*, 23/5/87.
5 *MEED*, 14/10/88.
6 *Al-Ahram*, 30/12/86.
7 *MEED*, 28/3/87.
8 *MEED*, 6/12/88.
9 *MEED*, 26/3/88, 27/5/88 and 15/7/88.
10 *MEED*, 26/3/88.
11 *MEED*, 27/5/88.
12 *MEED*, 15/7/88.
13 *MEED*, 6/5/88.
14 *MEED*, 3/6/91.
15 *MEED*, 15/7/88.
16 *MEED*, 23/9/88.
17 *MEED*, 30/9/88.
18 *MEED*, 27/1/89.
19 *MEED*, 11/11/88.
20 *MEED*, 27/1/89.
21 *MEED*, 9/6/89.
22 *MEED*, 14/4/89 and 28/4/89.
23 *MEED*, 28/4/89.
24 *MEED*, 26/5/89.

25 *MEED*, 2/6/89 and 16/6/89.
26 *MEED*, 25/8/89.
27 *MEED*, 28/4/89.
28 *MEED*, 9/6/89.
29 *MEED*, 14/7/89.
30 *MEED*, 9/6/89.
31 *MEED*, 13/10/89.
32 *MEED*, 23/6/89.
33 *MEED*, 2/6/89.
34 *MEED*, 13/10/89.
35 *MEED*, 22/9/89 and 3/11/89.
36 *MEED*, 8/12/89.
37 *MEED*, 15/9/89.
38 *MEED*, 12/1/90, 23/2/90 and 30/3/90.
39 *MEED*, 2/2/90 and 23/3/90.
40 *MEED*, 13/4/90, 4/5/90 and 8/6/90.
41 *MEED*, 18/5/90 and 8/6/90.
42 *MEED*, 8/6/90.
43 *MEED*, 29/6/90.
44 *MEED*, 29/6/90 and 20/7/90.
45 *MEED*, 28/9/90.
46 *MEED*, 19/10/90.
47 *MEED*, 9/11/90 and 18/1/91.
48 *MEED*, 18/1/91.
49 *MEED*, 8/3/91.
50 *MEED*, 7/6/91.
51 *Mideast Mirror*, 21/12/90.
52 *Al-Wafd*, 20/12/90.
53 *Al-Ahram*, 17/4/91.
54 *Al-Ahram*, 21/4/91.
55 Sutton (1982).
56 Sutton (1978).
57 Central Bank of Algeria (1982).
58 *MEED*, 15/11/86, 21/10/88 and 12/1/90.
59 *MEED*, 24/1/87.
60 *MEED*, 14/3/87.
61 *MEED*, 14/3/87, 18/7/87 and 27/5/88.
62 *El-Moudjahid*, 30/12/86.
63 *El-Moudjahid*, 30/12/87.
64 *MEED*, 12/9/87, 9/1/88 and 3/6/88.
65 Sutton (1990), pp. 15–16. See also Bedrani (1989).
66 *MEED*, 20/2/88.
67 *MEED*, 7/3/89.
68 *MEED*, 14/10/88 and 21/10/88.
69 *MEED*, 4/11/88 and 24/3/89.
70 *MEED*, 5/5/89.
71 *MEED*, 16/6/89.
72 *MEED*, 5/5/89.

73 *MEED*, 23/2/90.
74 A good account of the government's overall liberalization policy in the middle of 1990 can be found in the speech which the Algerian minister of the economy, Ghazi Hidouci, delivered in London on 26/6/90. Text from the Algerian Embassy, London.
75 *MEED*, 28/3/87.
76 *Al-Thawrah*, 12/2/87.
77 *Al-Thawrah*, 12/3/87.
78 *MEED*, 28/3/87 and 15/8/87.
79 *MEED*, 15/8/87.
80 *MEED*, 8/8/87, 15/8/87 and 30/9/88.
81 *MEED*, 2/9/88.
82 *MEED*, 9/9/88, 16/12/88 and 12/5/89.
83 *The Guardian*, 24/3/89.
84 *MEED*, 7/10/88.
85 *Al-Thawrah*, 21/4/89.
86 *MEED*, 1/6/90.
87 *Al-Thawrah*, 8/6/87.
88 *MEED*, 31/3/89.
89 *Al-Thawrah*, 13/4/89.
90 *MEED*, 14/7/89.
91 *MEED*, 15/9/89.
92 *Al-Thawrah*, 16/12/88.
93 *Al-Thawrah*, 12/4/89.
94 *The Guardian*, 24/3/89.
95 *The Guardian*, 24/3/89, and Chaudhry, (1991), p.18.

5· AUSTERITY PROTESTS IN RESPONSE TO ECONOMIC LIBERALIZATION IN THE MIDDLE EAST

David Seddon

Over the past two decades, a great wave of popular unrest has swept through the Middle East, manifesting itself in a variety of forms – including strikes, marches, street demonstrations and 'riots' – and generated by widespread anger and outrage at the austerity measures associated with government policies of economic liberalization. In most cases, the state has responded with considerable violence and there have been many casualties. Only the desert states of the Gulf and North Africa (including Libya and Mauritania), and the Ba'athist regimes of Syria and Iraq remain so far little affected.

The first of these protests took place in 1965 in Morocco, following the government's introduction of austerity measures in response to a deepening economic crisis. Strikes by dissatisfied teachers led to large demonstrations, joined by students and unemployed workers; clashes between protestors and security forces led to hundreds of deaths. The King responded by dissolving parliament and declaring a state of emergency, which was to remain in effect until 1977.

For a decade, the Moroccan protest appeared to be an isolated incident, but from the mid 1970s onwards such austerity protests were to become more common. In January 1977, the decision by the Egyptian government to raise food and petrol prices by over 30 per cent, as part of a programme of financial stringency and economic reform (designed under the auspices of the IMF) provoked long and fierce rioting in several major Egyptian cities. During the remaining few years of the decade, four other countries (Morocco again, Tunisia, Turkey and Iran) were to experience massive urban protest, leading in the last two cases to a military coup and a revolution respectively.

In the 1980s, numerous Middle Eastern states (Sudan, Tunisia, Morocco, Egypt, Algeria and Jordan) were shaken by outbreaks of popular protest against the effects of government economic reform programmes. Even Lebanon, in the midst of a civil war, was affected when demonstrations took place in Beirut in 1987 against the effects of devaluation. There were significant political consequences in several cases. These included the overthrow of the regime in Sudan, and political reforms in Tunisia, Jordan and Algeria. The reforms introduced in Algeria were to contribute to the effective disintegration of the power of the ruling FLN and to the rise of the Islamic Salvation Front (FIS). In Tunisia, the political liberalization did not include recognition of the main Islamic opposition movement, which continued to experience severe state repression.

At the beginning of the 1990s, it was clear that austerity protests would continue to accompany the process of economic reform. In Morocco, Algeria and Turkey, 1990 was marked by continuing demonstrations against the effects of government economic reform and liberalization. During the Gulf war, moreover, the massive demonstrations which were organized in the Maghreb in support of Iraq (and against the US-led coalition) were closely linked to protests over the effects of government economic reforms, and raised demands for domestic political liberalization (Seddon, 1991). In 1991, in Algeria, political reforms only accelerated the decline of the FLN and this, together with the unpopularity of government economic reform measures, made possible the dramatic successes of the Islamic Salvation Front at the polls.

But if popular protest has become increasingly associated in many parts of the Middle East with the rise of Islamic movements, no simple link exists between Islamism and social unrest. In the Islamic Republic of Iran, for example, several major cities witnessed demonstrations during 1991 in protest against government policies of economic liberalization. This chapter will examine this great wave of popular protest – the strikes, the demonstrations and the 'food riots' – and seek to suggest what factors have shaped it. It will be suggested that, over the last 20 or so years, major shifts in macro-economic policy (and the associated redefinition of the role of the state in Middle Eastern economy and society) have generated and/or sharpened structural contradictions, and with them the potential for social conflict. The two decades constitute a major period of transition in the region. Government policies have shifted from a commitment to nationalist development under state capitalism to the widespread espousal of private capital accumulation under a regime of economic liberalism and internationalism. This transition has threatened and destroyed previous 'arrangements' between state, economy and society, has generated new economic and social tensions, and has given rise to new patterns and forms of popular protest (see Walton and Seddon, 1992).

The starting point

In the Middle East, as elsewhere in the developing world, the achievement of national independence was succeeded by an even more difficult task; that of initiating national economic and social development. Throughout the region it was recognized that reliance on the private sector was unlikely to provide an adequate basis for such development. Even in those countries where there existed a significant indigenous bourgeoisie (as in Morocco, Egypt, Syria, Iraq), it was expected that the state would actively provide the framework for private capital accumulation. In general,

> the Middle Eastern state took upon itself the challenge of moving the economy onto an industrial footing, shifting population to the urban areas, of educating and training its youth wherever they lived, raising agricultural productivity to feed the non-agricultural population, redistributing wealth, of building a credible military force, and doing battle with international trade and financial regimes that held them in thrall. These were goals widely held, if poorly understood, by the citizens at large. There were no impediments then to the expansion and affirmation of the interventionist state (Richards and Waterbury, 1990: 187).

In general, it should be added, the interventionist role of the state was facilitated and reinforced by the monopoly (or predominance) of a single party over the political process.

An early example, if not a model, for many of the other states in the Middle East, was that of Turkey where, from 1923 onwards, political independence was succeeded by far-reaching economic and social change, constituting what has often been referred to as 'a revolution from above'. In April 1931, Mustapha Kemal 'Ataturk', former military leader and nationalist and now head of state, issued a manifesto containing six principles which were to provide the basis for the 1937

Constitution of the Republic. The Turkish state would be republican, nationalist, populist, secular, étatist, and revolutionary. He declared:

> we desire to have the government take an active interest, especially in the economic field, and to operate as far as possible in manners that lend themselves to the safeguarding of vital and general interests, or, in short, that the government ensure the welfare of the nation and the prosperity of the state (Hershlag, 1968: 69).

While supporting private enterprise, the ruling Republican People's Party prescribed state intervention in agriculture, industry, public works, commerce, health and education; and Turkey became one of the first developing countries to conduct an experiment in planned development, with its first five year plan in 1934.

Around the same time as Turkey was embarking on its distinctive path to 'modernization', Colonel Reza Khan of the Persian Cossacks was taking effective control of Persia/Iran. It was his intention to proclaim a republic, have himself made president, and build a 'developmental state' like that of Ataturk in Turkey. The Shi'ite clergy strongly resisted the plan for a republic, however, and persuaded Reza Khan to proclaim himself Shah in 1925 and found the Pahlevi 'dynasty'. During the 1930s and 1940s, while neither populist nor revolutionary, the Iranian state established itself as the central force for economic development in the country, much as the Turkish state had done. The first national plan was launched in 1944, and in the postwar years, Reza Khan's son, Mohammed Reza Shah, further consolidated the state's control over the direction of economic development. After 1953, following the nationalization of the Anglo–Iranian Oil Company, strong state intervention in key areas of the economy was combined with a professed economic liberalism and commitment to the promotion of capitalist development. The objective, as in Turkey, was 'a revolution from above'.

During the 1950s and 1960s, the governments of several newly independent Middle Eastern states adopted strategies for national economic and social development which broadly resembled the Turkish model, but which used the term 'Arab socialism' to designate their objectives (Iraq, Syria, Sudan, Egypt, Algeria and Libya). As in Turkey, the governments of these states were often formed by military officers who had taken power in the name of the popular masses.

What all of these radical populist regimes had in common was a commitment to rapid economic and social transformation, with the state as a dynamic force and instrument for 'revolutionary change' on behalf of and in the name of the people. Under regimes of this kind, the role of the state was to dominate the commanding heights of the economy in order to direct a process of state (or public) capital accumulation and to intervene where necessary to assure the social welfare of the people. Iran since 1979 has, despite the distinctiveness of the Islamic Republic, broadly followed this strategy of nationalist development, although there have been indications in the last few years of a degree of economic liberalization, culminating in the economic reforms under President Rafsanjani in the early 1990s. Despite effective criticisms of their socialist credentials, and talk of economic liberalization since the late 1970s, Iraq and Syria have both adhered by and large to this model of economic and social development. Libya has probably gone further (since 1975 in particular) than any state in the region, apart from the avowedly Marxist PDRY, to strangle the private sector.

In several states, however, a somewhat different strategy was developed, in which the explicit role of the state was to actively protect and nurture private capital accumulation. This handmaiden role has been played by the state in Morocco, Jordan, Turkey (since 1950), Iran (between 1963 and 1979), Tunisia (since 1969), Sudan (since 1972) and Egypt (since 1974). In some of these cases, the crucial interventionist role of the state has tended to be camouflaged by a rhetorical commitment to economic liberalism and private enterprise.

Thus, through the decade of the 1960s and into the 1970s, the vast majority of states in the region could be characterized broadly in terms of state capitalism, and their strategy for economic and social development as essentially that of nationalist development (involving, most crucially, import substitution industrialization). That there were significant variations within this general form is undeniable; but in virtually all cases, the state came to be, and to be seen by the population as, a key element in the process of national economic and social development. In all of the states of the region there was also a public commitment to social development and social welfare, even if the benefits of increasing public expenditure and the growth of the state apparatus were by no means equally distributed. Whether the dominant political ideology of government was liberal, socialist or Islamic, a form of social contract between state and people was forged, in which the state was identified as the guarantor of basic welfare as well as the promoter of economic and social development. Although political power was highly concentrated, opportunities for political expression limited and in most cases the effective monopoly of a single party, the government claimed to act on behalf of the people as a whole and, by and large, this claim was not widely or openly challenged.

Economic crisis and the introduction of economic reform

During the 1970s and 1980s, a series of global recessions and the process of international restructuring affected the states of the Middle East, as much as any part of the world. At the same time, government policies of adjustment and austerity, adopted to respond to the deepening economic crisis, themselves generated new contradictions and conflicts. It may be argued that the very strategy of economic and social development widely adopted in the region (as elsewhere in the developing world) during the preceding period itself generated structural contradictions whose resolution would in any case have required significant revisions and adjustments. Richards and Waterbury, for example, explain the deepening crisis of economies within the region largely in terms of the consequences of domestic development strategies, rather than in terms of the external forces of the global political economy:

> the process of state intervention has led to the demise of some classes . . . and promoted others . . . The process of intervention has also resulted in deep-seated crisis in the state sector itself, and in the economy in general, calling into question the feasibility of continued intervention on the same scale as in the past. We are witnessing in several Middle Eastern societies a cautious retreat of the state and hence a gradual weakening of the state bourgeoisie (Waterbury and Richards, 1990: 217).

While the writer does not ascribe the same weight as do these commentators to domestic policies alone, there can be no doubt that macro-economic strategies (often adopted, it must be said, under considerable domestic political pressure) were partly responsible. Growing import bills coupled with stagnant exports, resulting in part from the nationalist development strategy and in part from secular changes in the international terms of trade and protectionism by the advanced capitalist states, led to rapidly increasing trade and balance of payments deficits. Many governments continued to invest significantly more resources than were saved domestically, and as a result economies came during the 1970s to rely heavily on external sources of investment capital and began to accumulate large external debts.

On the whole, following the oil price increases of the mid-1970s, the oil exporting countries were in a better position to avoid large-scale external borrowing, but a significant number of oil importing states – Sudan, Morocco, Tunisia, Egypt, Syria, Turkey – developed substantial resource gaps (investment minus domestic savings) and associated external debts. The major world recession of the late 1970s and early 1980s made these problems significantly worse, and the burden of debt increased the pressure to introduce economic reforms. The reforms, however, failed in most cases to resolve the problem of indebtedness, which continued to grow throughout the 1980s.

Particularly in countries where revenues from oil exports did not exist, or were insufficient to provide a cushion against the growing tensions in economy and society, governments were faced during the second half of the 1970s with the stark choice between attempting to maintain the nationalist development strategy by further external borrowing, or implementing austerity measures as part of a programme aimed at liberalizing and internationalizing the economy. The second alternative risked domestic unrest, in response to rising prices and declining real incomes and to the evident withdrawal of the state from its previous commitment to safeguard the citizens' basic economic and social welfare. Nonetheless, it was increasingly pressed on governments by the international financial institutions as a precondition for further lending or for debt rescheduling.

Government measures to promote economic reform, often adopted under the auspices of the IMF and World Bank, began to be implemented during the second half of the 1970s. But the reforms introduced tended to be less stringent than external creditors and the international financial institutions, or indeed often the government itself under pressure from the more powerful fractions of capital at home, would have liked. The programme actually implemented represented an attempt to respond to increasing economic pressures without giving rise to major political dissent and social unrest. Two examples – those of Turkey and Morocco in the late 1970s and early 1980s – clearly illustrate the powerful constraint applied by the threat (and reality) of social unrest.

Economic reform under pressure: Turkey and Morocco

Turkey

Towards the end of the 1970s, Turkey found itself in a deepening economic and political crisis. Inflation climbed from 30 per cent in 1974 to 64 per cent in 1979; the foreign trade deficit stood at $2.8 billion in 1979, having been reduced from a massive $4 billion in 1977 only by simple inability to pay for imports. Servicing the foreign debt of around $13 billion had become a major burden and the debt itself had to be rescheduled in 1978. Governed through the mid-1970s by fragile and changing coalitions, none of which could risk actively promoting economic austerity for fear of the political reaction, Turkey drifted into crisis, pursuing expansionary policies. It has been argued that 'from the mid-1970s, an increasingly militant and organised working class movement became a major obstacle to the success of the government's crisis management policies' (Margulies and Yildizoglu, 1988: 145), but this movement was unable to prevent a decline in real wages and a deterioration in living standards for large sections of the urban population during the latter part of the decade.

Eventually, in 1979, as the economic crisis deepened, the social democratic government resigned, to be replaced by the conservative Justice Party, which began to introduce an economic reform programme, with the support of the IMF and the benefit of martial law. In the short term the programme involved devaluation, the abolition of stamp and import duties, and export promotion, combined with tight monetary control, restrictions on wage increases and the elimination of subsidies. In the longer term the programme aimed at a substantial restructuring of the economy, transforming it from one based on import substitution to an export-oriented one.

The response from abroad (from the IMF, the World Bank, the commercial banks and Western governments) was very positive: fresh loans were acquired, existing debts were rescheduled and Turkey obtained a net foreign aid inflow of over $1.5 billion in 1980. At home, however, the result was powerful opposition from a broad spectrum of interests, expressed in parliament, within the state bureaucracy, and in a massive increase in public social unrest and political violence. The first nine months of 1980 witnessed the largest strike wave in Turkish history and widespread popular protest as real daily wages slumped and consumer prices soared. In September 1980, the army took power, suspended parliament and banned all political parties, student organizations and trade unions. With the army in power, a state of emergency declared and major restrictions on civil liberties imposed, the new regime was able to implement far-reaching economic reforms. Under the repressive conditions established by the military at the beginning of the decade, popular protest was effectively stifled for nearly a decade. Only in 1990 and 1991 did large scale popular protest break out again against the effects of the government's economic reform programme.

Morocco

In 1978, the Moroccan government introduced a three year stabilization programme, after more than a decade of heavy repression under a state of emergency (declared following the austerity protests of 1965). Substantial foreign borrowing had been undertaken during the previous decade to cover a growing balance of trade and balance of payments deficit. The stabilization programme involved stricter import controls and cuts in public expenditure. The austerity measures, although relatively mild, were met by a wave of strikes and a significant growth in trades union opposition. The strikes, involving organized workers in both the public and private sectors, continued through 1978 and 1979. Strikers' rallies were often dispersed with considerable brutality, but the actions gained limited wage concessions and the unrest was contained.

At the beginning of the 1980s, the Moroccan government faced growing pressure from its international creditors to implement more far-reaching measures to reduce public expenditure, encourage private enterprise and investment, and promote greater efficiency in the allocation and use of resources. When in 1980 and 1981 attempts were made to cut public expenditure and reduce subsidies on basic goods, however, the resulting social unrest was widespread and severe. In June 1981, price increases in basic goods provoked a general strike by the major trade union federations, and in Casablanca the strike developed into a more general demonstration against the effects of government economic policies as workers in both the public and private sectors were joined first by small shopkeepers and then by students and the unemployed. The riots brought special police units, the national guard and finally the army into action. In two days of clashes throughout the city some 600 people were killed and many more injured. Faced with this opposition to the austerity measures, the Moroccan government hesitated to push ahead with the full reform programme, thereby incurring the disapproval of the IMF and World Bank, and the withdrawal of their support (Seddon, 1989a: 247).

Throughout the latter part of 1981 and during 1982, the government was mainly concerned with containing political dissent. By 1983, however, it had regained confidence in its ability to contain opposition, and with the economic crisis deepening it initiated a new programme of stabilization involving a 10 per cent devaluation, fiscal and credit restraints, cuts in public expenditure and reductions in food subsidies. The measures adopted encouraged Morocco's creditors to provide effective support, in the form of debt relief and rescheduling. But a second round of price increases was implemented in December, and at the same time the draft budget for 1984 (containing proposals for further austerity measures during the coming year) was made public. In January 1984, massive demonstrations of popular protest broke out in towns and cities across the country; during the two weeks of civil unrest, as many as 400 people were killed in clashes between demonstrators and security forces, while an estimated 9,000 were arrested for their part in the unrest.

For the remainder of the decade, the Moroccan state maintained very tight control. No national elections have been held since 1984, and all unofficial political parties and movements have been brutally suppressed. Some opposition was still able to find expression, however. In November 1986 the Democratic Labour Confederation denounced the government's economic policies and the country's dependence on the IMF. A year later the official opposition declared the government's commitment to further austerity measures in pursuit of economic restructuring to be 'anti-social'. But it was not until 1990–1 and the Gulf crisis that popular demonstrations against government policies broke out once again. On that occasion, support for Iraq and against the US-led coalition in the Gulf was explicitly linked to criticism of the Moroccan government's economic and social policies at home, as well as to its support for the coalition abroad (Seddon, 1991).

These two examples provide some indication of the ways in which the governments of Middle Eastern states have confronted the dilemma shared by virtually all of the developing world over the past two decades: how to reconcile the growing pressures for economic adjustment with increasing political opposition and social dissent.

But to appreciate the full significance of popular protest, we must go beyond individual case studies and recognize its prevalence throughout the region. On at least 20 occasions in at least nine countries in the Middle East over the last quarter century, major outbreaks of popular protest over the economic and social effects of government policies have occurred, often with significant political consequences. To understand the extent to which popular protest against austerity measures is a general feature of economies and societies in transition from 'nationalist development' to 'internationalist liberalisation' (see Walton & Seddon, 1992), we require a broader 'comparative anatomy of protest'.

The scale and significance of popular protests

In all of the austerity protests discussed in this chapter, the scale is substantial; often tens of thousands of protestors are involved, in numerous demonstrations, usually across several towns and cities in the country concerned. It is quite probable that many smaller incidents, which generally go unreported, have been missed. The impression may be conveyed that popular protest is something that only occurs on a grand scale, but there is no intention of excluding the undoubtedly numerous local instances of small-scale protest. These constitute an important part of the pattern of popular protest, and they are referred to wherever possible.

In the case of Iran, where it is even more difficult than usual to disassociate popular protest against government economic policies and deteriorating economic conditions from other more obviously political issues, it has been estimated that during 1978 there were nearly 2,500 mass demonstrations and urban riots, involving a total of 1.6 million people, and over 1,200 strikes. More than 3,000 people were killed and over 12,000 injured (Ashraf & Banuazizi, 1985: 22). In the last two months of 1978, demonstrators were joined by an estimated 5 million workers and public sector employees in strikes. Clearly, this was exceptional, and no other country in the region has experienced such a massive uprising and revolution. But elsewhere also, the scale of popular protest has been substantial.

In Turkey during 1979 and 1980, over 100,000 people were involved in nearly 350 separate strikes, while tens of thousands took to the streets in the major cities of western Anatolia, including Istanbul, Ankara, Izmir and others. Some 2,000 people were killed in clashes between protestors and security forces and in inter-factional violence during the seven months from February to September 1980 alone, with many thousands arrested and jailed, before the scale of civil unrest precipitated a military coup.

In Morocco, officially 'scores', but in fact as many as 200–300 people, may have been killed in the 1965 clashes with security forces and many more hurt. 'Hundreds' were reported to have been arrested. Tens of thousands of workers were involved in the strikes of 1978–9, and tens of thousands again were involved in the general strikes and mass demonstrations of 1981, with over 600 people killed in Casablanca alone. In 1984, large crowds took to the streets in most of the major cities throughout the country and were met with heavy repression: 150 people were killed in one northern town (Tetuan) and a total of 400 were conservatively estimated to have died throughout the country during the two weeks of protest, with many more injured and thousands (estimates vary between 2,000 and 9,000) arrested. In 1990, mass demonstrations clashed with security forces in several major cities, after a largely successful general strike which had involved hundreds of thousands of workers. The strike had been called to demand better pay and working conditions and to oppose the government's economic reform policies. In Fes, some 20,000 demonstrators clashed with workers who refused to strike, and with 'blacklegs' brought in to operate the public services (including transport), as well as with the security forces. Official figures on the casualties resulting from clashes over a two-day period in Fes alone were: 5 killed, 127 injured and 212 arrested. The trade unions reported over 25 killed by the end of the first day, while anonymous medical sources put the dead at over 30. The final official death toll was 65, but local estimates suggest well over 100.

In October 1988, Algeria was rocked by the most serious unrest since political independence in 1962. The demonstrations began in the poorer quarters of Algiers and the shanty town areas, but soon spread widely through the city. Popular protest was also reported from other cities, including Oran and Annaba. Probably tens of thousands were involved in all, and clashes with security forces left several hundred dead in the six days of rioting (conservative official estimates put the number killed at 159). Even when the protest was crushed in Algiers, there continued to be clashes in other, smaller towns, like Tiaret. The state responded to the unprecedented social unrest with unprecedented violence. Security forces in large numbers used live ammunition against the crowds and arrested thousands of protestors.

In Tunisia in late 1977, growing dissatisfaction at the deterioration in pay and working conditions led to a wave of strikes which effectively brought whole sectors of the national economy to a standstill. The army was called in to deal with the strikers. In response, the Union Generale des Travailleurs Tunisiens (UGTT) called a national strike for 26 January 1978, which was observed throughout the country. The hardliners in the cabinet voted for massive repression of the strike movement, with a view to destroying the power of the trades union movement. When there were disturbances in Tunis during the general strike, the army was given *carte blanche*. Estimates of the number killed in clashes vary between 46 and 200; some 800 people were arrested at the time, and shortly afterwards thousands of trade unionists were sentenced by summary courts.

In Egypt, in 1977, demonstrations involving 'thousands' (usually between 2,000 and 4,000) of protestors were reported in Cairo, with numerous 'large' demonstrations in other cities. The scale of the demonstrations in Cairo was such that the government imposed a curfew and ordered armed police and the army to shoot anyone found out of doors without a permit. The sounds of explosions continued to interrupt the curfew, however, with demonstrators fighting police after nightfall in two densely populated suburbs. These latter clashes added 13 to the death toll which, according to *Al Ahram* eventually reached 43 (with 600 injured) in Cairo alone after the first two days. The final official death toll (widely considered extremely conservative) was 73. At least 600 people were arrested in Cairo during the demonstrations and many more detained in Alexandria.

In cases like these, the very size and scale of the protests and the numbers of those killed and injured was politically significant. The protests could not be ignored. Where the numbers involved and the scale of violence were substantially smaller, the political repercussions could still be significant; especially when the popular protest gave rise to more organized forms of protest and opposition, involving an even wider spectrum of social forces. Cases in point include Sudan in 1985, Algeria from 1988 onwards, and Jordan in 1989 (see below).

The geography of protest
It has been suggested that over-urbanization is a significant variable in the comparative analysis of contemporary austerity protest (Walton and Ragin, 1990). Certainly urban growth in the Middle East has been extremely rapid, particularly during the 1960s and 1970s; and the rate of growth in urban employment has failed to keep pace with

the supply of labour, just as the development of the urban infrastructure has signally failed to keep pace with the increasing demands of a growing urban population. Shanty towns have sprung up and spread around the major cities of the region, while the pressure on the inner cities has increased dramatically. The expansion of the so-called informal sector of the urban economy has been particularly marked. Urban population growth, the growth of the informal sector and the growth of urban inequality have gone hand in hand across the region. High levels of unemployment, low and unreliable incomes and often appalling living conditions have combined to create a massive problem of urban poverty and deprivation.

This is the case even in some of those countries whose economies received a massive increase in revenues as a result of the increase in oil prices of the mid- and late -1970s, such as Iran. In Iran, by the late 1970s up to half the population was living in the towns. The population of some urban areas doubled in a decade and the population of Tehran in particular soared. The boom of the mid-1970s accelerated a process of economic and social transformation which had begun in the 1960s, involving a massive exodus from the rural areas and the mushrooming of the towns and cities. While the gap between rural and urban incomes grew, so too did the inequalities within the urban areas. By the mid-1970s it was estimated that the top 20 per cent of the population accounted for 40 per cent of the expenditure. The urban poor also suffered acutely from the housing shortage, as population growth outstripped available accommodation. The result was that some had to spend up to 70 per cent of their income on rent, while others simply constructed their own shacks where land was available.

In Tunisia, the 1970s saw a massive increase in urban population, most of it the result of the growth of shanty towns and slums. Roughly 21 per cent of the population of greater Tunis was estimated to live in shanty-town areas at the beginning of the 1980s, with 12 per cent in special 'housing projects'. The 'city' of Etthatmen, for example, which had a population of 7,000 in 1975, had grown to 28,000 by 1979 and by 1983 had reached 65,000. Inequalities in the distribution of wealth and income within the urban areas also grew as unemployment increased: real wages for the majority declined and the cost of living soared. Wage rises for formal sector workers in the early 1980s had little impact on the incomes of those in casual employment or out of work. The total number of those unemployed in Tunisia in the early

1980s was around 300,000 (approximately 20 per cent of the active labour force). A large proportion of these lived in the shanty towns and slums.

The growing urban problems of the 1970s and early 1980s were made more acute by the introduction of austerity measures, as governments struggled to respond to the deepening economic crisis of the period. In countries where there have been major outbreaks of social unrest (notably Egypt, Turkey, Algeria and Morocco), urban living conditions (housing, infrastructure and transport) appear to have been as important in causing the unrest as the more frequently cited problems of cost of living, unemployment and declining incomes. In Algiers in 1988 and in Fes in 1990, for example, it was clear that a combination of population pressure, declining living standards and the well-documented deterioration of the very fabric of the city itself contributed crucially to the outbreak of popular protest.

Popular protest is, without doubt, an urban phenomenon. But, contrary to what one might expect, austerity protests do not always start in the major cities or the capital, but have in some cases begun in smaller urban centres in historically disadvantaged but politically significant regions. Certainly, in the majority of cases, the mass demonstrations have begun and continued in the largest urban agglomerations. There the rapid growth of shanty towns and the overcrowding in the slums of the old cities and poor quarters ensures a critical mass of the urban poor, who constitute the major source for spontaneous popular protest. But in Tunisia in 1984, the unrest started in the small towns of the semi-arid southwest; in Morocco in 1984, the most violent demonstrations were in the underdeveloped north of the country; and in Jordan in 1989, it was unrest in the small town of Ma'an in the south that sparked off a wave of popular protest throughout the country. These three cases are worth considering in more detail.

In Tunisia, the unrest began in the Nefzaoua, a semi-arid region in the southwest of the country, which is historically the poorest region of Tunisia, and then caught on in other parts of the south. The southern interior generally has a high unemployment rate, and many men leave the area for work in the more prosperous towns on or near the coast; some 60,000 were employed as migrant labour in Libya in the early 1980s. The region also suffered considerably from the drought of 1983–4, which substantially reduced the local harvest. After the outbreak of mass protest in January 1984, a local observer in

Kebili (one of the small towns of the south where violent demonstrations occurred) remarked that 'it was not for bread that the young demonstrated, but because they were the victims of unemployment'. But this was not all. The south was an area where Libyan influence was known to be considerable, and where political opposition to the government had been openly manifested in the recent past. The popular protests of 1984 in Tunisia thus started in the small towns of the south and subsequently spread to the larger towns and cities of the north.

In Morocco, in 1984, the earliest demonstrations also occurred in the south, particularly in Marrakesh, where the drought of 1983–4 had seriously affected food availability and the cost of living. But the region in which mass protest developed on the most significant scale, and generated the greatest violence, was the north. This region, which had remained seriously underdeveloped under Spanish occupation until 1956, suffered acutely during its subsequent integration with the rest of Morocco between 1956 and 1960. During 1958 and 1959, largely in response to the economic hardship and political marginalization of the north, there had been serious social unrest and even a major rebellion. Furthermore, the north, and particularly the northeast where popular protest in 1984 was most severe, had been the source of open opposition to the regime since the 1920s and remained a politically volatile region. During the 1960s and 1970s the region was both economically and politically marginal, despite efforts to invest in agricultural development. The majority of the population depended for their livelihoods on remittances from migrant workers in Europe and elsewhere, and from smuggling. In the late 1970s and early 1980s, unemployment was high, remittances were declining as the recession deepened in Europe, and even the small towns of the region experienced a dramatic growth in population, without a corresponding increase in jobs. It came as no surprise to those familiar with the region's history and contemporary problems that, when popular protest broke out in Morocco, the north and northeast were particularly affected (Seddon, 1989c).

In Jordan, in 1989, less than 48 hours after the government announced price increases for fuel and other basic commodities (as part of the IMF-sponsored economic reform programme), demonstrations in Ma'an – a small town in the south – sparked off a wave of popular protest across the country. It was the fact that anger exploded first in Ma'an, and then other small towns in the south, that transformed a protest against price increases into a nationwide struggle for a fairer distribution of wealth, social justice and political reforms. The significance of Ma'an was that the late King Abdullah had chosen it as a base when hc first came to Transjordan; and since that time the south had been the bedrock of support for the regime. This bond was strengthened by the large-scale employment of young men from the region in the administration and the army. The direct dependence of Ma'an's inhabitants on the state for their livelihoods meant that they were hit hard when public expenditure was slashed, with many losing their jobs. In addition to its reliance on public sector employment, the south was also heavily dependent on incomes from other activities hard hit by the economic reforms. The price increases were simply the last straw. Unlike the cases of Tunisia and Morocco, then, the south of Jordan was politically significant not because of its economic marginality and tradition of political opposition, but precisely because of its economic dependence on, and its identification with, the regime.

Although protest against austerity programmes may initially break out in small towns, however, in virtually all cases it subsequently spreads to larger towns and cities. Sometimes this is because the protestors themselves actually take their protest from one place to another. More frequently, it is caused by the spread of news triggering off a simultaneous protest in several places, based on the same factors as led to the initial unrest. In Egypt in 1977, for example, the demonstrations started in the industrial town of Helwan, where steel workers stoned cars and buses before ordering lorry drivers to take them into Cairo. Cairo then experienced the largest protests, with every railway line between Cairo and Alexandria, Suez and the South being torn up in Cairo's suburbs, but there were also large demonstrations in many other major cities, including Alexandria, Aswan, Kena and Menia (where a new textile factory was badly damaged). In Sudan, in 1985, although the capital, Khartoum, and its suburbs constituted the major focus of popular protest, other town also were involved. There was rioting in Nyala, al-Fasher and al-Geneina in the west; in Atbara in the north; and in Port Sudan in the east. In Turkey, when 50,000 coal miners in Zonguldak on the Black Sea coast went on strike in December 1990 – to be followed in January 1991 by hundreds of thousands of workers in other industries – the striking miners and their wives actually marched on the capital, Ankara. They intended to press their demands for better working conditions, improved pay, and the resignation of Turgut Ozal (the architect of the government economic reform programme) and his government. They were stopped outside Bolu on their 150-mile march by a massive display of strength by the security forces.

It is rare for major cases of popular protest to be confined to a single town or city, as was the case with the Casablanca riots of 1981 in Morocco. Generally, if protest is limited to a single centre, it is on a small scale. More often, while demonstrations take place in several towns across the country, one centre in particular experiences major riots. This occurred in Morocco in December 1990, when a general strike gave rise to demonstrations across the country, but the city of Fes experienced particularly serious disturbances.

The physical pattern of protest within the towns and cities, while evidently linked to the social origins and location of those who take part, is difficult to generalize. Often, the major demonstrations take place in the streets and squares of the town's central areas, where the government buildings, office blocks, luxury shops and hotels that are the major targets of the crowd tend to be concentrated, but frequently the protests originate in the poorer quarters and shanty towns and then spread to other areas of town.

In Algeria in 1988, the riots started in the Bab el Oued, a slum district of Algiers, and in the neighbouring Kasbah, and in the Peripherique on the outskirts of the city where the major shanty towns are situated. In Algiers, a city designed for 850,000, the population now numbers over 3 million. It is not suprising that the riots broke out first in the poorer, overcrowded parts of the city. But other factors were involved. The people of Bab el Oued, for example, have a long tradition of defying authority; the quarter constituted the focus of some of the fiercest resistance against the French. There were also major demonstrations in El Biar (the district of diplomatic and government residences), Hussein Dey (an eastern industrial area), and Jouba Qadim. The latter two are known as Islamist strongholds. If the demonstrations were not orchestrated, they were not without distinctive socio-political roots.

The sociology of protest
In most instances, it seems clear that the majority of those involved in street demonstrations and riots are the unemployed and casually-employed from the shanty-town and slum areas. Rioters tend to be young, with the majority probably in the 16–30 age range. In some instances, observers have reported youths of between 12 and 15

involved in stone-throwing and other activities. But, on the basis of reports of those injured or killed, it also appears that the crowds often include the elderly. The majority of those involved in all forms of protest, and perhaps particularly in the street demonstrations and riots, are male. There is, however, evidence to suggest that women are also involved to an important extent, usually in 'supportive' roles (shouting from the rooftops, for instance) but sometimes more actively (Daines and Seddon, 1991).

In virtually all cases, significant increases in the cost of basic goods and services (or the threat of these on top of increases already experienced) have preceded and may be said to have precipitated the outburst of popular protest. The price of bread or flour and other staple foodstuffs appears to be particularly significant. This is in part because of the importance of these goods in household expenditure, especially for the urban poor, and in part because of their crucial symbolic value (particularly of bread) in Middle Eastern society. Looting is common, and often explicitly justified in the language of 'the moral order'. In Algiers in 1988, voices in the crowd that gathered outside the burned-out Monoprix supermarket after the weekend of rioting suggested that 'the kids did it . . . because they are hungry'.[1] The language of hunger was frequently used to underline the justice of the protests, and as a rallying cry. In Cairo in 1977, when riot police opened fire on crowds marching towards the National Assembly, 'this did not deter the crowds, who replied by shouting in unison: "we are dying of hunger now, so go ahead and shoot us, Sadat"'.[2]

Other crucial items include cooking oil, fuel (whether for cooking or for transport) and rents, again largely because of their importance in household expenditure and the lack of substitutes. Increases in taxes or in fees, particularly important in the case of students, have also been significant in provoking unrest (Morocco in 1984, for instance). In general, increases in the cost of living, especially when felt to be unreasonable or discriminatory, are the major stimulus to austerity protests. In so far as increases in the cost of basic goods and services have the greatest impact on the urban poor (the unemployed and the low paid), it is not surprising that the latter are universally involved in these protests.

It is worth noting that the sections of urban society most active in protests are those who enjoy least support and representation from organized groups and institutions. The trade unions generally represent the workers in the relatively protected areas of the economy, whether in the private or public sector. The professional and middle classes often have not only the trade unions but also their own professional associations through whom they can obtain support and through which they can express their grievances. Political groupings and movements may claim to speak and act on behalf of the ordinary people, but tend to involve primarily activists from relatively privileged backgrounds, generally relying heavily on intellectuals and students for their core membership. They often fail to articulate or represent the interests of the urban poor. This is perhaps less true for the Islamic groups than for those on the left, but even the Islamic movements often rely heavily on activists from petty bourgeois backgrounds.

In the majority of cases, the street demonstrations or riots involve predominantly unemployed and casually-employed young men, usually from the shanty towns and urban slums; the strikes involve workers in the private and public sector; and marches and petitions the more organized groups, including trade unions and professional associations and their members. Students may be involved in all three kinds of protest. There appears to be a very general tendency for the more organized groups and those of the middle classes to become involved after the 'spontaneous' demonstrations of the urban poor, taking advantage of these to orchestrate more systematic and coherent opposition. Such a tendency is, however, very general. It is clear from the instances presented above, that popular protest may have a dynamic or bandwaggon effect, so that those social groups initially involved may be joined by others, or even replaced by them as the protest finds new forms and patterns of expression. What starts out as a strike or march, may turn into a demonstration or riot; what starts out as a street demonstration may give rise to more orchestrated and organized forms of protest. Furthermore, several forms of protest, involving different social groups, may take place simultaneously.

If the 'faces in the crowd' are various and change as the protest evolves, so too does 'the language of the crowd' and its targets. The demonstrations of popular protest discussed here were, in most cases, spontaneous, in the sense of not having been orchestrated or previously organized by established groups or movements. But the actions of the crowds in the streets were by no means random. If violence against property was common, and some immediate targets – such as places of work, vehicles in the street and shops – were almost routinely identified, more substantial destruction was usually directed towards the symbols of affluence (banks, luxury hotels, airline offices, expensive stores) or towards the offices of institutions representing the state or the party.

The politics of popular protest

In several cases, the hostility towards the one-party state was demonstrated by attacks on the local authorities and the offices of the party itself. In Egypt in 1977, for example, crowds of dockworkers in Alexandria burned shops and two cinemas, and then went on to set fire to the Arab Socialist Union building. In Sudan in 1985,

> demonstrators smashed shop windows and car windshields, overturned vehicles and set them on fire, and blocked the streets with chunks of concrete and other heavy objects. Three buildings suffered particularly heavy damage: a branch office of the official Sudanese Socialist Union (the only party permitted under Numairi), the Faisal Islamic Bank (preserve of the Muslim Brotherhood), and the luxury Meridien Hotel (Seddon, 1989b: 120).

In Algeria in 1988, in Kouba district to the east of Algiers, residents reported that the mayor's office had been burnt down. In Oran, the FLN party headquarters was set on fire and there were official reports that mobs had attacked two offices of Air Algerie, an Air France office and the Spanish consulate.

In many instances, elements in the crowd showed that they recognized the role played by external forces in the adoption of austerity measures. In Sudan in 1985, 'students chanted, "We will not be ruled by the World Bank, we will not be ruled by the IMF", as the unemployed urban poor in the crowd protested at the increasing cost of living' (Seddon, 1989b: 120). In Omdurman (part of greater Khartoum), hundreds of women took to the streets in a large demonstration to protest against rising food prices; 'many were shouting, "Down down with the IMF"' (Seddon, 1989b: 122). Demonstrators also alleged that external agents were helping to suppress the unrest. In the protests in Egypt in 1977, one group of demonstrators chanted anti-American slogans, claiming that all the teargas came from the United States. Many of the empty canisters retrieved did indeed bear the label, CS 518 Federal Laboratories Inc. of Saltsburg Pennsylvania.[3]

To argue that the many instances of popular protest discussed in this chapter were essentially spontaneous, in the sense of not having been planned or organized beforehand, does not mean that the actions of the crowd were random or irrational. The widespread moral indignation and anger directed towards specific targets suggests a concern with social justice and with broad social and political issues beyond the simple matter of cost-of-living and prices. Furthermore, elements in the crowd were clearly prepared openly to criticize the regime and the political leadership, and to draw attention to the external forces behind government policies.

Some involvement of organized political groupings in the protests can not be denied. Frequently, unofficial leftist groups were involved. In almost all instances, particularly after the Iranian revolution, Islamic groups participated in the demonstrations. It is possible that the much-reported shouting of 'Islamic slogans' came from the latter, although it is more likely that such chants were spontaneous. In the case of Tunisia in 1984, some commentators have suggested that growing Islamic fundamentalism enabled agitators to encourage violence against property representing the symbols of luxury, corruption and foreign influence, and to adopt such slogans as 'there is but one God and Bourghiba is the enemy of God'. It is true that Islamist pamphlets were circulated during the demonstrations, and that minarets were used to chant '*allahu akbar*'. Generally, however, the Islamic groups (like the opposition political parties and trades unions) seem often to have been taken by surprise by the outburst of popular protest, and were sometimes surprisingly slow to respond. In Algeria in 1988, reports suggested that some Islamic groups may even have played a significant part in averting violence after prayers, and were waiting for a response from the government to a letter from the grand imam before acting.

Despite the manifest involvement of political activists from opposition groups in most of the instances of popular protest, there is little support for the notion that they played a key role in orchestrating the social unrest, except in the specific case of Iran in 1978–9. Some groups did claim responsibility, but usually their claims can be discounted. In Tunisia in 1984, a group calling itself the Tunisian National Opposition Movement (MONT) claimed responsibility (from Brussels) for the demonstrations, and denounced 'the repression by the Tunisian security forces of the hunger rioters'. But the recognized left-wing parties (officially outlawed but tolerated) clearly intervened only after the outbreak of mass protest, and then only to call on the government to resolve the crisis. The Tunisian Communist Party wrote to the prime minister demanding that there be consultations with all national forces to find a solution to the situation, but otherwise confined itself to condemning the violence. The Social Democrats (MDS) criticized the state for its deployment of the army and laid the responsibility at the door of the government, but did little else. As to Morocco in 1984, the writer has elsewhere outlined the political character of the protests as follows:

> while there is little doubt that Islamic political groups and some of the leftist movements – notably Ilal Amam – were certainly involved, these [riots] were essentially demonstrations of popular protest, involving spontaneous actions by young unemployed or casually employed individuals from the poor neighbourhoods of most towns where the 'riots' occurred (Seddon, 1989a: 250).

In Algeria in 1988, a group calling itself the Peoples' Movement for Algerian Renewal claimed responsibility for the popular protests; in a telephone call to a newsagency. The group demanded the resignation of the government, the dissolution of parliament, the abolition of the FLN, the revision of the constitution, the election of peoples' committees and an end to martial law. It was widely believed that the group was linked to anti-government groups within the FLN, associated with the former Communist Party and strongly opposed to the government's economic policies. The objective was to use the riots, and the earlier strikes at Rouiba and in Algiers, to bring pressure to bear on the government to revise its economic strategies or stand down.

Effects on economic policy
Often, despite the efforts of the state and the security forces, the protests could not be contained by repression alone. In many such cases – Egypt in 1977, Tunisia and Morocco in 1984, Sudan in 1985, Algeria in 1988, and Jordan in 1989 – governments felt obliged to revoke publicly the price increases that had triggered off the protests.

Measures to increase minimum wage levels or to increase real wages by a certain percentage have also commonly been adopted, in some cases after direct discussions with trade union representatives, as in Morocco in 1978–9 and in Tunisia in 1984. In Morocco in

1990, the government attempted to pre-empt the general strike threatened for December by announcing in the National Assembly plans to implement 'substantial rises in wages and other benefits' for workers, and by holding 'peace talks' with the union federations concerned. But all too often government-sponsored wage increases affect only those in formal sector employment, within the protection of the law and the scope of the trades unions, and fail to meet the needs of the majority of the urban poor. Deals with the unions are not, therefore, likely to affect popular dissatisfaction among the urban poor.

In most cases, efforts by governments to effect a tactical retreat by revoking the price increases and effectively recognizing the social costs of the austerity measures have been largely successful in bringing popular protest to a halt. Just as the price increases symbolized for the urban poor a denial of the state's responsibility for their basic needs (as well as a real increase in the cost of living and therefore increased deprivation), so the withdrawal of the price increases symbolized a recognition by the state of the 'justice' of the protestors' case. In Jordan in 1989, for example, Crown Prince Hasan (who was temporarily in charge while King Husain was in Washington), flew immediately to Ma'an to listen to the people's grievances. When Husain returned, he pledged himself to 'address the problem at its roots as soon as possible'. He then dismissed the prime minister, al-Rifa'i, who had been identified by the protestors as the architect of the economic reform programme, and appointed new economic advisers critical of the al-Rifa'i government's policies.

Often, however, the withdrawal of the austerity measures was only temporary, a dramatic and visible response to popular demands. In the majority of cases, government economic reform programmes had acquired a momentum (for reasons associated both with domestic and with external forces) which could be brought to a halt only with enormous difficulty and could only be temporarily slowed down. In most of the countries which have experienced major upsurges of popular protest, economic reforms have been pursued, even in the face of growing social dissatisfaction, as the economic pressures to implement far-reaching adjustment continue to grow. Morocco is a case in point; Algeria is another. In both countries, despite a history of popular protest, the governments have continued to pursue programmes of economic liberalization. In Tunisia also, after the public statement by President Bourghiba that the price increases would be revoked, the government continued (albeit more circumspectly) to pursue the economic reforms which had given rise to the dramatic price rises of January 1984.

Despite the evident political risks, the deepening economic crisis experienced by many Middle Eastern states during the 1980s, and the pressures from outside for more liberalization, have ensured that governments have continued to pursue economic reform programmes. The stated objective of these reforms has been to restore the conditions for renewed capital accumulation. Growth, it has been generally argued both by the reforming governments and international financial institutions, is the precondition for economic well-being and for the adequate provision of social welfare. This economic regeneration, however, has proved elusive and problematic, even under the most stringent of reforms implemented in the most draconian fashion by the most repressive of strong governments. The reforms have in fact threatened the livelihoods and welfare of large sections of the population, notably the urban poor, and have generated widespread bitterness and anger at what has been seen as a betrayal of the state's obligations. The reform measures, designed to promote growth and development, have so far failed to do either and have come to constitute a key element in the growing dissatisfaction of increasingly large sections of the population with their governments.

Conclusion

As long as the goverments of Middle Eastern states continue to pursue programmes of economic reform which fail to provide sufficient tangible benefits for the majority of the urban population, and are seen to create unreasonable social and economic deprivation and inequality, popular protest remains likely. While popular protest can often be contained, it can not always be. The development of more orchestrated political opposition is always a possibility, even under the most repressive of states. Political reforms can be introduced to prevent the development of widespread discontent, but political reform itself may also engender more far-reaching political changes which challenge the regime which introduced the reforms. Social programmes may have a role, but these tend to be ineffective in their stated objectives of improving the well-being of the poor.

In many Middle Eastern states, Islamic movements have been gaining support from those most adversely affected by economic liberalization. Since the Iranian revolution in 1979, popular urban protest has come to be increasingly associated with the rise of Islamism and Islamic political movements. The relationship between austerity protests and Islamism is, however, quite complex. In Iran itself, the economic reform programme of President Rafsanjani led in August 1991 to large demonstrations in several cities. This suggests that popular protest against the effects of economic liberalization does not respect or adhere to any particular political ideology. Austerity protests are clearly political in the sense that they involve collective action in opposition to government policies, and are directed against both specific and more general targets; they are, however, not associated intrinsically with any particular political movement or political ideology. In that sense, and that sense only, they are not political.

Popular protest is not merely a response to economic and social adversity, it is also a demand for social justice and for renewal of the social contract between state and civil society, in which the role of the state is to ensure the economic and social welfare of all in society. Significantly, it is Islamism, with its emphasis on the indissoluble relationship between economic, social, political and moral issues, and its explicit appeal to the notion of community ('*umma*), that provides a suitable discourse readily acceptable to the mass of the population of Middle Eastern societies.

Only when secular movements and political parties within the Middle East are able to develop a comparable coherent moral philosophy and appeal, as well as economic and social policies capable of ensuring the economic and social wellbeing of all citizens, both individually and collectively; and only when they develop the organizational capacity to involve and promote the active and continuing participation of those who have so often felt obliged to take to the streets to express their grievances and demand justice, will the strength of Islamism be effectively challenged.

Notes

1 *The Independent*, 10/10/88.
2 *The Times*, 20/1/77.
3 *The Times*, 19/1/77.

6· THE PRACTICAL RECORD AND PROSPECTS OF PRIVATIZATION PROGRAMMES IN THE ARAB WORLD

Paul Stevens

The object of this chapter is to assess the contribution which privatization might make to the improved economic performance of the countries of the Arab world.[1] Privatization carries many different meanings, and one source (Pirie, 1985) identifies more than 20 methods of privatization. For the purposes of this chapter discussion of privatization is confined to the selling off of state owned enterprises to the private sector, either domestic or foreign.

Assessing the potential contribution of privatization hopefully achieves two objectives. First, it provides a set of criteria by which the practical record can be judged. At this stage in the privatization programme of most countries in the region, this is all that can be done. To date, most programmes have involved more rhetoric than action (Stevens, 1989) and in the few cases where enterprises have actually been sold off, it is too early to make an assessment. Second, assessing the contribution may indicate whether or not the proposed programmes will continue, thereby covering the 'prospects' dimension of the chapter title. If the criteria for success are desirable and are being met, then the programme is likely to continue. If the criteria are either undesirable or unattainable or both, then the programme is likely to fall by the wayside or at least change its character and focus.

The issue of privatization in the Arab world is inextricably tied up with political issues ranging from ideology to power group relations. This chapter, however, seeks to set the criteria and their evaluation in terms of economics and to try and cut through much of the political rhetoric assigned to the motives for privatization. Official motives for privatization have been many and varied. In Morocco, in March 1988, the King emphasized the need to reduce the absorption of state investment and expenditure and to improve management and efficiency. In Iraq, in June 1987, Saddam Husain talked in terms of trimming bureaucracy, liberalizing imports and currency controls and deregulating the labour market. In Turkey, the head of the Mass Housing and Public Participation Agency (MHPPA) emphasized efficiency, productivity and the promotion of the capital market. In Jordan, the Prime Minister's office stated that the aims were to increase efficiency and productivity and to rearrange the roles of public and private sectors 'to get the best out of them' (Arab British Commerce, 1989).

The purpose of this chapter is to try and translate such vague objectives into specific economic objectives in the light of some of the existing literature on privatization (especially Beesely & Littlechild, 1983; Brittan, 1986; Cook & Kirkpatrick, 1988; Hanke, 1987; Haile-Mariam & Mengistu, 1988; Johnson, 1988; Kay & Thompson, 1986; Klein, 1984; Littlechild *et.al.*, 1988; Ramanadham, 1989; Swann, 1988; Veljanovski, 1989; Vickers & Yarrow, 1988). The next stage is to consider whether in the Arab world, with its given characteristics, such objectives are feasible.[2]

There are many reasons why goverments choose to privatize. These can be categorized under three headings. First are selfish political motives. For example, the programme may be aimed at rewarding family, political friends and allies. Alternatively, the programme might be part of a 'democratization' process aimed at reinforcing the political positions of a flagging regime. Second, the programme might be simple window dressing to secure the approval of the IMF and World Bank as part of debt rescheduling negotiations. Between 1980 and 1984 some 67 countries were involved in 94 adjustment programmes negotiated by the IMF. In 23 of the countries, the programme involved the selling of public assets to the private sector (IMF, 1986). Currently, the region's debt situation is very ominous and a large number of IMF negotiations are likely to occupy the next few years in addition to those already underway. Third, the government may be seeking to optimize the country's social welfare. Selling off state-owned enterprises is seen, in this perspective, to improve the economic performance of the enterprise.[3]

Analysing the argument that privatization optimises social welfare

It is the third of the possible motives for privatization outlined above, optimizing social welfare, which constitutes the most substantial and respectable argument for a government to undertake a privatization programme. To assess the strength of the argument requires an analysis which proceeds through several stages. First what precisely is meant by 'to improve the economic performance of the enterprise'? Secondly, what is required to achieve such 'improvements'? Thirdly, what features of the existing enterprise and its operating context have previously inhibited the achievement of such requirements? Finally, how might privatization reverse such inhibitions?

Definition of 'improved economic performance of the enterprise'
The optimal economic performance of an enterprise is initially defined as the production of an output which the economy requires, at least cost. In addition, the enterprise should be dynamic, innovative and flexible to allow it to continue to produce relevant low-cost output in a world where circumstances are constantly changing. These features could be described under the general heading of performance efficiency.

There is, however, another dimension to enterprise performance which cannot be ignored in the Arab world. The enterprise may well have an important role as a tool to generate improved equity. Public enterprises can provide employment and can provide subsidized goods or intermediate inputs. Such a role can be imposed by government decree.[4] Economic textbooks would argue that this is a sub-optimal way of achieving equity because of the distortions it introduces to market signals and because there are better ways of achieving improved equity which avoid many of these distortions (such as direct payment to the poor). However, the practical economic and political context of the Arab world rules out many of these alternative approaches. For example, all of the well-known problems associated with government tax collection in the Third World apply equally to any provision of direct payments to the poor (Bird & Oldman, 1975; Eshag, 1983; Newbery & Stern, 1987). For the Arab countries, certain public enterprises may provide the only route to improved equity. This equity role differentiates the arguments for privatization in Arab (and other Third World) countries from those which apply in industrialized countries. In the latter, the text book alternatives to improve equity become practically feasible.

What is required for the improved economic performance of the enterprise?
How is relevant, low cost output produced dynamically from an enterprise? The requirement is that the enterprise is responsive; responsive to the needs of the consumer and responsive to changed circumstances with respect to input prices, technology and the institutional operating context. The responsiveness is required primarily from the management of the enterprise. Responsiveness is a circular phenomenon. The first stage is to see and read the signals directing the decisions of the firm with respect to such factors as output and investment in capacity. The second stage is to make the correct response to those signals in the form of decisions. The third stage is for those responses to be rewarded if correct, and punished if incorrect. The fourth stage is to see and read the signals. In a market environment the signals are prices of both inputs and output. The reward is profit and income. The punishment is reduced profit and income and ultimately the threat of takeover or bankruptcy.

Why has the economic performance of the enterprise been sub-optimal?
Most Arab countries have a significant number of public enterprises. In 1983 a World Bank Study listed, for 24 developing countries, the percentage involvement of state-owned enterprises in manufacturing. The list of 24 countries included four from the region: Egypt, Syria, Tunisia and Turkey. The top two on the list were Rumania and Hungary, with figures in excess of 90 per cent.[5] The next three in the list were Egypt (65 per cent), Tunisia (60 per cent) and Syria (58 per cent). Turkey was tenth with 30 per cent. Many other examples could be cited to provide support for the assertion of a high level of state involvement, which arose for a variety of historical reasons (Beblawi & Luciani, 1987). In general, it is reasonable to assert that the role of state enterprises in the region's economies is large relative to many other Third World countries.

There is a widely-held view that these enterprises, for the most part, have failed to be responsive and have had a poor record of performance efficiency. This has certainly been the message of many of the politicians who wish to justify privatization programmes.[6] The writer is prepared to accept such a view, based upon his own observations of the last 20 years.[7]

Many explanations can be offered to explain this poor performance efficiency. Before these explanations are considered, one argument which is commonly heard and is highly relevant to the privatization debate can be eliminated. This is that public enterprises, because they are state-owned and controlled are congenitally incapable of being efficient. There are some theoretical perspectives in economics which would support this view, associated with economic theories of agencies (Vickers & Yarrow, 1988) and the economics of public choice (Institute of Economic Affairs, 1978; Peacock, 1979). The empirical evidence, however, points in a different direction. There has now been a considerable amount of empirical work to evaluate comparative efficiencies of public and private enterprises (some of which has encountered significant problems of comparability, usually linked to the enterprises facing different objectives). The results are mixed (Aylem, 1988; Haile-Mariam & Mengistu, 1988; IEA, 1985; Kay and Thompson, 1986). One may be tempted from this to conclude, as many do, that the evidence is therefore inconclusive. However, the writer would suggest that there have now been a sufficient number of serious studies to assert that there are no empirical grounds to assume that private enterprise is automatically superior to public enterprise. This implies that superior performance is essentially determined by the environment in which the enterprise operates, rather than ownership *per se*.

There are better explanations of poor performance. These can be categorized into two schools of thought which can be described thus:

1. In the economies, the signals to the enterprises are distorted or indeed non-existent and have been replaced by government command motivated by narrow political interest. This arose because governments interfered with the existing market mechanisms. In general there have been three areas where government control has created problems for enterprises: price controls; rigidity in pay and promotion; and finally financing and liquidity shortages. Political interference in the running of public enterprise in the Middle East has without doubt been a major disadvantage to efficient operation. Many examples exist. In September 1968, Aziz Sidqi, the Egyptian Minister of Economy admitted that:

My opinion as the minister responsible for some of the units of the public sector, or a large part of them, is that we practised an excessive control and an excessive intervention, for the results which we expected did not occur as a result of increased intervention, which led to an increase in difficulties . . . Also . . . it led to an increase in avoiding responsibility. (Asad & Owen, 1983)

Such interference was frequently initiated with the intention of destroying the power base of a particular group, landlords and merchants, for instance. The enormous economic impact of such moves tended to be ignored.

2. The system of management (classically described as bureaucratic) provides neither incentive nor reward. The capital markets impose no discipline on management by means of takeover or bankruptcy because the enterprises have no publicly quoted shares. Management payments are generally non-performance based which tends to deter the entry of more able managers and to protect those who are incompetent. In such a context, state support plus the lack of incentive generates a cost-plus mentality among managers. An issue of key importance here with respect to privatization concerns problems associated with asymmetry of information which brings together economic theories of agencies and the economics of public choice. The regulating politicians (the principals) face the management of the enterprise (the agents). However, knowledge of the enterprise and its operations lies with the agent, while the principal might be assumed to be relatively ignorant of such matters. Given this information asymmetry, the principal can not effectively ensure that the agents perform, irrespective of the objective set. Thus the agents (managers) are in a position to pursue their own objectives without hindrance. If the system encourages risk aversion to extreme levels this will lead to stagnant poor performance.[8]

Frequently, these two explanations are linked together. Logically, however, they are alternatives since one asserts that control causes confusion, poor decision-making and low morale, while the other asserts that managers pursue their own objectives without control and that this is inimical to performance efficiency. The only obvious link is the creation of an environment where decision-makers have very high levels of risk aversion. The distinction of causation is important if cures (such as privatization) are to be considered.

How is privatization supposed to secure an improvement in the economic performance of the enterprise?

There are three areas in which, according to supporters of privatization programmes, privatization is supposed to improve the performance efficiency of a state enterprise: improving the quality of the signals available to managers, improving the ability of managers to respond to those signals and improving the managers' willingness to respond to the signals. For the sake of clarity, the arguments employed here will be outlined with little critical comment.

There are two ways in which privatization might improve managerial signals. First, the change in property rights affects the relationship between principal and agent. The agent is the management of the enterprise. The principal will be the shareholders in the case of a private enterprise and a ministry/department in the case of a public enterprise. It is argued that the objectives of the ministry may be many and conflicting given the self-interest of the ministry bureaucrats and politicians, plus the genuine requirement that the enterprise meet social welfare needs. The signals which are transmitted by regulation or command are therefore blurred and contradictory. The private owner, however, is assumed to have a simple profit-maximizing objective which can be clearly transmitted to management. Targets can therefore be clearly set and monitored. Second, once outside the public sector, subsidies on inputs may be expected to disappear, leaving the management facing full costs.[9] Equally, it is argued that once outside the public sector, regulations affecting output prices may no longer apply. Thus the profit margin becomes a real figure both to the enterprise and the economy as a whole.

Privatization may be expected to improve the ability of managers to respond to signals in several ways. First of all, removal from the public sector may free the enterprise from regulation and command. Thus the management will be free to take decisions based only on the constraints of profit maximization. A variant of this is the improvement which occurs where management functions better in a decentralized way.[10] If privatization is linked to decentralization, managers may be able to manage more effectively. Furthermore, the management will theoretically be free to focus upon the enterprise rather than on wider national goals associated with social welfare. In effect, the objectives of the principals and agents should coincide. As previously outlined, because of information asymmetry the principal may still have a monitoring problem, but this is where the disciplinary role of the capital market and competition (discussed below) comes to the rescue.

Finally, privatization should improve the willingness of management to respond to the signals. There are three aspects to this. First, the management is directly exposed to the discipline of the capital market. The company, now quoted on the stock exchange, can face takeover – with the usual subsequent removal of existing management. Less dramatically, poor performance leading to low return to shareholders may persuade them to vote out senior management. Equally, a company borrowing funds from the market can face bankruptcy if creditors decide to foreclose because of poor managerial performance. This is only possible if the enterprise's safety net when in the public sector has been removed or at least reduced.

Second, management may now face the discipline of competition. Privatization which involves a switch of ownership and the generation of competitive forces are separate issues, but the two issues have become linked in the public debate about privatization. There are good reasons why public enterprise is likely to be associated with the absence of competition. First, public ownership has been seen as a solution to the problems of natural monopoly, where the efficient scale of operation requires only one supplier. Second, bureaucrats have a strong vested interest in fending off competition to protect their interests. Finally, in developing countries, infant industry arguments have strongly reinforced the linkage between a state company and monopoly. In so far as privatization is linked to increased competition, so it is argued, this provides a strong incentive for minimizing production costs by efficiency and technical innovation.

Competition and the discipline of capital markets are seen by many economists as able to overcome problems of asymmetry of information between management and owners. In effect the market can ensure that the agents fulfil the wishes of the principals providing that those wishes are reasonably quantifiable (for example the maximization of shareholders' return).

Finally, managerial willingness may be affected by the changes in the incentive structure which may be associated with privatization. Moving out of the public sector may well change the employment contract towards performance-based reward and punishment. It is without doubt true that in many cases management in public enterprise have looked forward to privatization, given the almost universal pay differential which exists between the public and private sectors.[11]

Barriers to privatization providing the conditions necessary to secure an improvement in the economic performance of the enterprise

To achieve the improvements identified in the last section – better signals plus greater ability and willingness to respond – privatization must be associated with four factors. These are improved competition; reduced government interference; the development of capital markets; and finally changes in the incentive structure. This sector considers whether these four conditions are likely to be associated with the privatization programmes of the Arab world.

The potential for improved competition

Politicians tend to use the word competition as a sort of mantra or talisman. In economics, the significance of competition is that it generates rivalry between producers, which forces them (as profit maximizers) to be responsive to consumer needs at least cost. If they are not, then someone else will so respond. In traditional economic theory, competition required a large number of sellers on the grounds that a small number of producers will be likely to collude. This immediately creates a conflict between efficient scale of operation and market size. In situations where the scale of operation is large, the market may not be able to support more than one 'efficient' producer.

In the Arab world, the problem is especially relevant. In many cases (but by no means all) the national markets are either too small or too fragmented to justify the existence of more than one plant supplying particular goods. In a study (Badr, 1983), the Gulf Organization for Industrial Consulting (GOIC) looked at 26 projects and found that only 9 had a minimum efficient plant size in relation to the Gulf markets to justify even one plant. Thus it might be argued that in many Arab countries, many of the industries would be natural monopolies due to small market size.[12]

Since the early 1980s, economists have developed theories of contestable markets (Baumol, Panzar & Willig, 1982). In essence this argues that it is the threat of competition which matters. Fear of a hit and run raid by a new entrant will generate the discipline needed to encourage low-cost responsiveness. The concept of 'potential competition' has proved very popular with proponents of privatization, since it provides grounds for allowing an enterprise to remain a monopoly without tight regulation, provided entry is free. Although this idea has not yet permeated the discussion in the Arab world, one can see the attraction of such an argument in a society used to the give and take of the bazaar where hit and run entry has been a characteristic of business for centuries.

There is, however, a problem with the contestable markets argument if the industry is characterized by sunk costs. These are costs which are transaction-specific and can not therefore be recovered outside of their operating context. Thus large sunk costs for supplying will deter entry, since if you 'run' you forfeit the sunk costs. Most of the enterprises being mooted for privatization in the region are characterized by such sunk costs, especially heavy industry. There is also the problem that potential entrants must have easy access to the technology available to the incumbent. In a Third World country with its skill shortages and control of technology by multinationals this is extremely difficult. In addition, more recent theoretical work on strategic entry deterrence and predatory pricing behaviour suggests that if entry does take place it is more likely to lead to exit or collusion rather than competition.[13]

A central point to much of the discussion over the ability of competition to enforce discipline, whether by a number of sellers or by potential contestability, concerns rivalry. A key element behind the creation of rivalry through privatization is, who buys the shares? If they are bought up by one family or grouping, then it is plausible to expect that rivalry will be limited. Even without there being such a blatant eventuality, a small number of sellers are expected normally to collude to overcome the disadvantages associated with market uncertainty. This is precisely why countries have, in one form or another, anti-trust legislation to prevent collusion. The ability and willingness of Middle East governments to introduce such legislation, let alone ensure its implementation must remain extremely doubtful.

Assuming that competition by numbers or contestability is absent, it is only desirable to leave the monopoly as a monopoly provided some sort of regulation is applied which forces the equivalent effects of a competitive market. However, there are many well-known problems with regulation.[14] Of particular importance, once again, is the issue of the asymmetry of information between the regulator and the industry. In a context where skilled manpower is in short supply, such as the Arab world, this presents a real problem.[15] Thus a reason for privatization – to circumvent the information asymmetry problem – re-emerges in the form of regulation by the regulator of the private owner, rather than the ministry controlling the manager. In the case of a contrived monopoly, the purpose of regulation is to hold the fort until competition rides to the rescue. It is not obvious why many of the contrivances behind the monopolies in the Arab world, which stem from political factors, will necessarily go away to allow new entrants. Ultimately, there is no substitute for an effective competition policy, which faces severe practical constraints in the region.

Given this, the benefits of competition for the region may well prove to be non-existent. Privatization of itself can not produce a competitive environment, nor does competition require all enterprises to be privately-owned. The two are essentially separate issues and although they tend to be lumped together under the heading of liberalization, to do so is extremely dangerous. The result is likely to be a series of privately-owned monopolies which need to be neither responsive, low-cost nor dynamic.

There is, of course, one simple and practical way of developing competition and in particular of providing the entry threat required for contestable markets. That is to allow uncontrolled imports. Such a move is administratively easy, and would provide a definite check on any threat from a domestic monopoly.[16] There are of course problems in adopting such a policy. Unfettered imports may lead either to direct balance of payments problems, or problems stemming from the adoption of policies designed to alleviate balance of payments problems.[17] There are all the arguments associated with infant industries and strategic industries, pointing to the need for protection. Furthermore, in the development of the theory of contestable markets much has been written on problems associated with the hit and run entrants 'cream-skimming', leading to sub-optimal results. Nonetheless, if a government is really committed to a privatization programme, liberal trade regimes provide a simple answer to many of the problems over competition cited above. Such moves of course would lay the private owners open to (for them) undesirable pressures. If privatization has primarily a selfish political motive, therefore, liberalization of trade regimes is unlikely to follow. It could be suggested that a government's willingness to link privatization to free trade is an acid test of their real motivation.

Barriers to the removal of state control
Privately-owned enterprises are not immune from government interference.[18] They operate in a legal environment which is set by

government and can be used to control all aspects of enterprise operation. Whether newly privately-owned enterprises may still face administrative or regulatory interference from governments is very much a function of why the industry was originally brought under state control. In the Arab world this is a complex and contentious issue. Two extremes can be taken to illustrate the range of possibilities. The first asserts that such control/interference was an integral part of a political system based on client-patron relationships, with interlocking circles of control and influence. While such a political system remains in place it is difficult to see any diminution of intrusive government policy. This is reinforced if the buyer of the enterprise is in fact not a large number of small shareholders but a single individual or corporation who is close to the central circle of control.

The second interpretation asserts that state control/interference was to protect the poor and disadvantaged.[19] Few of the regimes in the region are sufficiently secure to be able suddenly to abrogate that role on any scale. Two issues are especially sensitive. First is the employment provision role of public enterprises (Handoussa, 1990a). In 1988, for example, Tunisia slowed down its privatization programme because of severe drought. The official explanation given by the Governor of the Central Bank was that it was important not to exacerbate unemployment at this stage by selling state companies with surplus labour. In view of such considerations, it seems likely that even after privatization, enterprises may remain subject to labour laws which provide for security of tenure. The second sensitive issue is price control in conditions of severely repressed inflation. In some areas, such as tourism, this is less important since the burden does not fall on the poor. In other areas, such as agriculture, it is crucial. Iraq is a good example. Prior to privatizing agricultural output, prices were decontrolled. This led to increasing prices which created significant popular unrest. In June 1989 this in turn forced the reimposition of price control.

The issue is essentially one of degree. It may be possible to reduce interference in certain areas such as financial control (including investment decisions) which may benefit an enterprise. There is, however, a strong 'catch 22'. With a limited and specific privatization programme it is possible to relax direct control without necessarily incurring the anger of the mass of the population. However, the newly privatized enterprises are still indirectly controlled, in so far as they are operating in a broader economy where state control remains. This will certainly lessen the gains from reduced government interference. Alternatively, a large-scale programme to free large parts of the economy (hence removing the indirect control) is likely to produce unacceptable political consequences.

Barriers to developing capital markets
Unlike the situation in many Third World countries, the availability of funds in the region is likely to be less of a problem. There have been a number of instances in Third World countries when privatization programmes have been postponed because they are simply too large for the domestic capital market to swallow (Hemming & Mansoor, 1988). Taking the Arab world as a whole however, there is surplus liquidity in the system. For example, in the Saudi banking system alone it has been estimated that there are 70–80 billion rials of surplus liquidity.[20] This is roughly equivalent to the privatization proceeds of the British government up to the end of 1987.

There is obviously a variation between countries, and some may find themselves short of domestic investors. This raises questions about the willingness of governments to allow non-nationals to participate. Foreign investment is a sensitive issue in the region, but a number of countries have already created the legal framework necessary to allow it. In particular, the type of debt-equity swaps popular in Latin America might be of interest. If the 'foreigners' are other Arabs, local hostility may be reduced. Many of the supporters of privatization in the region see the potential repatriation of Arab capital as a major gain from such programmes. The experience of the 1970s, however, suggests that such enthusiasm may well be premature since the record of Arabs investing in other Arab countries has not been good (Rumaihi, 1986).

The income distribution in the region is such that it is unlikely that a privatization programme would bring forth the small investor. However, this is not a necessary condition for the development of a capital market. Selling to a few rich individuals could well assist capital market development, although this would at the same time reinforce the existing concentration of economic (and hence political) power. It could also create a very unstable market, if a few players dominate. Markets with a few large players encourage the sorts of irregular behaviour characterized by the Suq Al Manakh crisis. Such capital markets do not provide the discipline required.

A possible mechanism to avoid negative distribution effects and to encourage smaller investors would be to privatize by giving preference to the workers; the co-operative route. This can also be used to resolve the problems caused by the absence of any capital market (Hemming & Mansoor, 1988). This route raises a number of problems in the Arab world. Many of the likely privatization candidates are capital intensive projects, which means that the workers could not afford to purchase the enterprise unless the selling price was significantly below market value. There is also a problem over the national and ethnic identity of the workers. Clearly, if expatriates predominate, as in the Gulf, selling to them would be unacceptable, especially at 'give-away' prices. Equally, the predominance of minorities in the workforce could inhibit such a route. In many Third World countries, this latter point has been a serious stumbling block to such programmes.[21]

The development of capital markets faces many problems in the region. In virtually all the countries, the capital markets are new[22] and very small.[23] For example, in Turkey, the Istanbul Exchange only opened in 1986, and this was specifically for the privatization programme. Forty companies are quoted and trading is negligible. Smallness gives rise to two problems. The first is volatility. Small markets on which little is traded can be subject to enormous fluctuations in share price, either as a natural consequence of trading or as the result of deliberate manipulation. The result is that shareholders, especially small ones, are likely to get hurt. This adds significantly to the existing inhibitions against the holding of paper, which is a necessary condition for an expansion in the capital market. Recent Turkish experience demonstrates the difficulties.

A second problem is that of short-termism.[24] Firms may be forced to take decisions to keep the financial markets happy which could be against their (and the economy's) long-term interest. After all, in many of the countries the state-owned enterprises were created precisely because the private sector would not undertake projects of a similar nature. In the industrialized countries, research suggests that short-termism is much less of a problem than many believed (McConnell & Muscarella, 1985). Research is needed now to assess whether such a conclusion can legitimately be carried over to the Arab world. Much of the discussion of the role of merchants in the region and their relatively short time horizons, suggests that short-termism could be a problem. A linked problem occurs if the market for the good is comparatively small and spatially dispersed. In such a context, 'the costs of upfront investment are bound to be recovered over periods which exceed by far the planning horizon of private entrepreneurs' (Teplitz-Sembitzky, 1990: 32).[25]

In general, it is likely that any boost to local capital markets and their consequent disciplinary role is overstated. This is particularly true if the block sale approach is adopted where the enterprise is simply sold to another enterprise. Equally it is fair to argue that the process of developing capital markets must begin somewhere and that privatization could be a useful starting point.[26]

The disciplinary role of an active capital market may face other restrictions. It is well known in the economics literature that takeovers face limitations. In particular there is the problem of free-riding, whereby it is in the interest of an existing shareholder to reject a takeover offer since the buyer will offer a price for the shares below what it is believed will be the eventual value. If existing shareholders hang on, they can benefit from that higher price. Hence takeovers would never occur. This problem can only be solved by the creation of sophisticated regulations concerning takeovers. Moreover, taking over very large companies is almost impossible in the absence of leveraged buy-outs. Such buy-outs require a degree of sophistication in capital markets which may be unrealistic in the region for some time to come. Finally it may well be that the harshness of market discipline, ultimately bankruptcy, may be alien in the Arab world where such extremes are unacceptable given the prevailing ethic.

Barriers to the provision of adequate incentives

A key source of managerial incentive derives from competition and the control of the capital market. The extensive literature on this subject suggests that managers in a large private firm do not necessarily have a strong interest *per se* in profitability for shareholders. Rather they, like any bureaucracy, are more concerned with issues such as salary, survival, growth and prestige (Aylem, 1988; Kay & Thompson, 1986). What is crucial to force an improved performance is pressure for accountability from competition and the capital markets, as previously discussed. In the words of one observer, it is 'not ownership as much as market environment, firm's organisation and managerial incentives that determine the performance of companies' (Aylem, 1988: 128). For such pressure to work to enhance performance, efficiency requires competition and active financial markets. Simply switching ownership is not enough.

It may well be the case that enabling an enterprise to escape from government labour regulations and restrictions could generate an environment where the workforce at all levels is better motivated to perform. An obvious point, but one worth making, is that such improvements can be achieved equally well by keeping the enterprise in public ownership and changing the regime of labour regulation. If labour law is to be reformed however, the equity role of the public enterprise does need to be considered. This creates a genuine dilemma. Casual empiricism suggests that countries which adopt a gradual approach to the restructuring of their economies fail. This is because the reforms are too slow to produce benefits. Hence opposition to reform is likely to outweigh support for it. On the other hand, countries which adopt the 'short, sharp shock treatment' are more likely to survive and prosper because the benefits of reform come more quickly to assuage the pain. This of course assumes they do not fall apart in the process.

It is a truly difficult dilemma and one which underlies much of the procrastination which now characterizes the region's privatization plans.

Conclusion

The analysis has presented a fairly negative view of the prospects for privatization in the region, at the micro level of the enterprise.[27] To ensure that selling state enterprises improves economic performance requires certain conditions to be met. These are increased competition, reduced harmful interference from the state, the development of capital markets and a new incentive system for labour. All face significant obstacles in the Arab world. This suggests that the record of existing programmes is likely to be poor and that their prospects in their current form may be limited. Many of these obstacles are derived from the nature of politics in the countries concerned. It is likely that political reform is a necessary condition if privatization is to contribute to improved economic performance in the Arab world. In the jargon of the debate, 'perestroika' is not possible without 'glasnost'.

Notes

1 Turkey is also referred to in the study since it was one of the first countries in the Middle East to introduce a privatization programme.

2 As the chapter will show, there is a distinctive Third World dimension to the privatization debate. However, it has been difficult for the author to identify a specifically Arab dimension to the issue. This is an area that needs more consideration.

3 This chapter adopts a very micro approach to the issue, by concentrating on the impact on individual enterprises. A more macro evaluation of privatization in the Arab world can be found in Stevens (1989).

4 Government decree can of course also require privately-owned enterprises to follow a similar path. An obvious example might be the requirement for positive discrimination in the enterprise's hiring policy.

5 Given the ideological imperative, this is not surprising.

6 This constant attack upon the public sector has, in many cases, had a very negative effect upon morale in the public sector; one of the costs of the privatization programmes which is less publicized.

7 There are a number of important reservations attached to this view. First, generalization is dangerous and there are many examples of public enterprises which do turn in respectable performances by conventional financial criteria. Second, as already discussed, many public enterprises have without doubt performed an equity function for which there was no practical alternative.

8 Alan Peacock (Peacock, 1980) quotes the Irish poet Louis Macniece in 'Bagpipe Music': 'sit on your arse for fifty years and hang your hat on a pension'.

9 This ignores the fact that there may well be external costs and benefits associated with the activity of the enterprise, which remain outside of the managerial signals.

10 In Egypt tourism has been cited as such an example (Handoussa, 1987). However, in the latest corporate management thinking, 'customer responsiveness' is generally accepted as crucial in virtually all businesses. For many this requires decentralized decision-making, since the employees on the 'front-line' (those dealing with customers) must be able to take decisions. Only where transactions involve large indivisible items (such as heavy industry) would such decentralization not apply.

11 Such enthusiasm frequently fails to take account of equally important changes in employment tenure.

12 This is a classification of monopoly used by economists to distinguish from a contrived monopoly. In simple terms, if a monopoly is a natural monopoly, competition would not emerge nor should it emerge in terms of efficiency criteria since more than one supplier would increase costs unnecessarily. A contrived monopoly, on the other hand, precludes competition by some sort of barrier to entry. In such a case competition can not occur if the barriers are effective, but competition would be desirable.

13 An excellent discussion of these issues with respect to electricity utilities in developing countries can be found in Teplitz-Sembitzky (1990). This provides a valuable antidote to the lobby in favour of privatizing electricity utilities in the Third World. It is significant because it is a World Bank paper, albeit suitably disclaimed.

14 For example, see Kay and Thompson (1986); Teplitz-Sembitzky, (1990).

15 Even in the industrialized world this is seen by many to be the main barrier to effective regulation.

16 Even where the commodity is a high-volume low-value item, which provides some degree of natural protection by means of the high proportion of c.i.f. element in the final price, at least some cap exists on the monopolist's suppliers' ability to secure excess profit. There are very few goods where import may simply be impractical. The only obvious examples are (in most cases) electricity and water.

17 For example domestic inflation fed by devaluation.

18 Equally it is perfectly possible, in theory, to have publicly-owned enterprises which are insulated from government interference. For example, Algeria has created state-sponsored trust companies in eight sectors (fonds de participation), whose function is to hold shares in state-owned companies, specifically to protect them from government interference.

19 Of course this could equally be for motives connected with the first explanation – the maintenance of political control.

20 This number is based on private discussion.

21 Kenya and Malaysia are frequently cited in the literature.

22 Those that are old, such as the Cairo Stock Exchange, are effectively defunct.

23 Traditionally in the Third World, companies tend to rely more on debt than equity. For example, Aylem (1988), cites the Seoul Stock Exchange where at the end of 1985 the 340 companies listed had an equity capitalization equal to only $6 billion, with an average gearing ratio of 350 percent.

24 This is where exigencies of the capital market force companies to make decisions not to undertake activities/investment which on any long term basis would be beneficial.

25 Although the quote relates to electricity utilities, it would apply to any capital intensive project.

26 For example, Hemming and Mansoor (1988), claim that in Turkey sales of bonds secured by revenues from the Bosphorus bridge and the Keban dam have been a major influence on the growth of the domestic capital market.

27 An attack on other aspects of privatization, such as the benefits to the government budget, can be found in Stevens (1989).

7· FOREIGN INVESTMENT AND ECONOMIC LIBERALIZATION IN THE MIDDLE EAST

George Joffé

The role of foreign investment

In the recent enthusiasm for the restructuring of Middle Eastern economies, commentators have directed relatively little attention towards the issue of direct private foreign investment and the role it might play in the process of economic liberalization.

Attention has been focused, instead, on issues such as foreign trade and domestic price structure liberalization, currency convertibility and the removal of restrictions on international capital flows, reduction of the domestic role of the public sector and export-oriented growth. Much of this attention has, furthermore, resulted from the over-riding preoccupation with external debt and the conditions imposed by the IMF and the World Bank (not to speak of the Paris Club or the London committee) for debt-rescheduling and reduction.

There is little doubt that this relative lack of interest on the part of commentators reflects the minor role played by direct private foreign investment in the economies of the region. As Tables 7.1 and 7.2 show, only Egypt has consistently relied on direct private foreign investment, as part of the *infitah* process introduced by President Sadat in 1974, to generate more than 10 per cent of direct investment.[1] Foreign/domestic investment ratios in Egypt ranged between 0.095 and 0.229 over the period 1979–89. Only Saudi Arabia came close to these levels, with ratios of 0.137 in 1984, 0.098 in 1983 and 0.112 in 1981. In Saudi Arabia's case, this was largely because of its elaborate joint venture arrangements with foreign multinationals in the refining and petrochemicals sector. Otherwise, oil-rich states have themselves tended to invest abroad rather than to seek inward investment, as was particularly clear in the cases of Kuwait and Libya in the first half of the 1980s. The overall pattern, then, has been that direct foreign investment has constituted only a minor proportion of gross domestic investment.

The most frequently-cited reason for encouraging foreign direct investment focuses on the need to boost capital inflows. For non oil-exporting countries, capital inflows are required to counter chronic deficits on the current account. Oil-exporting countries may also require such inflows, if they are undertaking major construction projects (Saudi Arabia and Algeria are cases in point).

Foreign direct investment, however, has constituted only a small fraction of the overall capital inflow into Middle Eastern states, except in the cases of Egypt and Turkey. Much greater amounts have come in the form of official development assistance (for the poorer states) and of public sector loans or publicly-guaranteed loans to the private sector. This can be seen by comparing the figures for direct foreign investment, given in Table 7.1, with the figures for public external capital inflows and development assistance, given in Tables 7.3 and 7.4. It should be borne in mind that foreign investment can also generate a capital outflow, through the repatriation of profits. Direct foreign investment, then, is not only a small part of total investment, it is also a small part of capital inflows.

The most recent (provisional) balance of payments statistics to emerge from Morocco make the point very well. In 1990, the Dh1.602 billion deficit on the current account was compensated by net capital inflows of Dh15.126 billion, leaving a surplus in the balance of payments of Dh13.524 billion ($1 = Dh8.80442). Actual capital receipts from both official and private sector totalled Dh23.936 billion, while foreign debt repayments totalled Dh8.810 billion. Net private capital inflows, however, only totalled 4.294 billion and net foreign direct investment was only around Dh1.9 billion, less than 4 per cent of gross fixed capital formation.

Despite this, the rhetoric of virtually all states in the region, particularly those states which are not oil exporters or which are high capital absorbing states, stresses the importance of foreign investment to the national economy. This is especially true of the Maghreb. In Morocco, for example, King Hassan II found it necessary to make public in 1990 a formal letter to his prime minister in which he instructed that, if the government did not publish its decision on applications for foreign investment within two months of such applications being lodged, it was to be assumed that they had been

Table 7.1: *Net Private Foreign Investment in the Middle East, 1979–89** (*Selected years – $ million current*)

Country	1970	1979	1981	1983	1984	1985	1986	1987	1988	1989
Algeria	45	72	315	−14	−14	2	290	−20	−48	−59
Bahrain	na	na	na	na	na	na	na	na	na	na
Egypt	–	1,211	746	845	713	1,175	1,208	869	973	1,586
Iran	25	–	–	–	–	–	–	–	–	–
Iraq	24	–	–	–	–	–	–	–	–	–
Jordan	–	26	143	30	71	23	21	33	0	0
Kuwait	–	145	36	−241	−125	−57	−288	−93	−262	–
Lebanon	–	–	–	–	–	–	–	–	–	–
Libya	139	−319	−1,079	−335	−329	−316	139	−80	43	–
Morocco	20	39	59	46	47	20	1	57	85	167
Oman	na	na	na	154	157	175	138	138	33	–
Qatar	na	na	na	na	na	na	na	na	na	na
Saudi Arabia	20	−1,173	3,376	3,653	5,228	2,513	964	−1,175	−1,175	–
Sudan	–	–	–	–	9	–	–	–	0	0
Syria	–	−52	–	–	–	–	–	–	0	–
Tunisia	16	49	294	186	115	107	159	92	59	74
Turkey	58	129	150	72	113	99	125	110	352	663
UAE	na	na	–	–	–	–	–	–	–	–
Yemen**	–	−5	40	8	7	3	5	−10	–	0

Note:
* Net investment by non-residents in enterprises over which they exercise significant managerial control, including investment by residents abroad. For 1989, investment by an investor above 10 per cent of total equity in a country other than that in which the investor is resident.
** Including both North and South Yemen.
– no figures available.
na (not available) – not recorded because population below 1 million.
SOURCE: World Bank, (various years), *World Development Report*, Oxford University Press.

automatically approved. This was passed into law in mid-1990.[2] Regulations governing foreign investment in Tunisia are similarly liberal.[3] In Algeria, the March 1990 money and credit law permitted foreign investors to take a majority stake in most sectors. The oil sector was initially excluded on grounds of 'national sovereignty', and it was subsequently confirmed that the oil sector would not be open for foreign investors to acquire majority stakes.[4]

The situation in some eastern Arab states is similar. In Jordan, for example, restrictions on foreign investment were removed in the mid-1980s and ventures with 100 per cent foreign ownership are now permitted. In Egypt, in October 1989, a new law streamlined foreign investment application procedures, placing foreigners and private Egyptian investors on the same legal footing (something which was

Table 7.2: *Gross Domestic Investment in the Middle East, 1960–89*
($ million)

Country	1960	1965	1979	1981	1983	1984	1985	1986	1987	1988	1989
Algeria	1,176	697	13,116	15,477	17,464	19,262	20,945	19,443	18,734	16,089	12,332
Bahrain	–	–	–	–	–	–	–	–	–	–	–
Egypt	504	819	5,286	6,933	7,818	7,515	7,638	7,762	6,549	6,866	7,579
Iran	700	1,049	–	–	–	–	–	–	–	–	45,675
Iraq	316	389	9,956	–	–	–	–	–	–	–	–
Jordan	–	–	898	1,046	1,452	1,098	897	960	1,110	1,014	704
Kuwait	–	336	2,796	4,124	4,906	4,559	4,342	–	–	3,994	4,471
Lebanon	133	253	–	–	–	–	–	–	–	–	–
Libya	–	435	5,160	9,316	7,213	7,031	–	–	–	–	–
Morocco	204	295	3,439	3,399	2,793	3,059	2,607	2,952	3,183	5,278	5,374
Oman	–	–	–	–	2,163	–	2,646	–	–	–	–
Qatar	–	–	–	–	–	–	–	–	–	–	–
Saudi Arabia	–	322	24,440	30,012	37,374	38,283	29,466	21,190	16,438	19,607	16,987
Sudan	209	133	1,070	980	−70	763	485	–	903	1,124	–
Syria	–	147	2,551	3,658	3,876	3,823	3,929	4,176	4,558	2,542	1,490
Tunisia	131	246	1,760	2,201	2,036	2,221	1,955	1,870	1,775	1,663	2,052
Turkey	1,411	1,149	11,857	13,478	10,046	9,492	9,764	13,155	15,813	15,446	15,752
UAE	–	–	–	8,420	8,806	7,787	8,717	–	6,404	6,201	7,068
Yemen AR	–	–	–	1,219	−742	617	777	1,000	641	768	–
Yemen PDR	–	–	–	–	–	–	–	–	–	–	–

SOURCE: World Bank, (various years) *World Development Report*, Oxford University Press.

done in Morocco in 1985). The procedures ensured approval of applications within 20 days and protected investment against nationalization.[5] Yemen, too, introduced a new investment code in 1989, guaranteeing foreign investment against nationalization without compensation, providing five-year tax holidays and allowing foreigners to own property in the republic.[6]

In the oil-rich states of the Gulf, attitudes are not quite so welcoming. Oman does permit foreign majority holdings up to 65 per cent of total equity in joint ventures.[7] Similar regulations exist in the UAE and in Saudi Arabia, but nationals in both of these countries must have at least a nominal position of control in any joint venture. In Kuwait, nationality and property legislation makes it essential for foreign investment in a commercial undertaking to be under formal Kuwaiti control.[8]

Even the more radical states of the Middle East have adapted their attitudes towards foreign investment. In Iraq, Arab investment in some sectors (such as tourism) has been welcomed for some years.[9] Before the Gulf crisis, moreover, the Iraqi government was moving towards

Table 7.3 *Net Inflow of Public External Capital into the Middle East, 1970–1989**
($ million)

Country	1970	1979	1981	1983	1984	1985	1986	1987	1988	1989
Algeria	278	2,467	382	−371	−255	68	−475	653	1,388	−197
Bahrain	na	na	na	na	na	na	na	na	na	na
Egypt	87	1,489	1,918	765	995	735	516	513	832	734
Iran	705	1,089	–	–	–	–	–	–	–	–
Iraq	46	113	–	–	–	–	–	–	–	–
Jordan	12	193	234	325	450	119	247	15	167	830
Kuwait	–	–	–	–	–	–	–	–	–	–
Lebanon	10	45	58	−13	−11	−16	22	−4	5	5
Libya	–	–	–	–	–	–	–	–	–	–
Morocco	131	1,046	1,103	229	690	127	653	612	476	644
Oman	na	na	na	416	147	559	567	−94	66	184
Qatar	na	na	na	na	na	na	na	na	na	na
Saudi Arabia	–	–	–	–	–	–	–	–	–	–
Sudan	31	194	489	385	139	45	165	139	329	191
Syria	29	307	113	94	188	263	261	287	176	−53
Tunisia	42	591	283	151	247	314	258	215	212	243
Turkey	203	3,763	1,306	423	1,246	470	1,697	1,441	1,859	835
UAE	na	na	na	–	–	–	–	–	–	–
Yemen AR	–	116	245	297	153	139	156	15	124	na
Yemen PDR	1	92	158	274	145	398	480	172	171	na
Yemen Rep.	na	na	na	na	na	na	na	na	na	386

Note:
* Net public external capital inflows are all disbursements annually of all public and publicly guaranteed foreign long-term loans less amortisation (repayment of principal). They thus exclude direct private investment and private non-guaranteed long-term loans.
– no record.
na – not available/applicable.
SOURCE: World Bank, (various years), *World Development Report*, Oxford University Press.

permitting Western oil companies to engage in joint exploration and development ventures in the oil sector. Syria also now provides limited encouragement for foreign private investment, although the investment law is very out-of-date and new legislation is being developed to encourage foreign investors.[10] Only Libya actively prevents any kind of foreign private investment at all, but even here there have been hints that the rigid ideological purity of the *jamahiriyah* may soon be rendered more flexible.

Prospects for attracting more foreign investment
Since the current economic role of direct private investment in the region seems to be relatively marginal, it seems strange that regional

Table 7.4: *Official Development Assistance to the Middle East, 1979–89* (*$ million – net from all sources*)

Country	1979	1980	1981	1982	1983	1984	1985	1986	1987	1988	1989
Algeria	102	176	163	137	95	122	173	165	214	171	153
Bahrain	na	na	na	na	na	na	na	na	na	na	na
Egypt	1,450	1,387	1,292	1,417	1,463	1,794	1,791	1,716	1,773	1,537	1,578
Iran	6	31	9	3	48	13	16	27	71	82	89
Iraq	18	8	9	6	13	4	26	33	91	10	5
Jordan	1,299	1,275	1,065	799	787	687	538	564	579	415	280
Kuwait	2	10	9	6	5	4	4	5	3	6	4
Lebanon	101	237	451	187	127	77	83	62	101	141	132
Libya	5	17	11	12	6	5	5	11	6	6	11
Morocco	473	896	1,034	771	398	352	785	403	447	481	443
Oman	165	174	231	132	71	67	78	84	16	1	16
Qatar	na	na	na	na	na	na	na	na	na	na	na
Saudi Arabia	11	16	30	57	44	36	29	31	22	19	16
Sudan	671	588	681	740	962	622	1,128	945	898	937	760
Syria	1,803	1,727	1,495	952	813	641	610	728	684	191	139
Tunisia	210	233	252	210	205	178	163	222	274	316	247
Turkey	594	952	724	659	356	242	179	339	376	269	122
UAE	7	4	1	5	4	3	4	34	115	−12	−6
Yemen AR	268	472	411	412	330	314	–	–	–	–	–
Yemen PDR	76	100	87	143	106	85	–	–	–	–	–

Note:
These figures are for all grants and loans on concessional terms made by all bilateral official agencies and multilateral sources. They do not include loans raised on international capital markets or from other sources.

SOURCE: World Bank, (various years), *World Development Report*, Oxford University Press.

governments should invest so much legislative effort in preparing the appropriate investment climate, given that other sources of external finance are far more important. The effort expended appears to be out of proportion with the results obtained.

One reason why Middle Eastern states are apparently so anxious to attract foreign investors may be precisely so as to counter the currently marginal status of direct foreign investment in their economies. We now need to examine, therefore, whether they have any realistic prospect of attracting a substantially higher level of investment. The real potential for investment in the Middle East should be seen against the background of the way in which direct private foreign investment has expanded elsewhere in the developing world. The basic source of direct foreign investment has traditionally been the multinational corporation (MNC) – an enterprise that owns and controls productive activities in more than one country.

Worldwide direct foreign private investment has risen, in current price terms, by 29 per cent annually between 1983 and 1989, reaching an annual total of $196 bn in 1989 – a far higher rate than growth in world gross domestic product (7.8 per cent annually) or in world trade (exports rose at 9.4 per cent annually). The developing world has been losing in the struggle for access to these investment flows. Its share of the total fell from 28 per cent of the total in the late 1970s, to 25 per cent in the first half of the 1980s and to 18 per cent during the second half of the 1980s. Moreoever, ten developing countries alone mopped up 75 per cent of the available funds; five in Asia, four in Latin America and only one (Egypt) in the Middle East.

For the Middle East the picture is even more gloomy, for there was a persistent decline in investment during the 1970s[11] and no significant rise in the 1980s. This means that the current drive for direct foreign investment starts from a much lower base than is the case in Asia and Latin America. Much of the decline in foreign investment during the 1970s was, of course, an effect of Middle Eastern countries taking control of their oil industries. The World Bank has recently argued that the developing countries will gain a higher proportion of direct foreign investment over the 1985–95 period than they did between 1980 and 1989. Yet, even here, it is made clear that it is Asia and Latin America which will draw most of the benefit. In the future, the World Bank argues, direct private foreign investment flows will grow, but they will be concentrated in 'globally integrated, middle income countries with well-developed infrastructure'.[12] Few Middle Eastern countries possess these characteristics.

The only Middle Eastern states which may be able to anticipate an increase in investment are those offering opportunities which cannot be matched elsewhere; the oil exporters. Yet even here the prospects might not be very bright. Although international oil companies may well be seeking new investment opportunities, to which the current rash of proposals for participation arrangements and joint ventures in Middle Eastern oil have been designed to respond, they may not wish to repeat the uncomfortable experiences of the 1970s, when virtually all their assets were nationalized. They are also aware that political instability may undermine whatever guarantees host countries are prepared to offer for the protection of direct foreign private investment within their borders.[13]

It may be argued, furthermore, that Arab economies are not sufficiently oriented to manufacturing, the preferred sector for direct foreign investment. The other major sector of interest to foreign investors tends to be the service sector and here the emphasis is usually placed on tourism, particularly in Morocco and Tunisia. The major industries which tend to attract direct foreign investment, such as textiles, food processing, light industrial assembly, pharmaceuticals, white consumer goods and, in some cases, electronic assembly and plastics, are relatively immature in Middle Eastern economies.

Foreign investment and economic liberalization

With little foreign investment having reached their economies, and little prospect of more coming, the causes of the eagerness of Middle Eastern states to make legislative changes so as to attract foreign investment must be sought elsewhere.

The theoretical literature suggests that foreign investment carries with it some further advantages, besides those which flow directly from the inflow of capital. The 'advantages', however, are seldom clear-cut. It can be argued that, by creating another commercial entity (which presumably generates a profit), government tax receipts will increase, thereby generating additional resources for domestic investment. Potential investors, however, will be seeking arrangements which minimize tax payments. If they believe that the balance of fiscal advantage will turn against them and towards the host country, they may find the investment unattractive. Claims are also made that direct foreign investment can speed the process of technology transfer and the transfer of other commercial skills and stimuli, and may promote employment creation. However, modern technology and manufacturing techniques tend to be capital- rather than labour-intensive, such that the wrong technology is transferred, and little employment is created. Counter claims have been advanced that foreign firms distort local wage levels and absorb the better-educated elements of the labour-force, disadvantaging indigenous enterprises. Firms are also accused of diverting domestic investment away from more appropriate objectives.

In the case of the Middle East, the marginal nature of the impact of direct foreign investment on the Arab economies suggests that these arguments are of secondary concern, and that another dynamic may be at work. The primary reason why Middle Eastern countries have chosen to give such emphasis to foreign investment in their economic liberalization programmes lies in their need to show some concurrence with the perceptions of the IMF and World Bank. Other chapters of this book provide information on the specific agreements which individual Middle Eastern states have reached with these bodies. More important than the individual agreements, however, is the 'world view' of the IMF and World Bank. The World Bank argues that 'openness – the free flow of goods, capital, people and knowledge – transmits technology and generates economic growth across nations'.[14]

Within developing countries, the process of engaging in economic restructuring and 'openness' involves adopting, popularizing and legitimizing a new ideological and philosophical attitude towards the issue of economic growth. The result is that the conventional economic panaceas, such as privatization and the reduction of state sector expenditure, become very public objects of policy, whatever their real economic significance may be. Governments tend, therefore, to adopt and proclaim new economic orthodoxies as part of their attempts to persuade international opinion of the validity and durability of their economic reforms. The specific encouragement of direct private foreign investment by developing governments is more an affirmation of their acceptance of the new economic orthodoxies than it is a statement of realistic intent.

Even though countries in the Middle East may enthusiastically seek direct private foreign investment, the factors which ultimately decide whether or not they are successful may lie outside their own competence and control. MNCs have their own reasons for their foreign investment decisions, based in their own organizational behaviour and commercial practice. The objective conditions offered for investment by a particular country will not play a major role in the decisions that are actually taken unless they coincide with the MNC's own interests and objectives.

Notes

1 EIU (1990), *Egypt, Country Profile 1990–91*, Business International, p. 58.
2 EIU (1990), *Morocco, Country Report*, No. 3, Business International, p. 10.
3 EIU (1990), *Tunisia, Country Profile 1990–91*, Business International, pp. 26–7.
4 See Economic Intelligence Unit, (1991), *Algeria, Country Profile 1991–92*, Business International, no. 14, pp. 46–7.

   The new Ghozali government, under the prompting of Petroleum Minister Nordine Ait-Laoussine, has proposed the sale of $6–$7 billion worth of Algeria's hydrocarbon assets in order to reduce the country's foreign debt. The assets concerned are said to be 25 per cent of the Hassi Messaoud oil field and potential buyers include French and US oil companies. See *Africa Confidential*, vol 32.

5 EIU, (1990), *Egypt, Country Profile 1990–91*, Business International, p. 59.
6 EIU, (1991), *Oman, Yemen Country Profile 1991–92*, Business International, pp. 58–9.
7 *Ibid*, pp. 30–1.
8 McLachlan K.S. (1990), *Kuwait in the 1990s: a society under siege*, EIU Special Report no. 2035, Business International, pp.32–3.
9 Joffé G. (1990b), 'Developments in Iraq since the ceasefire' in Davies C. ed. (1990), *After the War: Iraq, Iran and the Gulf*, Chichester: Carden, p. 240.
10 EIU, (1990), *Syria, country profile 1990–91*, Business International, pp.5–56.
11 Andersson T. (1991), *Multinational Investment in Developing Countries*, London: Routledge, pp. 15–18.
12 World Bank, (1991), *World Development Report 1991* Oxford: Oxford University Press, p. 24.
13 In a recent publication, the UNCTC argues that developing countries are now willing to collaborate with transnational corporations in order to encourage direct foreign investment and that, as a result, the threat of nationalization has become a minimal risk. See UN Centre on Transnational Corporations (1990), *The New Code Environment*, UNCTC Current Studies, Series A, no. 16, New York: United Nations, p. 16.
14 World Bank, (1991), *World Development Report 1991*, Oxford: Oxford University Press, p. 88.

PART TWO

8· EGYPT

Robert Springborg

Al-infitah (the opening), the term now generally employed to designate economic and political liberalization throughout the Arab world, was first used in this context in Egypt. Initially describing the role of foreign investment in the housing and construction sectors in a government document in April 1973, the term entered Eygpt's political lexicon the following year via the October Paper, the manifesto of Egyptian liberalization (Dessouki, 1982: 75). Almost a generation of Egyptians has come to maturity under successive governments whose official proclamations have steadfastly reiterated their commitment to *al-infitah*. The adjective *intaji* (productive), added as a qualifier in the wake of President Sadat's assassination, was not intended by the new Mubarak government to signal a radical departure from the goals of the original liberalization, but rather to disassociate the process from previous errors and excesses and to amend its methods in order to preserve it. The Egyptian *infitah*, having demonstrated longevity, adaptability, and transportability, and having captured the sustained attention of domestic and regional publics, to say nothing of international bankers, IMF officials, and Western academics, provides a rich source from which observations and lessons about the process of economic liberalization and its political and social effects can be drawn.

Initiating liberalization
As Nazih Ayubi has correctly observed, 'Egypt's open door policy represents the outcome of developments on three distinct levels: the domestic, the regional and the international'. (Ayubi, 1982: 349). At home Egypt's socialist experiment could not continue, according to Ayubi, because those directing it were not socialists. At the regional

145

level the quasi-integrated Arab oil economy, brought about by the post-1973 oil boom, nurtured Egypt's opening by creating the conditions for greatly increased transnational flows of capital and labour. Among the international factors conducive to liberalization were the perceptions of Egyptian decision-makers that a US hegemony had been established in the region, and the conviction in Washington that Egypt could play the dual role of peacemaker with Israel and model for other political economies of the region which the US hoped would abandon Soviet methods and alliances.

The voluminous secondary literature on Egypt's *infitah* is mostly in harmony with Ayubi's account of the inauguration of the process. Egypt's economy is generally agreed to have entered a crisis in the mid-1960s, as signalled by the severe foreign exchange shortage of 1965 and the attempts by the Muhi al-Din government to negotiate an IMF standby agreement in that year. The protracted crisis has been widely interpreted as an indication that Egypt had reached the turning point which invariably confronts import substitution industrialization. The state either needs to 'deepen' the experiment by extracting savings from the middle classes (which hitherto have prospered), or turn away from economic nationalism and seek closer integration into the world capitalist system. The latter path ensures that the state can retain the support of the politically vital middle classes. In Egypt's case the leftward path was blocked by the increasingly comfortable state bourgeoisie, by the private bourgeoisie still entrenched in the political economy, by the degeneration of the single party and its appendages into a patrimonialism aptly described as 'sultanic socialism' (Moore, 1980: 54), and possibly by the predilections of the *ra'is* himself (Waterbury, 1983: 317–26). Instead of admitting the defeat of Arab socialism, however, Nasser first prevaricated and then, after 1967, hung on grimly, buying doses of political support from the middle classes by cautious liberalization measures (such as those announced in the March 30 Programme of 1968) and by gradual relaxation of import controls.

Sadat had a clear preference for the abolition of much of the economic edifice Nasser had created. This was indicated, for example, by Law 65 of 1971, which granted tax concessions to foreign investors and provided for the creation of free zones, and by the inclusion of the term *infitah* in the government's economic programme put before parliament in April 1973. Nonetheless, the new president possessed insufficient political resources to implement fundamental change.

Those resources ultimately became available to him as a result of the October War. Endowed for the first time with legitimacy, able to offer the carrots of Arab petrodollars and Western technology, and gleeful in his revelations of Nasserist excesses and Soviet perfidy, Sadat so skilfully orchestrated this happy coincidence of events that the inflated promises for the *infitah*, and the policy itself, went virtually unchallenged until months after the enabling legislation had been put in place in June 1974.

Sadat did not confront his off-balance and divided domestic opponents single-handedly. Arrayed around him (in order of their relative contribution to formulating and promoting the policy-components of the *infitah*), were his new American friends, many Arab *shaikhs* recently engorged with petrodollars, and the agglomeration of Egyptian *ancien régime* and state bourgeoisies, leavened by self-made hustlers who together comprised the *munfatihun* (openers) who John Waterbury has described so well (Waterbury, 1983: 172–6). In succeeding years the Arab *shaikhs* displayed ever-diminishing interest in using their petrodollars to pry open the Egyptian political economy, and the domestic coalition that first emerged triumphant in 1974 fissured and weakened. But, along with the Americans and other heavyweights of the world capitalist order, Egypt's leaders remained committed to the project. So far that combination has been sufficiently potent to ensure that the project has not been abandoned, that its viability and necessity have become grudgingly accepted in key domestic constituencies, and that uneven but real progress has been made toward establishing a free market economy.

The process of economic liberalization

In no other country of the Middle East has the promise of economic liberalization so captured the hopes of such a large percentage of the population as did Sadat's *infitah* in its early stages. Disillusionment with the Nasserist experiment in state capitalism had engendered a widespread feeling of despair, when Sadat suddenly offered a new equation for Egyptian development: Arab petrodollars + Western technology + abundant Egyptian labour = exports of finished goods (to the Gulf region). For the equation to work, restrictions on imports and exports had to be eased (especially those pertaining to movement of capital), trade had to be reoriented in a 'northwest' direction – away from the East bloc (Abdel-Khalek, 1981) – the institutional capacities of the public sector and government administration had to be improved, and more scope had to be provided for private economic activities. In some circles the public sector was deemed to be beyond redemption, requiring complete privatization. In these heady days little thought was given, and virtually no words spoken, about the need to generate investment capital through domestic savings. Arab money would obviate the need for further Egyptian sacrifice, which, after all, had been in blood in the long struggle to defend Arabs from Israel.

In 1975 Sadat, unwilling to hear any words of caution about the pace and extent of reforms, swept aside Prime Minister Abd al-Aziz Hijazi, a principal architect of the *infitah*. Almost two more years passed before it was revealed to Egyptians and the world at large that Sadat's new equation for development did not add up. In the interim, Sadat's handpicked economist-technocrats, overly influenced by the new orthodoxy of development which offered the miracle cure of export-led growth, threw political caution to the wind. The *infitah* had generated a flood of imports, but capital investment (especially in tradable goods sectors) had lagged. Domestic savings would have to be mobilized to fill the gap. With the military having already tightened its belt, the only other major source of funds was that earmarked for subsidizing basic consumer commodities. The government's economic team, working with IMF officials but in isolation from the more politically sensitive members of the Sadatist élite, gave sanction to a standby agreement which called for sudden and drastic price increases. The response, which took the form of the January 1977 riots, was equally sudden, and far more enduring in its consequences.

When the magnitude of the threat posed by the riots became apparent, Sadat rescinded the price rises. The principle established was that the pace of reforms, especially when the reforms related to subsidies, would be dictated by the tolerance of the people. Never again would the IMF and its Egyptian fellow travellers be allowed to elevate economic over political rationality. President Mubarak relearned this lesson in September 1984, when worker unrest caused him to cancel belt-tightening measures far less draconian than those which stimulated the 1977 riots. As a consequence of political caution engendered by fear of further riots, the progress of the *infitah* since 1977 has traced a zig-zag pattern, moving inexorably forward but with lateral diversions and frequent rests.

There was no alternative to incremental reformism. Sadat may have been tempted to crush the unrest with the Central Security Force which he had inherited from Nasser (and had then greatly expanded). But to impose austerity with troops would have been a parlous course of action, and neither Sadat nor Mubarak attempted it. The mutiny by Central Security Force conscripts in February 1986, underscored the risks associated with such a strategy.

Acceptance of policy outcomes can only be contained through adequate participation in policy formation. But, lacking the political infrastructure for such participation, the government has been compelled to use security and intelligence agents to monitor the popular pulse. This substitution of administration for politics helps to account for the erratic course of economic reform. Standard operating procedure is for the government to float a trial balloon in the form of a leak to the media that an initiative is soon to be taken. Intelligence operatives charged with monitoring reactions report how the news has been received on their beat. Depending on the depth of antagonism to the proposed change, the government delays, amends or proceeds with it.

An associated tactic is reform by stealth, which takes various forms. One is that of policy implementation in the absence of public policy-making (or even of official announcement). Having learned in 1977 that governmental declarations can spark reactions, political elites have subsequently ordered prices to be increased surreptitiously. In this manner school fees have been raised, the price of postage, electricity and telephone services increased, and subsidized goods removed from the market place. The financial burden of subsidizing basic commodities, moreover, has been lightened through their debasement. The ever-shrinking loaf of bread, inclusion in it of larger amounts of exogenous materials, and repacking of commodities such as rice in smaller containers (but sold at the previous price), are some of the ingenious means that have been employed.

Obfuscation has also surrounded the process of privatization. The legal cornerstone of the *infitah*, Law 43 of 1974, made it possible for public sector companies to invest their funds in joint ventures with private concerns, the resulting enterprise being wholly private. Total investments under the provisions of Law 43 and its successors, Law 32 of 1977 and Law 230 of 1989, amounted to some LE5.2 billion over the decade 1977–87. This comprised almost one half of gross fixed non-agricultural investment over the period (Handoussa, 1990b: 154). Two-thirds of these investments were made with purely

Egyptian capital, and about one-third of the latter investment came from public-sector firms (Handoussa, 1990b: 162). Thus the public sector, itself suffering from inadequate capital investment, has made a major contribution to privatization, especially in manufacturing. The backdoor nature of this privatization process suggests that government strategy has been to placate potentially hostile constituencies, such as organized labour, by adamantly and repeatedly reaffirming its commitment to the public sector. In reality, however, government policy has been to allow that sector to wither in the shadow of a newly-emerging private economy which the state is itself financing.

Backdoor privatization has not been confined to manufacturing. The financial sector has also received a transfusion of capital, with the public sector participating in 42 banks and 52 investment companies. Public monies are thus invested in almost 65 per cent of all banks and over 36 per cent of all investment companies licensed to operate under Law 43 (Handoussa, 1990b: 159, 162). Annual reports issued in early 1991 by representative banks of the public and private sectors illustrate how the socialization of losses and privatization of profits has damaged the interests of government-owned banks while invigorating private ones. In the first week of January 1991, the Banque du Caire, one of the big four public sector banks, released its results for the 1989–90 financial year. On total assets of LE3.6 billion, net profits were LE37.5 million, a return of about one per cent. A fortnight later the Export Development Bank of Egypt released its results for the same period. It announced a 20 per cent dividend to shareholders in the wake of a 26 per cent rise in profits. In its fifth year of operation, the bank earned LE20.4 million on assets of LE787 million, a return on average assets of 3.2 per cent.[1] The bank is owned by none other than the venerable Banque du Caire and the other three public sector banks, as well as by a few private investors. Banque du Caire's progeny, outperforming its parent by better than three to one, indicates that privatization is working, at least for some.

That a substantial shift of resources from public to private sectors has occurred, while the president and most of those around him have staunchly defended the public sector, suggests that word and deed may well be purposely discrepant. It also raises the question of whether the process currently underway is leading to the ultimate privatization of the public sector or, as Ahmed El-Ghandour claims, to the publicization of the private (El-Ghandour, 1990: 184). El-Ghandour implies that backdoor privatization is a means whereby the public sector, hence the government, extends its control into the private sector, ensuring that 'rents' will continue to be collected by those who straddle the two sectors. This issue will be taken up below. The subterranean character of much of the privatization process, and the ambiguity about the objectives of those engaged in it make it difficult to determine the true extent of reform and unwise to accept public pronouncements at face value.

In Egypt, then, the process of economic liberalization involved an initial attempt to achieve a simultaneous, rapid breakthough on virtually all fronts. Following the failure of this, the government fell back to a strategy of gradual reform, conducted with as little fanfare as possible and with only as much haste as was permitted by a closely monitored, potentially volatile public. As a result, the economic reforms have not been presented as a coherent package. Instead each component (reducing subsidies, raising interest rates, floating the currency, energizing capital markets, removing existing barriers to trade, and privatizing at least some portion of the public sector while enhancing the capacity of public administration) has retreated and advanced according to its own schedule.

The ultimate objectives of those directing the *infitah* are ambiguous not only because of tactical considerations surrounding the implementation of reforms, but because of differences of opinion about their substance. Among Egyptian neo-classical economists and their political patrons, the solution to public sector ills is not decentralization, but complete privatization. Yet many members of the political élite known for their support for economic reform generally, do not take such an uncompromising stance. Deputy Prime Minister, Secretary General of the National Democratic Party (NDP), and Minister of Agriculture, Yusif Wali, for example, described the government's programme in the campaign preceding the November 1990 parliamentary elections, as one which was committed to 'protecting public, private, and co-operative ownership'.[2] The statement was consistent with Wali's known preferences and behaviour (Sadowski, 1990: 144–153). Following the 1990 elections President Mubarak declared a 'thousand days campaign', during which reforms required to stimulate exports would be undertaken. The reforms focused on freeing the economy from red tape and planning economic growth coherently. The president did not mention privatization. The long-awaited cabinet reshuffle on 20 May 1991, moreover, left the incumbent economic team intact, rather than bringing in staunch advocates of reform as had been hoped for and predicted by the supporters of liberalization. Mubarak's group of economic advisers includes those known for their ardent support of virtually all aspects of economic liberalization, such as Minister of Tourism Fuad Sultan and Deputy Prime Minister Atif Ubaid. It also includes powerful spokespersons for the retention of the public sector and other components of state capitalism, such as Minister of Planning Kamal Janzuri. While the government's commitment to liberalization is no doubt more profound than is indicated by its public statements, differences of opinion within the élite about the method and ultimate objectives of liberalization clearly persist.

International involvement in Egypt's liberalization

Egyptian political economists frequently emphasize economic factors as being the key determinants in the integration of their country into the world capitalist order (Abdel-Khalek, 1982; Amin, 1982). Egypt's major attraction to Western suitors, however, is its geo-political centrality. A US tactic while pursuing the strategy of subordinating Egypt to Washington's regional imperatives has been to hold out the hope of rapid economic development facilitated by Western participation in a liberalized economy. Tangible evidence of the US strategy is found in the visits to Egypt in the mid-1970s by literally thousands of business persons (Gillespie and Stoever, 1988: 33).

But the promised flow of private Western capital and technology did not develop, at least not at the level which Sadat had been led to believe. In relation to GDP, total foreign private investment in Egypt at the end of the 1970s was around one per cent. The proportion was the same as that achieved by Algeria, which had not yet undergone any significant liberalization. It was about half that of Morocco or India; and about one-fifth of Pakistan's (Weigel, 1990: 71). Non-Arab capital, virtually all of which was Western, 'decelerated its investment effort following the general slowdown in the economy starting in 1984/85' (Handoussa, 1990b: 165–6). Multinational corporations, outside of the petroleum sector, have yet to respond in a significant manner to Egypt's inducements. Just as the visits to Egypt in the wake of the October War by prominent US business persons, such as David Rockefeller, were prompted by the US government, so have subsequent initiatives by many US-based corporations been taken as a result of government urgings. In the 1980s, for example, the Cairo office of the United States Agency for International Development (USAID) attempted to mediate between General Motors and the ministry of industry, offering the inducement to GM of several hundred million dollars of Egypt's economic assistance package to establish a car assembly plant. Never enthralled by the prospect of working with Nasco, a public-sector firm, GM finally backed out in the wake of the May 1987 IMF standby agreement. It offered the excuse that the currency devaluation specified in the agreement undermined the project's viability.

While the international private sector has played only a marginal role in Egypt's liberalization, Egypt's relations with Western governments, and especially with the US, may actually have retarded the pace of the *infitah*. In their political rhetoric virtually all Western governments, and especially that of the US, have urged Egypt to liberalize. Increasingly they have predicated components of their economic assistance programmes on Egyptian willingness to undertake specific reforms. Since the mid-1980s they have coordinated efforts to assert maximum pressure on Egyptian decision-makers. But these persistent efforts by Western governments to induce change through policy dialogue have been undermined by the same political considerations which first attracted the US to Egypt in the wake of the 1973 war. The US and the West in general want a politically stable Egypt, at peace with Israel and pursuing an overall foreign policy conducive to Western interests in the region. While stability over the long haul requires economic development, which most Western decision-makers believe can only be achieved with further liberalization, over the short-term, these decision-makers have been aware that too much pressure could destabilize Egypt. Since political decision-makers operate in the here and now, they have generally chosen the safe, soft option. Whatever the warnings and however tough the rhetoric of USAID and IMF officials, Egypt has on some critical occasions been able to count on favourable political interventions to avert disaster.

The recent history of Egypt's economic relations with Western governments and public international financial institutions is one strewn with unfulfilled threats and promises; threats by the IMF, World Bank, USAID among others to withhold assistance, and promises by the Egyptian government to undertake reforms in order to obtain funds. In May 1987, for example, after several years of negotiations, the US executive leaned on the IMF to conclude a standby agreement on terms so favourable to Cairo that a key IMF negotiator resigned in protest. In the fall of 1990, after almost a decade of bitter negotiations over Egypt's military debt to the US,

President Bush pushed through Congress measures necessary for the cancellation of a major share of the outstanding principal, thereby drastically reducing the crippling interest bill. Egypt's creditors in the Gulf followed the American lead, resulting in nearly \$14 billion of debt reduction in a matter of weeks. In May 1991, the member-states of the Paris Club, formed in 1977 of Egypt's major creditors, agreed to halve Egypt's debts by 1994.

Because most economic assistance is provided directly to the government, it reinforces the state's centrality within the political economy and provides 'rent' to enable it to emulate allocation states (Luciani, 1990). Patronage generated by foreign assistance is doled out by governmental bodies, including the NDP. The institutional interests of the latter are to retard entrepreneurialism and reward parasitism. While some foreign assistance resources are awarded directly to private enterprise, these are proportionately small and in some cases pass through the controlling hands of government officials (Sullivan, 1990: 75).

In sum, the rhetoric of 'Egypt's friends', as those who formed the Paris Club were dubbed, has become unremittingly harsh in its criticism of Egypt's failure to implement far-reaching reforms more quickly. But deeds have not matched words. Urged on by a host of outsiders, Egypt has progressed toward a free market economy at a pace more or less determined by domestic political conditions. Egypt's 'friends', nevertheless, have been useful. They have dutifully played the role of the 'tough cop' in a 'soft cop – tough cop' act. President Mubarak, the soft cop, has mastered the role of appealing to his people to accept reforms on the grounds that if they do not, the tough cop, in the form of the IMF, will force them to yield to yet more punitive measures. Whether this drama is an orchestrated one, or whether the players act out their roles extemporaneously, matters not to its success, which may well be the most important contribution Egypt's 'friends' have made to the *infitah*.

Stimulating and channelling capital investment

Because of Egypt's comparatively lengthy experience with liberalizing a command economy, and its having commenced that experiment during the great oil boom of the 1970s when the regime was awash in petrodollars, its record of attracting investment capital has broad relevance. Egypt has learned two basic lessons the hard way. First, that however plentiful capital is in the region, it is the propensity of one's own citizens to save and invest that is of ultimate importance; second, that the obstacles which impede investment are structural rather than procedural, hence difficult to remove.

Egypt has encountered two main problems with foreign private investors: they are concerned with economic return rather than social profitability, and their investments are irregular and volatile. Foreign private investment in Egypt is concentrated in urban real estate, tourism, banking, and in the petroleum sector. All of these have had compartatively high rates of return, but none generate the package of social profits (including job creation, the development of backward and forward linkages, and the production of exportable surpluses) which are associated with agricultural and industrial expansion. In mid-1988 foreign capital constituted 64 per cent of the investments in Law 43 companies in petroleum, 44 per cent in tourism, 40 per cent in services and 37 per cent in the financial sector. But in manufacturing and agriculture, foreign capital accounted for only 28 and 27 per cent, respectively, of investments under Law 43 (Handoussa, 1990b: 179). Throughout the period of the *infitah* Egyptian capital has been overwhelmingly dominant in agriculture and industry, and its share has been increasing. Egyptian capital accounted for 11 per cent more of manufacturing investment in 1988 than it had done a decade earlier, while in agriculture it was 3 per cent higher (Handoussa, 1990b: 179).

Arab investment has been strongly influenced by regional politics. The deterioration of Egypt's relations with the Arab states, therefore, has a depressing effect on capital inflows from the region. While that episode is now history, so too are the massive reserves of the oil-exporting states and their citizens (Sadowski, 1991). Egyptians are known to possess very significant private savings, possibly exceeding the $50 billions in total foreign debt which the country once carried (Springborg, 1991: 233), and their investment preferences are unlikely to be affected by the vagaries of inter-Arab politics. It would seem eminently sensible, then, for the government to seek to attract Egyptian capital into domestic investments.

Obstacles which deter potential Egyptian investors may differ somewhat from those which impede investment by multinational corporations and other foreign companies. Generally, however, domestic and non-Egyptian investors remain reticent not because of any specific policy the government has or has not enacted, but because of the structure of the political economy as a whole. More than any other

Arab government, that of Egypt has constantly amended laws regulating capital investment in the hopes of attracting such investment. The basic law governing private investment, Law 43 of 1974, was itself an amendment to Law 65 of 1971. Law 43 was in turn amended in 1977 and again in 1989. The key component of the 1977 revision was that it granted to domestic investors rights and privileges extended to foreigners by Law 43. Law 230 of 1989 further liberalized some conditions governing investments, abolishing the requirement that foreign investors have a local partner and the prohibition on landownership by foreigners. Law 230 also provided further tax exemptions and the assurance of more rapid approvals for investment applications. On the other hand Law 230 imposed new, stricter requirements on the repatriation of capital, on price setting, and on worker profit-sharing. It also endowed the General Authority for Investment with much greater discretionary power to accept or reject investment proposals than that body had previously possessed (an apparent move away from economic rationalism).

The legal structure within which the nation's currency has been managed has also been the subject of much tinkering. While there has been some backsliding, the basic trend has been to move slowly toward a unified, market-determined exchange rate. The most recent change was announced early in 1991. It eliminated the least realistic of the then three official exchange rates, provided for the licensing of previously illegal foreign exchange traders, and partially legalized forward contracts for currency dealings. To the dismay of the IMF these changes left intact the separate Central Bank pool of foreign exchange, fed by oil exports and Suez Canal revenues and used to subsidize government imports of basic commodities. At the end of 1990 a new banking secrecy act, designed to allay fears of depositors that the government might arbitrarily confiscate their savings, took effect.

The organizational context within which the public sector operates has also regularly been redefined. In 1975 an attempt was made to prepare the legal groundwork for privatization of at least a portion of the public sector. Presidential Decree 262 granted public sector companies the right to raise capital through stock issues. This provision, however, was never utilized. In July 1975, Law 111 established general assemblies for public sector companies, abolishing the *mu'assasat* system of centralized control that had been in place since the late Nasser years. Eight years later, the *mu'assasat* were reestablished. During the 1980s the Capital Markets Authority and the NDP undertook two major efforts to overhaul the public sector, but the changes they recommended remained dead letters.

The net effect of modifications to the legal framework governing foreign investment has been to reduce substantially the restrictions placed on investments. While Morocco and Tunisia have still fewer restrictions on foreign investment than Egypt, Cairo has succeeded in removing more barriers to foreign ownership than have Algeria, Iraq, Jordan, Kuwait, Libya, Saudi Arabia and Syria (Weigel, 1990: 74). Despite the creation of a legal environment hospitable to foreign capital, however, foreign capital in proportion to Egypt's GDP remains very low by Third World and even Arab standards (Weigel, 1990: 71). Ibrahim Shihata has, realistically, drawn the following conclusion from Egypt's experience: 'it is neither practical nor useful for a country to try to encourage foreign investments by means of tax exemptions and similar financial incentives.' (Shihata, 1990: 128). The key determinant of the flow of investment, both foreign and domestic, in any country is 'the degree of confidence in its national economic potential'. This in turn is most heavily influenced by 'macroeconomic policies and the extent to which they respond to changing realities'. Investment promotion ultimately rests on 'the country's management of its economic resources and the overall organization of production, distribution and consumption, both in the legislative context and, more important perhaps, in practice' (Shihata, 1990: 128). The best indicators of the strength of a country's macroeconomic framework are domestic savings and investment rates, and these have been extremely low in Egypt throughout the period of the *infitah* (Hansen, 1988: 267–70).

Instead of undertaking basic structural reforms which would create an environment truly conducive to private investment, the government of Egypt has been preoccupied by tinkering with the legal superstructure. The tinkering has introduced some more liberal conditions governing investment, but the gain is partially offset by uncertainty resulting from the tinkering itself. Moreover, even while seeking to entice private investment through special incentives, the Egyptian authorities have presided simultaneously over the further expansion of the state's role in the economy. Public revenue as a percentage of GDP climbed steadily during the *infitah*, rising from 34.4 per cent in 1975 to 43 per cent in 1984 (Hansen, 1988: 167). The state, far from withdrawing from the economic arena in favour of private enterprise, has occupied a greater share of it.

Egypt's difficulties in stimulating private investment have been compounded by an inability to channel capital into socially profitable ventures in the tradable goods sectors. The policy environment is largely to blame for this shortcoming. No master plan based on the principle of comparative advantage and the prioritization of sectors and/or projects has emerged, despite the *infitah* having been pursued for almost two decades. Unlike the newly-industrializing countries (NICs) of Asia, and to a lesser extent Saudi Arabia and some of the smaller Gulf states, Egypt has not produced a foreign investment code intended to channel investments into industry, facilitate technology transfer and promote exports.

Egypt's failure to prioritize sectors and projects according to rational and clearly-articulated principles probably reflects underlying structural resistance, not just shortcomings in the system of policy formation. A system of guided investments must rest on a relationship of trust, a partnership between business and government. This has been achieved in several Asian countries, now including Indonesia. A business–government partnership requires the government to commit resources to the physical and human infrastructure which will facilitate profitable investments in targeted areas, and of course to refrain from altering the rules of the game arbitrarily. Neither condition has thus far been met by the Egyptian government.

A related problem is that government policy has directed investments towards large capital-intensive undertakings, thereby aggravating unemployment and depriving small businesses of capital (especially enterprises in the amazingly resilient informal sector). According to Gouda Abdel-Khalek, these deficiencies are inherent in the dependent development which *infitah* has encouraged: 'the leading sectors will be oil, the Suez Canal and tourism, which are capital-intensive . . . Growth along these lines will fail to generate enough employment.' He predicts that social disparities will widen and may in fact invite 'social unrest and mounting political repression' (Abdel-Khalek, 1981: 406).

Whether this pattern of investment and its negative sociopolitical consequences are inevitable outcomes of the *infitah* is debatable. It is clear, however, that job creation has suffered as a consequence of inappropriate investment. According to Bent Hansen, Egypt's industrial investments have been 'excessively capital intensive' for a country at that level of development (Hansen, 1988: 78). Capital investment per worker in Law 43 companies has escalated from LE15,000 in 1979 to LE41,000 in 1989 (Handoussa, 1990b: 167). Law 43 companies have accounted for about 85 per cent of investment in private sector manufacturing, but only 18 per cent of jobs created in that sector (Handoussa, 1990b: 167). As Law 43 companies have accounted for almost half of gross fixed investment outside of agriculture over the past 15 years, and as the private sector's share of total investment from the mid-1970s to the mid-1980s was more than a half of the country's total expenditure on the importation of capital goods, it seems reasonable to conclude that the expansion of the private sector and the increase in the capital-labour ratio are directly linked. The private sector, however, is not alone responsible for the inadequacies in job creation. The government's encouragement of agricultural mechanization, for example, ignores the relative costs of capital and labour as factors of production. This policy contributes substantially to rural unemployment (Richards, 1989).

Unemployment has become a major problem. It more than doubled in the nine years up to 1986, when it reached 15 per cent (Handoussa, 1990b: 143). It has continued to escalate since then and was further aggravated by the Gulf crisis. In his opening speech to the new parliament in December 1990, President Mubarak's first comment on the economy concerned unemployment. He spoke of the necessity to create 500,000 new jobs annually.[3] If LE41,000 is required to create each new job (as it was estimated for Law 43 companies in the late 1980s), Egypt will have to spend LE20 billion annually to meet the president's target figure. According to Minister of Planning Kamal Janzuri, by the end of 1990 LE16.3 billion had been invested in the public and private sectors in the first three years of the five year plan.[4] This suggests that less than a third of the capital required for job creation is actually being invested.

There are two possible ways of resolving the problem of job creation. The first is to stimulate more investment. The second is to reduce the capital/labour ratio. Both strategies could be pursued at the same time through the expansion of the small-scale private sector. Small and medium investors have not been encouraged by government policy, and have actually 'been deprived access to the same attractive rules offered to large firms' (Handoussa, 1990b: 160). Whether this is an unalterable structural condition resulting from dependent development, or a policy which can be changed by the current order, is a key question. Fuad Ajami contends that the preference for large, capital intensive projects is because 'large commissions require grandiose projects' (Ajami, 1982: 498). If corruption does underlie the preference for large projects, can such corruption be checked? What are the possibilities for altering the rent-seeking behaviour that is both symptom and cause of Egypt's persisting inability to make the transition to a political economy in which the market determines a greater share of rewards and punishments, and political processes a lesser one?

Obstacles in the transition from rent-seeking to free markets

The bureaucracy is the body within the state which most resists the shift away from state-control of economic activity. The size and behaviour of the bureaucracy thus provide a barometer for the progress toward establishing a free market system.

The Egyptian bureaucracy has prospered during the *infitah*. Total public employment increased by four times, from 1.2. million in 1969–70, to 4.8 million in 1986, or from 3.8 per cent of the population to almost 10 per cent (Springborg, 1989: 137). But salary increases have not paralleled the growth in bureaucratic employment, nor have they kept pace with inflation. Rent-seeking behaviour, therefore, remains endemic. While its most obvious manifestation is the solicitation of bribes from the public, rent-seeking also takes the form of 'straddling', whereby bureaucrats divert the state's resources into private-sector activities within which they have an interest. Dennis Sullivan and Yahya Sadowski have provided numerous examples of such 'diversionary tactics' (Sullivan, 1990; Sadowski, 1990). Both observers rightly conclude that straddlers constitute a major source of opposition to liberalization, because they collect rents on behalf of more highly-placed patrons.

Two remedies are prescribed for political systems seeking to rid themselves of bureaucratic corruption. One is for the political elite to reassert rigid authoritarian control over the state and society, rooting out corrupt elements prior to entering into a partnership with business in the manner of the NICs of Asia (Sadowski, 1991). This remedy sees the basic problem as residing in the state's weakness, for the state has permitted rent-seekers to bleed it of resources. By gathering its strength and defending its interests, the state will serve the purposes of entrepreneurs who require protection from parasitical elements entrenched in the bureaucracy.

Alternatively, the state may rid itself of rent-seekers by democratizing (Brumberg, 1989). By encouraging political participation as a trade-off for increased taxation, the government will enhance its legitimacy and promote acceptance of its policies (Anderson, 1987). It can then dispense with the services of bureaucratic rent collectors. The need for political control is reduced, and hence the need for a large bureaucracy. This is why, according to Daniel Brumberg, economic stabilization agreements have a better record of success when they are implemented in tandem with democratic reforms, and why the transition to a free market economy must be preceded by democratization (Brumberg, 1989).

The struggle over economic liberalization is one that occurs mainly within the state, between different factions or trends, rather than between the state and society. The most powerful opponents of the process in Egypt are dug into the state apparatus. They seek to avoid drawing attention to the self-serving arrangements through which they extract rents. They do not, therefore, exert themselves to provide theoretical or empirical defenses of the status quo; they just defend it. On the other hand, the most vocal challengers of the status quo are reforming bureaucrats, many of whom have served apprenticeships with Western financial institutions, public and private, or who have worked closely with them in Egypt. Thus Fuad Sultan, Abd al-Muna'im al-Qaissuni and Atif Ubaid (politicized technocrats holding or having held ministerial portfolios) have reputations for being advocates of reform. Their influence, however, does not stem from their having identifiable political constituencies, but from connections upward into the inner core of the political élite around the president. As they do not have independent bases of political support, they are restricted to employing the tactics of bureaucratic politics in their quest for a liberalized political economy. Were they unambiguously to cross the vague boundary that separates state from society, such as by seeking to mobilize organized constituencies behind their person and their cause, their proto-political careers would be jeopardized.

The bourgeoisie's capacity decisively to affect economic policy is limited by its fragmentation and ambivalence toward liberalization. With regard specifically to the state bourgeoisie, the most thorough recent investigation of this grouping's attitudes suggests that its views are mixed, with cautious support for liberalization balanced by fear of the consequences of competition (Waterbury, 1991). The fragment of the bourgeoisie comprised of independent entrepreneurs who unambiguously advocate the state's withdrawal from broad areas of economic activity, disposes of too few economic and political resources to play a decisive role. Another fragment of the bourgeoisie, that comprised of traditional entrepreneurs active in the informal sector, tends not to be firmly committed to liberalization. Many traditional entrepreneurs prospered during the Nasser era, thanks to protectionist trade policies. Since then most have been exposed to increased competition from imports and local production of consumer goods by Law 43 industrial companies (Hofmann, 1986). While the Egyptian *suq* is not as central to the national political economy as is the Iranian bazaar, the attitudes of its denizens are similar. Bazaaris strongly opposed the Shah because of their concern that his efforts to modernize the economy (in co-operation with selected, patronized bourgeois élites) would undermine the income and influence of the bazaar. For the same reason the Egyptian *suq* is wary of the *infitah*.

Egypt's political structures are not conducive to the articulation of support for liberalization. The National Democratic Party, as the government party, is a major channel of political patronage. While it includes a faction that supports rapid, widespread reform, patronage ensures that a preference for étatism persists. The vigour of opposition parties is restrained by a host of restrictions placed on them by the government. The poor performance of those parties and their organizational deficiencies, however, suggests that even in the absence of restrictions, opposition parties would encounter great difficulty in attracting mass followings. The staunchest advocates of a free market economy, the Liberals, have consistently been the weakest of the opposition parties. The Wafd, considerably more sophisticated than the Liberal Party, does not endorse wholesale liberalization unanimously. Some of its leading members remain convinced that, at least for tactical political reasons, various components of state capitalism must be retained (Springborg, 1989: 206).

Islamist political organizations, chief of which is the Muslim Brotherhood, are in some measure vehicles for what might be termed an Islamist bourgeoisie. While this class fragment is unremittingly hostile to the state's involvement in the economy, it is simultaneously ill-disposed towards reforms proposed by Western financial agencies. While a reform coalition including the Islamist and secular bourgeoisies may eventually emerge, it is not as yet even in the process of being forged. The government's purposeful destruction of Islamic investment companies, a step widely supported by secular liberals, suggests that the latter feel closer to the state than they do to Islamized members of their own class.

Despite claims by some observers that the Egyptian bourgeoisie has in recent years constructed a relatively dense network of organized interest groups, the pursuit of individual interests appears not to have been supplanted by dedication to effecting significant policy changes. Law 230 of 1989, which substantially altered the conditions under which private investors operate in Egypt, was enacted virtually in the absence of inputs from organized business (Hill, 1989). Pluralism even for the bourgeoisie appears still to be a distant prospect.

The Egyptian government has adopted a 'distension' strategy, as Diniz has termed the process in the case of Brazil. The strategy entails reducing political tension through a partial liberalization (Diniz, 1986: 65). But whereas in Brazil and other Latin American countries, where middle sector groups capitalized on opportunities offered by partial liberalization, their equivalents in Egypt appear not to have done so. They have left vacant the political space made available by the political élite's decision to reduce tension through a partial liberalization. The pace of reform has been set by the state. The middle sectors have been unable to portray themselves as champions of a political liberalization which would benefit society as a whole, and to gain wider societal support by so doing.

The political vacuum surrounding the debate over liberalization raises the question of whether or not the *infitah* is bound to continue to unfold in slow, incremental fasion, with the government tailoring policy initiatives to the speed at which private economic activity can absorb a higher percentage of the labour force. As the political system appears to be in stasis, with the level of political institutionalization more or less matching the degree of social mobilization, the trend which has held sway for more than a decade seems likely to continue (unless the government galvanizes the street by some ill-considered initiative). But other scenarios should be assessed, at least cursorily, before too confidently projecting the past into the future.

Breakthrough or breakdown?

A sudden breakthrough, whereby the pace of economic liberalization would be dramatically accelerated, could result from either increased authoritarianism or democratization (Sadowksi, 1990; Brumberg, 1989). The former option appears the less likely of the two. For the regime suddenly to tighten up, to root out corruption and the parasitic rent-collectors who presently both plague and support it, would require a new political foundation. Since the entrepreneurial bourgeoisie is small in number and influence, it could not alone serve as that crucial new political foundation. Workers and peasants, on the other hand, have been so demobilized and are so estranged from liberalization policies that they could hardly feature prominently in the regime's thinking about radical new departures. A newly invigorated Nasserism, but one committed to Arab capitalism rather than Arab socialism, appears out of the question.

Democratization seems better placed than authoritarianism to provide a prelude or accompaniment to economic liberalization. There are two alternative scenarios in which political liberalization could make possible a more rapid and thoroughgoing economic liberalization. The first is a democratic breakthrough, whereby social forces (especially those of the middle sectors), empowered by social mobilization generally and inspired by some specific events, rush into the political space created by the partial political liberalization and demand that the state patronage networks be dismantled, and that the state release its grip on both political and economic affairs. This is not an altogether impossible outcome, especially if one envisages the development occurring under the banner or Islamic liberalism, or least as a result of a coalition of Islamist and secularist liberals.

Alternatively, one can argue that Egypt has now been brought to the brink of a new order, and that this new order will soon be set in place without any dramatic or traumatic political events. Existing liberalization policies, in combination with worker remittances, have resulted in the acquisition of substantial economic resources by individuals and organizations. Those resources are being invested in political infrastructure which is providing alternatives to the state. Before too long successful political careers will be made on the basis of this autonomous societal infrastructure and through appeals to liberalize, as Boris Yeltsin did in the USSR. If and when this happens, the incremental, subterranean process of economic liberalization will become the focal point for political debate and political mobilization.

Unfortunately, the democratic breakthrough scenarios are not significantly more convincing than the breakdown scenario. In this case, the government is overwhelmed as a result either of miscalculating popular hostility toward economic liberalization and moving too fast with it, or moving too slowly and ultimately being overtaken by economic crisis. Growing unemployment, social mobilization generally, and the continued frailties of political infrastructure all suggest that the political system remains vulnerable and could collapse as a result either of precipitate change or immobilism. Ilya Harik has contended that economic liberalization in a condition of poverty is practically impossible because the state is held accountable by the populace for the provision of a major share of its sustenance. The social contract is inviolable and it stands in the way of both democratization and economic liberalization. Harik has not so far been proven incorrect by the Egyptian experience. If the pace of economic liberalization and political pluralization over the past 17 years continues for an equivalent period into the future, however, he will have been shown to have been too pessimistic.

Notes

1 *MEED*, 11/1/90: 10; 25/1/91: 18.
2 *Foreign Broadcast Information Service, Near East and South Asia*, Washington, D.C.: US Department of Commerce, 28/11/91.
3 *Foreign Broadcast Information Service, Near East and South Asia*, Washington, D.C.: US Department of Commerce, 18/12/90.
4 *Foreign Broadcast Information Service, Near East and South Asia*, Washington, D.C.: US Department of Commerce, 27/12/90.

9· TUNISIA

Jon Marks

Compared with most Arab countries, Tunisia has enjoyed a good press in the West for its experiment in controlled political and economic liberalization. Despite periodic examination of its human rights record, Tunis has been able to provide political analysts and potential investors with a welter of positive reports from a variety of agencies (stretching from the IMF to *Jeune Afrique*) on its progress towards creating an open economy and a tolerant political culture.

A constant theme in the projection of Tunisia's image abroad has been the government's effort – and often its 'success' – in overcoming the problems inherent in cumbersome state structures which were developed during the colonial era, and which have since acted as a hindrance to growth. Liberalization was the order of the day through much of the 1980s, as debt problems and the prevailing economic fashion forced Tunisia to reassess its economic structures and priorities. The process was accelerated with the appointment in July 1986 of the administration led by Rachid Sfar (until October 1987), whose planning minister, Ismail Khalil, designed an IMF reform programme, the broad outlines of which are still being followed today.

The plaudits for the Tunisian brand of Arab liberalism became louder still after the problems surrounding the founding president Habib Bourguiba's increasingly wayward leadership were resolved at a stroke in November 1987. The most obvious contender for the succession, Prime Minister Zine el Abidine Ben Ali, took power in a bloodless 'constitutional coup'. Tunisia's allies, ranging from Algeria to the USA, breathed a collective sigh of relief. Many Tunisians and much of the international community had feared that civil conflict could not be avoided, after months of rising tensions surrounding internal battles for the succession and the authorities' struggle with radical Islam. This gave Ben Ali's presidency, and 'second republic', a great initial impetus.

The pattern of economic liberalization

It is clear that the Tunisian economy has indeed undergone important changes since 1986. The character of the policy changes which have occurred in Tunisia is sketched out in the sub-sections which follow.[1]

Moving away from state socialism, 1966–86

Despite the fact that Tunisia's economy had been one of the region's more open economies ever since the unravelling of Ahmed Ben Salah's socialist schemes in the mid-1960s, the extent of state direction and state control in the economy remained very substantial through to 1986. In 1986 there were over 300 enterprises in which the state had a stake (mostly a predominant stake). The public sector accounted for about two-thirds of GDP, and a similar proportion of new investment. The state controlled most prices, wages and rents, and was the leading client of many small businesses. The exchange rate, interest rates and overall credit policy was closely controlled by the government (usually through the central bank). Basic commodities were heavily subsidized. Appearances notwithstanding, the Tunisian economy was closely regulated and controlled.

The debt crisis initiates change, 1985–6

An acute debt crisis hit Tunisia rather earlier than it did some other regional states, such as Egypt, Jordan and Algeria. The fall in oil prices and a falling off of tourist revenue in the mid-1980s left Tunisia with an external debt of $5 billion in 1986. Debt-service payments of $1.2 billion were due, and the country had in that year a current account deficit of $618 million. Lacking the reserves to meet the debt service payments, the Tunisian government turned to the IMF in the summer of 1986, and an agreement was concluded in August.

Introducing fundamental economic reforms in conjunction with the IMF, 1986–91

The standby credit which the IMF made available to Tunisia in 1986 was accompanied by a mutually-agreed 'comprehensive economic adjustment and reform programme'. The extent of the programme, and the seriousness with which it was pursued, encouraged the IMF to make available to Tunisia a three-year extended fund facility (EFF) in 1988. The agreement for the latter, signed in July of that year, involved access to SDR207.3 million. The Tunisian government made clear its intention of proceeding with a specified set of reforms when the facility was agreed. In July 1991, the fund approved a one-year extension to the EFF when economic problems, due mainly to the Gulf conflict, meant that Tunis could not meet its targets.[2]

The comprehensive economic adjustment and reform programme comprised, in the words of an IMF publication, 'a comprehensive set of structural reforms, including price and import liberalization, tax reform, financial sector liberalization, and public enterprise restructuring and privatization, all of which are supported by prudent financial policies' (IMF, 1991: 242).

Over the period since 1986, the range of economic liberalization policies has been extensive. It has included the encouragement of joint ventures with local and international partners; the introduction of a programme of privatization, whose objective is to reverse the 60/40 public/private sector ratio;[3] the liberalization of trade, with import licenses having been removed from 60 per cent of all imports by 1988 (and the remainder to be removed steadily over the years through to 1991);[4] the introduction of an industrial investment code, giving equal treatment for foreign investment in manufacturing, and allowing full tax exemption and unrestricted profit repatriation for earnings from wholly export-oriented factories;[5] the removal of controls from interest rates on savings and credit for non-priority areas;[6] steady moves toward the abolition of foreign exchange restrictions;[7] the modernization of the financial markets;[8] the opening of maritime transport to private investment;[9] tax reforms to create greater incentives;[10] the creation of a free port at Zarzis;[11] and the cutting back of subsidies.[12]

While the practical effects may not have been as great as the measures might suggest, a substantial re-ordering of the Tunisian economy has occurred. An account given in an IMF publication sums up the main changes (from the IMF's perspective) as follows:

> The share of total imports free from quantitative restrictions was raised to 70% at the end of 1990 from 53% in 1988. In addition, by the end of 1990, approximately 70% of prices of manufactured goods at the production level were liberalised, while the share of distribution margins liberalised was raised to 40% in 1991 from less than 10% in 1988.
> . . . At the same time, most interest rates were freed, and the

scope of bank credits at preferential interest rates was significantly reduced, while the margin between preferential lending
rates and the money market narrowed.

In the area of public enterprise reform, about three-fourths
of the 75 eligible public enterprises have been privatised. The
enterprises that will remain public will be restructured on the
basis of performance contracts agreed between the government
and the enterprises, under which managers will receive greater
autonomy as well as incentives to improve productivity.

In the fiscal area, a comprehensive tax reform was
implemented successfully during 1988–90. A value-added tax
replaced a complex system of turnover and excise levies, while a
new system of direct taxes introduced a personal income tax and
a harmonised corporate income tax (IMF, 1991: 242–3).

Political change
Since Ben Ali took power in November 1987, the official media have
missed no opportunity to refer to the 'spirit of November'. His
accession was projected as the opening of a new political age in which
the existence of a multi-party system, with some six legalized parties,
and of independent human rights groups monitoring the state's
activities, enabled the Tunisian government for some time to claim
leadership in the small camp of Arab democracies. The Neo-Destour
party, now renamed the Rassemblement Constitutionnel Democra-
tique (RCD), was re-shaped in the course of its July 1988 party
congress, when Ben Ali brought in a younger, better-qualified generation of party cadres. However, in the wake of a concerted challenge
from radical Islam and mounting concern over alleged human rights
abuses, it is questionable whether the Tunisian government can still
afford to be so confident in its capacity to mobilize public support and
take the moral high ground.

Setting the reforms in perspective, and assessing future prospects
The economic downturn since the Gulf conflict has called into
question Tunisia's success story, with the country now struggling to
regain its position as the IMF's favourite pupil. Reform measures,
proposed with such confidence in the late-1980s, have encountered
severe difficulties when they have been put into practice.

It is the contention of this chapter that Tunisia's current economic and political problems are not due only to problems of recent making (the rise of radical Islam in North Africa and the Gulf crisis), but are rooted in a longer-term failure to put liberalizing theories properly into practice. The failure stems in part from a lack of belief in some policies, especially those, such as privatization, which seem to have been promoted mainly to satisfy international creditors. Another factor is the regime's inability to break down the power structure inherited from Bourguiba. Some reform policies challenge vested interests which, for all the talk of Tunisia's new face under Ben Ali, remain very much in control.

Tunisia can point to an impressive performance in several sectors. The nature of its political system and constraints in the day-to-day operation of business, however, act as a block on it achieving an economic breakthrough. This can, no doubt, be said about the other countries covered in this book. There are a number of reasons, however, why it is of particular significance in Tunisia's case:

i   The country has actively promoted itself as being in the vanguard of Arab political and economic liberalization.
ii Lacking the hydrocarbons base of its neighbours, Algeria and Libya, Tunisia has had to develop a coherent investment strategy to attract the sort of capital which will allow its economy to become efficient and productive. Tunisian planners do not have the luxury of being able to sit back on ideology and mineral resources.
iii The Tunisian government likes to compare the country's potential to that of the Asian tigers. If this is the league in which Tunisia want to play, it must accept to be judged by international standards. Comparative advantage, growth rates and employee costs must relate to those of Hungary or Malaysia, not just to those of Algeria, Egypt and Morocco.

In the two sub-sections which follow, the dynamics which have impinged on the economic liberalization process in two important fields are examined – those of tax reform and of privatization. The case studies point to the gaps between theory and practice in Tunisian liberalization.

Tax reform

The 1990 budget, building on top of an already ambitious programme of tax reforms, placed an upper limit of 35 per cent on the rate of individual and company taxation, and introduced tax breaks on reinvestment and other forms of productive enterprise. Such moves were intended to rationalize the tax system and widen the tax net. A system of 18 bands for personal income tax was reduced to six only, with the top rate payable on income over TD50,000, while those earning less than TD1,500 a year became exempt. To encourage reinvestment, firms were henceforth to pay only 30 per cent of the tax due on profits if those profits were reinvested in export-only projects. For reinvestment in projects for the local market, the profits tax would be only 50 per cent of the usual rate. It is hardly surprising that this programme received a positive response from local businesses and from international companies based in Tunis. Some of the latter had complained that the restrictive old system made it very costly to pay their senior employees properly.

The tax reforms were not without cost. The planning and finance minister, Mohammed Ghannouchi, calculated that in the first year of operation, the reforms would cost the state TD48 million in lost revenues from taxes paid by state employees alone. But in the longer term he was confident that the tax base would be considerably widened, increasing the contribution of tax receipts to the exchequer. In August 1991, Ghannouchi convened a press conference to say that value added tax (VAT) had come to represent some 30 per cent of all revenues, raising some TD620 million in 1990 (its first full year of operation). In the first seven months of 1991, 34 per cent of taxation came from indirect sources, compared with 13 per cent in 1988.

For all the initial welcome given to tax reforms by local business, opposition ensued. This emerged after Ghannouchi took measures to prevent tax evasion. The main instruments which he introduced for this purpose were new controls, a larger number of tax inspectors, and a *loi sur la transparence* which allowed the authorities to publish details of an individual's tax payments. Leading the opposition to the measures was the powerful employers' federation, the Union Tunisienne de l'Industrie du Commerce et de l'Artisanat (UTICA), which was headed by one of the country's leading industrialists, Hedi Jilani. UTICA argued that Ghannouchi's new measures constituted an 'inquisition' which would block new investment. The employers used the government's official figures against its claims of widespread fraud, arguing that the rise in payments of indirect taxation proved their own probity. No more controls, they maintained, were necessary.

As yet, there is no evidence that the tax base has been widened as a result of the reforms, nor that there has been a reduction of inequalities of payments,[13] the two main benefits which were supposed to ensue. Ghannouchi's position was weakened through the implementation of reforms which proved unpopular among the very group they were most intended to help. It is significant that previous efforts to introduce greater tax controls failed in parliament, under the administrations of Hedi Nouira and Mansour Moalla.

Privatization

This has been presented abroad as an important element of government policy. The IMF economist, Paul J. Duran has noted that: 'In the area of public enterprise reform, about three fourths of the 75 eligible public enterprises have been privatised' (IMF, 1991). The figure is impressive, underlining the state's commitment to disengage from day-to-day economic management. However, an analysis of the companies in question suggests that in practice privatization has not been as impressive as in theory. The bulk of privatizations have been of state holdings in hotels and other properties, which were in any case managed by private operators. The number of major industrial holdings to be turned over to private management is much lower, and senior planners have often displayed a marked lack of enthusiasm to proceed with privatization in this field.

The larger privatizations have tended to follow a model which was exhibited when Somotex Internationale, part of the Sogitex holding textile group, was sold off. The sale involved the participation of the World Bank's International Finance Corporation (IFC) with loan and equity capital, a powerful foreign purchaser (in this case Italy's Klopman International) and a detailed expansion programme.[14] A similar line-up was involved in the other two Sogitex privatizations to date, the major examples of Tunisian disinvestment. The government's model favours privatizations when the following three characteristics are present:

i Strong financial support, especially from the IFC, but also bringing in private funding sources such as the local arm of the Saudi Dallah al-Baraka group, Beit Ettamwil/Saoudi-Tounsi (Best Bank).
ii A substantial foreign partner capable of providing new investment and safeguarding jobs by raising production.
iii A company taking over which has the ability to secure new export markets and transfer technology.

This model has many strengths, ensuring that investment and a coherent business plan are brought in to industries with growth potential but lacking sufficient capital or management skills. The problem is that the conditions can only be met in a very few cases. Enterprises must wait for a suitable buyer, which can keep them in a state of limbo for years.

The pattern of Tunisian privatization shows that the government is extremely prudent: it does not particularly like the idea and consequently will only act when the maximum benefit can be achieved. This reluctance to push ahead with privatization may reflect the government's refusal to give up power, rather than the more positive perception that privatization is only valid if it brings tangible economic benefits.

The political dimension

To enable a liberalized economic system to work efficiently (and equitably), a higher degree of transparency and adherence to formal rules (rather than informal networks) is required than in the past. Political reform does, therefore, seem essential. President Ben Ali seemed to understand this in his early days, when it was even suggested that he might break with Neo-Destour Party structures which had proved resistant to reform. The 1988 RCD congress pointed the way forward (at least to a purged and reformed party), and overtures to the opposition suggested that a pluralistic political system would soon emerge. However, this opening has proved illusory. It is clear that al-Nahda is the only movement which could challenge the RCD's dominance, and this has been crushed by an active security machine. Rather than splitting with the RCD's grandees, Ben Ali has increasingly turned to long-term Neo-Destour supporters in filling senior positions. His early moves towards appointing moderate opponents has only fitfully been sustained (although some, such as Dali Jazi and Mohammed Charfi remain in government). The legalized opposition has yet to win a single parliamentary seat. To reverse this trend Ben Ali proposed that RCD candidates should stand down at by-elections to allow opposition deputies to compete alone and the opposition to enter the Chamber of Deputies. This was rejected by the opposition, which felt that under the existing system the electoral cards remained stacked against it. In elections there is evidence that local RCD leaders have acted as they did in the past, ensuring that the RCD candidate wins, no matter what the president does to organize a free and fair fight.

Moreover, a sycophantic cult of personality appears to be growing around Ben Ali. A reading of the official press produces an impression that Ben Ali, like Bourguiba before him, is the font of all decision-making and creative thought in the country. Ben Ali reacted against this when he first took power, but the pattern seems set to repeat itself. There has also been an increasing concentration of powers around the presidency. Ben Ali has appointed a full set of presidential counsellors and advisors, who at times seem to act as a shadow government. Junior ministers sometimes appear not to be acting on their government superiors' orders, but rather to be going 'above their heads' to the presidency. This indicates that personalized networks of power and patronage, firmly centred on the presidency, are active.

The rejection of the Islamist opposition remains a key element in local politics, as the Islamists in recent years have proved the only credible challengers to the RCD establishment's dominance. Conflict with al-Nahda reached a peak when nearly 300 alleged Islamist activists were arrested on 21 May 1991, having been implicated in a coup plot. Their number included about 100 military personnel. Official reports alleged that the Islamists had made plans to start uprisings in the country's universities, to infiltrate saboteurs from abroad and overthrow the government to create an Islamic republic. The faces of Rachid Ghannouchi, Hamdi Jebali and other radical al-Nahda leaders were displayed on 'wanted' posters around the country. More than ever, the Islamists were placed outside of the political process.

The failure of the legalized opposition to mount a serious challenge is a setback for liberalizers. The legal opposition parties, of which the Mouvement des Démocrates Socialistes (MDS) is the largest, will no doubt continue to push for a greater opening in the political system. Tayeb Zahar, the editor of *Réalités*, has sketched out a role which the oppostion could play in interaction with the government, to consolidate civil society:

Today a consensus seems to be established between the authorities and opposition parties on the need to consolidate and
develop the gains of the civil society. This is the wish of the
majority of Tunisians who have suffered from the spirit of single
party and exclusion (from the political process). But consensus

has nothing to do with unanimity, because each party has need – in the country's interest – to keep its personality, its autonomy and its specificity. Public opinion is waiting for a veritable public debate on the fundamental choices which determine the quality of life, the form of the society and the future of Tunisia. This debate, which could be televised, would cover essential questions like the economy, education, health and must take place outside the electoral field and without demogoguery.[15]

However, the opposition parties constitute little more than divided, intelligentsia-dominated groups with small membership. Logic suggests that they must come together if they are to provide a meaningful challenge for the RCD (and the Islamists). Whether this can be achieved remains to be seen. The MDS has in the past indicated that it does not want to be part of a united opposition. More significantly, the authorities have consistently worked to block any coming together of opposition groups, believing that this might eventually form a coherent challenge to be mounted to the regime. The media remains tightly controlled by RCD members.

It is clear that the Tunisian experience in political and economic liberalization is far from over, and can not be judged simply a success or failure. A new political formula is needed to create an environment in which economic growth can be sustained by the emergence of genuine consensus politics, whatever the risks for the established order.

The struggle with al-Nahda, the failure of an effective legal opposition to emerge and the continued dominance of an RCD establishment where, for all the efforts to bring in new blood, traditional party barons still wield genuine weight, all point to the fact that there is much to do before Tunisia can objectively claim to have a successful functioning pluralist political system. For pluralist politics to become rooted, the legal opposition must be allowed to develop as a credible alternative to the RCD; the groundswell of Islamist opinion must be accommodated within the system, except where the actions of radical Islamists fall outside the law; the judiciary must be seen to have greater independence and the police establishment must be seen to be less powerful than it is now.

However, this leaves unanswered the question of whether greater political pluralism would speed the development of a more effective, liberal economy, making Tunisia a 'new tiger' in the Mediterranean.

Privately many of Tunisia's creditors and investors argue that if the country is genuinely to develop along these lines, then like the Asian 'tigers' this can best be achieved with a relatively benign authoritarian government in place – exactly like Ben Ali's.

Notes

1 The author would like to thank Tim Niblock for his observations in drawing up this section.
2 *MEED*, 12/8/88 and 19/7/91; IMF (1991: 242–3).
3 *MEED*, 2/1/88.
4 *MEED*, 19/3/88. However, this target has yet to be achieved.
5 Investment code issued on 2/8/87.
6 *MEED*, 19/3/88.
7 *MEED*, 26/8/88.
8 *MEED*, 16/12/88.
9 *MEED*, 10/2/89.
10 *MEED*, 7/7/89.
11 *MEED*, 28/7/89.
12 *MEED*, 25/8/89.
13 See *Réalités* (Tunisian weekly), 5/9/91.
14 *MEED*, 12/5/91.
15 *Réalités*, July 1991, author's translation.

10· SYRIA

Raymond A. Hinnebusch

The apparent global triumph of democratic capitalism has had Middle Eastern repercussions from Jordan to Algeria. But many observers have been impressed by what appears to be the relative immunity of this region to the global bandwagon. Does the Middle East make up a world sub-system where the tendency toward global liberalization is short-circuited or is it simply a later developer, inevitably to be incorporated into the unfolding liberal world order?

This paper will examine the case of Syria. Liberalization first began in Syria two decades ago, but it advanced at a snail's pace and suffered reversals; today it appears to be accelerating. As one of the Arab states which has experimented with liberalization, yet has appeared most resistant to it, Syria's experience gives insight not only into the forces for but also the obstacles to liberalization.

There is a wealth of theory on the topic. All liberalization scenarios begin with an economic crisis which induces state elites to liberalize. Marxist theorists speak of a crisis of state capitalist accumulation resulting from private appropriation of the state economic surplus. Others stress the exhaustion of development strategies mixing populist redistribution and import-substitute industrialization; populist coalitions, possible in times of prosperity, are replaced under austerity by conservative ones repressing mass demands. There must, however, be a viable alternative to populist statism if capitalist development is to be adopted as a dominant strategy rather than a mere palliative. The credibility of capitalism, and some would argue democracy, depends on a bourgeoisie strong enough to lead capitalist investment and push for liberalization. In the view of critics, however, the Middle East bourgeoisie is too parasitic or comprador-oriented to play this role. Liberalization involves increased integration into the world capitalist market, but (as the controversy between liberal and dependency theory suggests), there is little consensus on whether integration will bring benefits such as investment and markets or increased dependency. Policy-makers are presumably moved to liberalize if they perceive economic opportunities, or if international economic pressures (such as debt), leave them little choice. The state does not, however, decide exclusively according to an economic logic, and presumably state élites must see liberalization as either in the state's political interest or that of some class or group for whom they act.

Is the state, then, an obstacle to or facilitator of liberalisation? In one view the state, responding to economic pressures, promotes capitalist development with legal–rational reforms and at least limited political liberalization, but in the opposing 'neo-patrimonial' view, the state can not pursue economic rationalization or democratization without undermining its own political base. The state must also calculate the reaction of society to liberalization. Without an ideology legitimizing the inequality and Western penetration which accompanies capitalist development, the result is likely to be social conflict. But can the dominant indigenous ideologies – nationalism, populism, and Islam – be adapted to capitalism, or will they continue to generate resistance to it? All of these factors must be addressed in any convincing explanation of the Syrian case.

The failure of Syria's liberal road and the rise of the Ba'th state

The Ba'th state arose in Syria as a direct response to the perceived failure of Syria's liberal road, propelled by those who had paid its costs but enjoyed few of its benefits. It is therefore hardly surprising that, in important ways, the state in Syria institutionalizes forces and ideas resistant to capitalism.

Syria's first attempt at capitalist development took place as an integral part of the world capitalist system: in part under foreign penetration or control, in part under a laissez-faire national regime. Syria had, by virtue of its position, historically been a centre of trade, giving rise to an age-old entrepreneurial tradition and a merchant bourgeoisie. After World War II, the Syrian bourgeoisie led an economic expansion in commercial agriculture and light industry, based almost entirely on indigenous capital (IBRD, 1955). This seemed to indicate that, despite its late start, Syria was embarking on a 'national–capitalist' road to development. But Syria's would-be capitalists proved too weak to sustain this promise amid profound structural imbalance and political instability. Unbalanced development was manifested in the state-driven expansion of a salaried new middle class, in excess of the economic base which would have been required to support it. Capitalist development was also accompanied by growing inequality and class cleavages, in particular by landlord–peasant conflict arising out of capitalist penetration of agriculture. The outcomes of early capitalist development were sharply uneven, the costs being carried by the 'have nots' while the benefits chiefly accrued to the 'haves'.

Inevitably, Syria's capitalist expansion reached a plateau. The period of relatively high growth was based on the exploitation of natural advantages that were exhausted by 1956 (Hansen, 1972). The very low incomes of the bulk of the population, especially those of the impoverished peasantry, provided little market for industry, and further industrialization required a totally new order of investment. The classic extroverted, dependent capitalist economy, in which foreign exchange from agricultural exports was spent on manufactured imports (dissipating local profits or funneling them abroad), limited both industrial investment and markets (Hilan, 1969: 227–50; Hilan, 1973: 158–68). Many Syrians believed that land reform was essential to create a rural market and generate an agrarian surplus, without which the backward agrarian sector would remain a drag on the whole economy (El-Za'im, 1967). By the late 1950s, it was widely believed (Jabbur, 1987: 89–90) that Syrian industrialists could not or would not make the much bigger investments needed for the next stages of medium and heavy industrialization, and hence that without massive government intervention and investment the road to industrial diversification was blocked. According to the widely accepted view among Syrian intellectuals, in a mature capitalist world where industrial competition requires huge investments, national capitalism can not hope to succeed without a major role for the state. The bourgeoisie failed to address these obstacles to development. It remained, in the view of critics, too closely linked to the landed 'aristocracy', or too imbued with the short-term 'merchant mentality', to lead national capitalist development or the deepening of capital in the short time-frame given to it (Arudki, 1972: 27–8; IBRD, 1955: 373, 399–401).

These contradictions might have been overcome were it not for the growing political crisis which engulfed Syria in the 1950s. A conflict of manifestly class character had come to separate the agrarian–commercial upper class from the new middle class. The latter came to perceive few opportunities under the laissez-faire system, and its interest in state-led development was blocked by the property-owning elite. The rural wing of the middle class, expressing the grievances of the peasantry against landlords and merchants, had a double grievance against the dominant classes. The old regime also failed to incorporate the middle class into the system politically, contributing to the discrediting of its embryonic democratic institutions. The post-independence nationalist crises, beginning with the establishment of Israel, de-legitimized the ruling elite and the capitalist model (which was seen as widening dependency on imperialism) and gave credibility to radical alternatives. When the first stage of capitalist development reached a plateau in the mid-1950s, the notion spread that the 'national bourgeoisie' had exhausted itself. This became a self-fulfilling prophecy for, as radicalism and instability undermined the bourgeoisie's confidence that it could keep its grip on the state, it began to de-invest.

The rise of radical ideological parties, particularly the Ba'th, manifested the political discontent of those left out of the capitalist model. The Ba'th party came to incorporate a 'populist coalition' made up of sectors of the military, intellectuals, the salaried middle class, minorities, workers and peasants. The party institutionalized an anti-capitalist socialist ideology, generated amidst the social conflict of the 1950s. The experience of perceived capitalist exhaustion shaped the political outlook of a whole generation, from whom the Ba'th party produced the political rulers of contemporary Syria. For the new élite the Ba'th brought to power in 1963, capitalism was associated with internal inequalities, international dependency, national weakness, and 'dead-end' development. The subsequent need to adapt to economic exigencies has led that élite to acknowledge that Syria had some early capitalist successes, fashioned by a bourgeoisie with entrepreneurial skills and a propensity to invest. But the socialization of its politically formative years excludes any strong ideological commitment to liberalization (Hinnebusch, 1990: 49–80).

The Ba'th state

Under the Ba'th, a powerful state was created at the intersection of the domestic and international arenas. In its drive to carry out a revolution from above and to make Syria a major player in the regional arena, the state made and unmade classes and harnessed the economy to its political requisites. But this state, in many ways overdeveloped relative to its resource base, eventually found itself buffeted by constraints which narrowed its autonomy and capacity to manipulate the environments it straddled.

Under the early Ba'th, the state was captured by radical leaders who for a period (1965–70) embarked on a populist–etatist alternative to capitalist development. Through land reform, nationalizations, and government control over the market, the regime narrowed the economic bases of the bourgeoisie and demolished its political power. The Syrian social structure was transformed. On the one hand, the social weight of the bourgeoisie, particularly the landed upper class, radically declined. Indeed, the bourgeoisie went into Beirut exile in the thousands. Landlords and industrialists suffered the most. Most industrialists affected by nationalization left business or emigrated. Merchants, without fixed assets to lose, were better able to weather the radical period and would thereafter emerge as the main component of the bourgeoisie.

At the same time, education and state employment broadened the salaried new middle class, and land reform transformed a large part of the landless proletariat into a small-holding peasantry. As fear of nationalization deterred the emergence of new large capitalist firms in industry, the gap was filled by the proliferation of tiny ones: the commercial and artisanal petty bourgeoisie, rather than contracting, actually flourished. There was, thus, a significant expansion in the social weight of elements which might be bracketed as the *petite bourgeoisie* (Longuenesse, 1979).

By 1970, the state-controlled public sector had become the core of the economy. The state development plan and budget were its main source of productive dynamism. In the 1970s, the public and private sectors each accounted for roughly half of NDP, but in industry the state sector towered over a multitude of small undercapitalized artisan and family enterprises: 98 per cent of the 40,000 or so private manufacturing enterprises employed less than 10 workers (World Bank, 1980, v.4: 53, 166). Despite the liberalization after 1970, this structure remained essentially unchanged through the 1980s, for although handfuls of middlemen were enriched they had no interest in industrial investment and, in any case, a government-imposed division of labour between public and private sectors long restricted private investment to low-investment light consumer sectors. In 1984, public industry employed a third of the labour force in industry but produced 78 per cent of gross industrial output (Syrian Arab Republic, 1989: 77, 170–1).

The public sector was a key to the state's autonomy and crucial to its interests: for example, public sector surpluses appear to have financed more than a third of all state expenditures and amounted to an average of 9.1 per cent of total GDP from 1966–76. Nevertheless, the central vulnerability of the Ba'thist political economy was the failure to make the public sector an engine of capital accumulation and investment that could substitute for private capital in the overall economy. The regime had therefore to live with a persisting and hostile bourgeoisie which, still controlling a disproportionate amount of Syria's capital and skills, would soon force the regime to come to terms.

In fact the political struggle of the bourgeoisie was a major factor in derailing the radical Ba'th from its 'socialist' course. The bourgeoisie did not accept nationalizations and land reform without a fight: the chambers of commerce and professional associations led campaigns of strikes and denunciations of the government. The *suq* carried on economic guerrilla warfare against the government takeover of foreign (and segments of domestic) trade, its restrictions on imports, and its efforts to fix prices and to regulate the market. The disinvestment of the bourgeoisie sent the economy into a tailspin. Religious leaders declared war on the 'godless Ba'th' while the urban artisans and small merchants of the traditional *suq* provided the shock troops of Muslim Brotherhood opposition. The regime had to repress no less than four major uprisings instigated by the bourgeoisie between 1964 and 1973, amidst an atmosphere of conflict and instability through much of the 1960s.

Syria's 1967 defeat by Israel, disillusioning and delegitimizing the left-wing Ba'thists, was the catalyst which set in motion the abandonment of the radical strategy. A 'realist' wing of the Ba'th regime emerged under Hafiz al-Asad, arguing that in the face of external threat internal class struggle had to be subordinated to national unity. The weakness of state economic institutions was exposed by the increased burdens of defence. The major investments of the radical Ba'th in infrastructure and import-substitute industrialization had resulted in debt but little revenue-producing exports, ending in a foreign exchange crisis. The competing demands of defence and development could not be carried without Arab aid and a reactivation of the private sector, and this required a retreat from radicalism. In 1970 Asad deposed the radical wing of the Ba'th.

Nevertheless the radical Ba'th period changed the political land-scape of Syria. The subordination of the heights of the economy to the state, the levelling and fluidization of the class structure, and the spawning or broadening of social forces dependent on the state created the social terrain for the emergence of an autonomous Bonapartist state 'above classes'.

Asad set out to reshape the state and its strategy. His first priority was to carry on the struggle with Israel. He led a reconciliation with the bourgeoisie and the Arab oil states, prepared for a war to recover the territories lost in 1967, and began constructing a powerful national security state. Asad used a combination of kin and sectarian solidarity, Leninist party loyalty, command of an enormous military apparatus, and oil 'rent' to concentrate authoritarian power in his hands and to consolidate the state's autonomy of society. High policy was shaped by reason of state, not dominant class interests: by an élite determi-nation to defend the legitimacy, capabilities, and resource base of the state. Lesser decisions emerged from bureaucratic rivalries over patronage or from the competing economic prescriptions of statist and liberalizing factions for addressing economic constraints. As access to state patronage began to define economic opportunities, class loyalties gave way to clientelism – partly organized on sectarian and regional lines – thus fragmenting solidarities below the state.

In economic policy the regime, pulled between the desire to control resources and the need to maximize production and gain a slice of the new oil wealth of the Arab world, combined statism and limited liberalization throughout the 1970s. On the one hand, this was a period of bureaucratic and public sector expansion. It was financed in good part by Arab aid which increased more than ten times, mostly to recompense Syria for its burdens in the Arab–Israeli conflict. Syria's own oil exports also climbed tenfold. Although much of the new wealth was channeled into the military, the regime used a part of it to embark on a second wave of import-substitute industrialization. At the same time, *détente* with Syrian and Arab capital and limited liberalization revitalized the private sector in trade, construction and light industry. Many enterprises in these fields, protected from the competition of large capital and sometimes enjoying a symbiotic relation with the state, flourished. Liberalization also allowed Syrians to take advantge of work opportunities in the Gulf, and the inflow of remittances leavened the economy. Economic boom combined with continued controls on imports made for growing smuggling. The dual public and private engines of the economy drove an impressive economic expansion in the 1970s: real GNP grew 8.2 per cent in 1970–5 and 6.8 per cent in 1977–80.

Syria's dual track policy, producing both economic boom and state expansion, seemed to work to the advantage of both its traditional populist constituency and of others who, benefiting from liberalization or work abroad, were partly co-opted by the regime. The state was able to stay above and balance off these various social forces, avoiding any decisive choice between statism and private capitalism. Thus, while the Ba'th's former ideological hostility to capital was abandoned under Asad, populist policies had been institutionalized and were not reversed; the state continued to protect its constituencies, such as co-operatized peasants and public sector workers, from bourgeois encroachment, thereby limiting the possibilities of surplus extraction and investment by private capital. While previously the agrarian bourgeoisie had dominated a weak state, now a strong state seemed to dominate a much weakened bourgeoisie, arbitrating between it and its own populist constituencies. The Asad regime was a classic Bonapartist state, far more an artefact of *raison d'état*, of a drive to maximize state power in a context of intense insecurity, than of class or communal interests. Its economic policy was less 'state-capitalist' than 'neo-mercantilist': one which promotes economic development but as merely one instrument of a broader project of state formation.

In the 1970s, the initial egalitarianism of state action began to reverse: instead of breaking down class barriers and inequality it began to reconstruct them. The state either generated or became the pole around which various fragments of a new bourgeoisie began to form. It generated a 'state bourgeoisie' as the political élite used office to acquire illicit wealth and went into business on the side. For example, in the 1980s, the military élite enriched itself on smuggling. The state also fuelled the development of the private bourgeoisie. The mediation of most state foreign trade by local agents of foreign firms, who earned illegal commissions, generated a parasitic wing of the bourgeoisie. A new state-dependent bourgeoisie, often of *petit bourgeois* origins and at least partly productive, was fostered through the expenditure of state revenues on contracts with private firms. Fragments of the old bourgeoisie also found opportunities to preserve or reproduce itself through similar connections. Various alliances – business, political, sometimes marriage – developed between these various state and private fractions, muting the former sharp antagonism between them. The core of this new class was a kind of 'military-mercantile complex', linking the Alawi political élite and the Damascene bourgeoisie. Seale, (1988: 457) speculates that Asad deliberately sought in this way to give his regime a class underpinning needed for stability.

This new stratum could be considered a coalition of favoured class fractions, perhaps a new bourgeoisie-in-formation, but it did not yet form a new ruling class. It remained too fragmented. Notably, the amalgamation of the new and old élites into a single class had not matured; Alawis had not produced a significant stratum of private businessmen, and intermarriage between them and the old oligarchy remained exceptional. *Détente* between bourgeoisie and regime was concentrated in Damascus, where the bulk of state patronage was dispersed, and did not much extend to the northern cities, a big factor in the Islamic revolt there in the early 1980s. Moreover, in this period of state expansion, conditions were not ripe for the bourgeoisie to widen control of the means of production. Plenty of wealth – mostly oil 'rent' – flowed into private hands from remittances, state expenditure, and parasitic activities. But it remained liquid, expended in conspicuous consumption, was channelled abroad, or into commerce and little was invested in productive assets. Risks remained too high, the public sector and protected peasant agriculture were off limits and no private banks or stock market existed to mobilize and concentrate capital. Nor was state policy deployed in the service of capitalist development: liberal–capitalist ideology had yet to overthrow populism and statism in either state or society. The paradox was that the state itself retarded the development and autonomy of the very bourgeois fragments it was reviving or fostering.

Ba'thism under pressure: retreating state, expanding society?
The Ba'thist state soon came under serious pressures, both political and economic, which had the potential to force a change of course on it. In the late 1970s and early 1980s, Islamic rebellion threatened the very existence of the regime and put forth a counter-ideology which challenged Ba'thi populism. Modern Islamic movements are typically ambivalent towards capitalism, accepting private property and a fair profit while attempting to contain its individualism, inequality and materialism by a strong all-encompassing moral code. Whether particular Islamic movements legitimize capitalism or express egalitarian

revolt depends on the nature of the state against which they mobilize and the social forces they incorporate. In Syria, the Islamic movement developed out of reaction to Ba'thist statism and populism, thus incorporating those social forces Ba'thism damaged (first of all, the Sunni urban establishment, the *ulama*, and the youth of the *suq*). This social composition shaped a movement which expressed resentment of Alawi and rural privilege but did so in the language of a particularly conservative rather than egalitarian variant of political Islam.

The economic order proposed by the Islamic movement in the early 1980s was unambiguously pro-capitalist. Private enterprise would be the basis of the economy 'as prescribed by the Quran'. Ba'thism was rejected for mixing the worst of the West (rampant materialism) and of the East (an unproductive state sector which destroys incentives and is corrupted to enrich a small political clique). An Islamic economy would encourage private ownership, investment, and the 'natural incentives' of a fair profit, and protect private investors from national-izations. Workers had to cease to malinger and to work for their wages; a sentiment clearly expressive of a bourgeois worldview. The state should not encroach on the trade sector, which is properly private, and should be allowed to freely import and export. The bloated bureaucracy must be cut and people encouraged to work in the private sector. Land reform was said to have ruined agricultural productivity, and state farms and co-operatives should be abandoned. The anti-statist, pro-market bias of most of this programme is unmistakable.

In the showdown, state power proved decisive over the Islamic movement which, in trying to turn the political clock back to the era of bourgeois dominance, could not sufficiently broaden its social base as to bring down the regime. But political Islam continues to represent a counter-culture, still very much alive in the *suq*, which, if its programme is any indicator, could help legitimize a return to capitalism.

Barely had the regime weathered the political rebellion when economic stagnation set in for much of the 1980s, seemingly sympto-matic of a failure of capital accumulation. The Ba'th regime had never succeeded in making the public sector into an instrument of capital accumulation which could really substitute for private capitalism. Over the whole period of Ba'th rule, domestic resource mobilization has only covered about two-thirds of expenditures on government, defence, and development. It fell well short of the state's ambitious development plans; for instance, public sector surpluses were projected to finance only 54 per cent of the fourth Five Year Plan (1976–80), and of this much was oil revenue rather than the profits of industry (World Bank, 1980, v.4: 101). Savings have never been enough to maintain high rates of investment. In the 1960s, under radical Ba'th dominance, savings covered about 84 per cent of investment but the regime could only mount relatively modest investment levels. Under Asad a big investment drive was undertaken, but between 1973 and 1986 savings covered barely a half of investment (World Bank 1980, v.2: 18; Syrian Arab Republic, 1984: 564; Syrian Arab Republic, 1989: 480–1).

The gap in the budget was filled by a combination of resources. Arab transfers have made up a large proportion of total resources, growing from about 13 per cent in the early regime years to nearly a quarter of the total in the 1980s. The balance has had to be financed by domestic or foreign borrowing. Deficit financing has varied from 6.6 per cent of the total budget in 1966–76, to a high of 22.5 per cent in 1976 when Arab aid dipped. External borrowing (from suppliers) has also filled the gap. (World Bank 1980, v.4: 88; Clawson, 1989: appendices 4, 5). Debt as a percentage of GNP increased from 10.8 per cent in 1970 to 25 per cent in 1988, interest payments from $6 million to $119 million, and long-term debt service as a percentage of GNP from 1.7 to 2.6 per cent (World Development Report, 1990: in Niblock, this volume). In short, the state-dominated economy has lacked the dynamism to sustain good growth rates without external assistance.

The vulnerabilities of Syria's statist economic strategy can not be divorced from the impact of Asad's power strategy: building a maximum-sized coalition required rewards for a wide range of actors. During its war with the bourgeoisie under the radicals, the regime had mobilized mass sectors through an 'inclusionary' and redistributive policy, fostering consumption at the expense of accumulation. Import-substitute industrialization increased consumption and dependency, without developing a strong productive state sector. The economic liberalization which appeased the bourgeoisie in the 1970s also fuelled a consumption boom at the expense of savings. The 'democratization' of patronage under the Ba'th widened the net of corruption from a few families to a larger portion of the population. Nationalist imperatives and the dominant military role in the regime dictated the diversion of public resources into a massive military machine. In short, the economic logic of accumulation was subordinated to the logic of state formation; of militarism, populism and patronage.

This strategy was only possible as long as economic expansion continued. But the expansionary impetus, being too dependent on Arab aid, came to a halt when aid inevitably declined. Bureaucratic over-development had meanwhile taken place, however, creating a state too large for the country's economic base. By the mid-1980s Syria was in an economic crisis which grew most immediately out of its over-dependence on external aid. Thus, Arab transfers fell from $1.8 billion in 1981 to $500 million between 1986–8 after Syria's foreign policy, notably its Iranian alliance, antagonized its donors in the Arab Gulf; aid may have wholly halted thereafter. The result was a foreign exchange and debt crunch. In 1988 Syria paid back to the Arab states and lending agencies $9.6 million more than it received, but it still fell $210 million in arrears to the World Bank, which cut off development assistance. This resource crunch brought internal growth to a halt: new factories, failing to produce revenue-generating exports, were dependent on aid for parts and raw materials, and they closed down when this shrank. These economic imbalances were manifest in inflation, balance of payments crises, a painful decline in GNP, and a seemingly intractable stagnation (Drysdale and Hinnebusch, 1991: 44–7).

Incremental liberalization under state dominance

Elite change combined with economic crisis generated pressures for liberalization. There was a growing ideological vacuum at the centre. As an embourgeoised elite itself went into business on the side, its residual commitments to socialism eroded. The austerity of the later 1980s, in forcing factories to close down, exposed the weakness of the statist industrialization effort. As the fiscal crisis forced the regime to reduce its economic responsibilities, it looked to private sector development as a safety valve. Syria's increasingly porous economic borders, open to smuggling, the movement of labour and remittances, and the transfer of capital, exposed the weakness of state attempts to manage the economy, especially given the complicity of regime élites themselves in illicit cross-border economic enterprise. The collapse of communism has not only accelerated the ideological crisis, but, in threatening to deprive the public sector of East European aid, technology and export markets, further undermines the viability of statism.

On the other hand, decision-makers have perceived opportunities as well as constraints. Syria's largest business families are, to a great extent, internationalized, their wings abroad accumulating capital which under favourable conditions could be invested at home. A certain petty peasant capitalism is emerging in the countryside, while the 'informal' urban sector certainly possesses some capital and entrepreneurship. Austerity has generated a greater receptivity toward free enterprise among the state's own constituency. Many small commercial or artisanal enterprises are run by families with one foot in the government and one in the village. As state expenditure contracted in the 1980s, these families had to diversify their resources by setting up petty businesses, often from capital accumulated working in the Gulf. The regime wants to channel this capital and energy into productive, not just speculative, undertakings. It may be on the way to deciding that substantial liberalization is the spark needed to unleash these potentialities.

So far, however, the state, far from being recaptured by a recon-structed bourgeoisie, remains ambivalent in its view of private capital. President Asad, the key player, is little Westernized and is committed to a stubborn pursuit of the national struggle against Israel even at the expense of economic development. He has so far been unwilling to allow the complete unravelling of the statist system he helped to construct, and he lacks any Sadat-like interest in undermining threat-ening state bureaucrats. Socialist residues are defended by a powerful array of interests; party apparatchiki, public sector managers, trade unionists, the co-operatives. There remains a perception in the regime that the private sector is only interested in short-term high profit enterprise and that the state must continue to undertake large-scale long-term investment. Thus, there is as yet no move to privatize the public sector which, in principle, continues to monopolize large and strategic industries as well as the production of key popular consump-tion commodities. Powerful regime figures continue to defend the public sector. Izz ed-Din Nasir, a member of the Regional Command of the Ba'th party and head of the trade union confederation, who is seen as a major opponent by private business, was the force behind a 1989 conference aimed at fostering the co-operation of public man-agers and labour leaders in the search for greater efficiency in public industry. His message was that there is no alternative to the development and reform of the public sector.[1]

Creating a suitable investment climate would require a revocation of populist practices such as subsidies and labour rights, but the regime is aware that its stability is hostage to a kind of populist 'social contract', that is, the expectation that it will cushion economic hard times and maintain a minimum standard of welfare. Syrian policy-makers are also aware of the Egyptian precedent where, as they perceive it, *infitah* generated an import boom, the proliferation of agents for foreign firms, a worsening of trade and foreign exchange imbalances, mounting debt, dependency and social instability rather than local industrialists and significant foreign investment. Thus, they seek to tailor policy to take advantage of opportunities while containing costs and they may have the leeway to do so. Compared to other Middle Eastern countries, Syria's debt is modest and it is thus less vulnerable to IMF pressures (World Development Report, 1990; Niblock in this volume). Syria's aid and oil prospects may also allow decision-makers to avoid the pain of major market reforms and, indeed, to keep alive the populist coalition through food and other subsidies cushioning inequality. New oil fields and the windfall reaped by Syria's stand against Iraq have increased its breathing room. Oil rent also keeps important sectors of society tied into clientalist relations with the regime and lacking in the independence or motive to seek liberalization.

The crisis of Ba'thism nevertheless began to create a more favourable climate for the bourgeoisie. By the mid-1980s, official policy explicitly aimed at trimming the role of the state, stimulating the private sector and adapting to the market rather than, as before, largely trying to constrain it. Asad reputedly declared that Syria's merchants were an 'honourable class' and backed a widened role for the private sector at the 1985 Eighth Regional Congress of the Ba'th Party (Seale 1988: 452; Sadowski 1985: 5–6). It took five years, but in the latest, post-Gulf war twist, the government press has started to promote the benefits of liberalization, to restrain populist and nation-alist rhetoric, and, seemingly, to give an unprecedented seal of approval to capitalists and capitalism. Step by step, policy has altered in line with rhetoric.

The regime pursued a fairly rigorous austerity policy in the late 1980s, meant to get budget and balance of payments deficits under control and create a more healthy economic environment (Heydemann, 1990; Perthes, 1990: 5). Deficit financing was reduced. Public hiring and wages were frozen, pushing down real wages. Subsidies on bread and fuel were curbed, driving up prices, and efforts were made to target them more precisely to the needy. While in some respects austerity was to evade international pressures for more thorough liberalization, it whittled away at the foundations of populism and, together with cuts in military spending and state industrialization, signalled a step back from the overdevelopment of the state.

As the public sector stagnated, the regime also made such significantly more serious efforts to encourage the private sector that some businessmen spoke of a 'second *infitah*' (Perthes, 1990: 5–6). While the principle of a public–private division of labour was not abandoned, the division has been rapidly eroding, with a declining number of fields reserved to the public sector: some 300 industries are now open to investment by the private and mixed sectors. In 1991, a major new investment law was promulgated which welcomed foreign investment in industry, permitted repatriation of profits, and waived import duties and taxes; it sought to bring in enough foreign investment to give local and expatriate capital confidence.

A major new policy initiative has been the encouragement of a joint public–private sector, so far most developed in the fields of tourism and agriculture. The agricultural investment companies are typical of this sector. While the state retains a share of assets and some control in the companies, management is in private hands. The companies are outside the state planning and price control system, enjoy a generous tax holiday, can deal in foreign currency outside official channels, may freely import and export, and are exempt from labour laws (Hopfinger, 1990). According to a leading private businessman, this approach, avoiding the opposition of the trade unions, is Syria's special road to privatization. Indeed, the provision by the state of large tracts of state-owned land to these companies may amount to a *de facto* 'privatization' of this land. The joint sector could be the womb of widening common interests between state and private élites.

Besides the joint sector, resource constraints have forced the state to reach arrangements which have in practice put certain public industries under private control. Because the lack of foreign currency to import scrap iron deprived it of the ability to run the Hama iron and steel works, for example, the regime permitted private sector entrepreneurs who could obtain scrap to rent the facility. Similarly, the end to the state's ability to pay for certain traditionally public sector-imported commodities has encouraged black market smuggling: in effect an unintended 'privatization' of a segment of foreign trade (Perthes, 1990: 14, 18). Responding to this reality, the regime now allows the private sector to import certain commodities which were previously state monopolies, such as rice and paper, timber and steel, provided this is financed by foreign currency held outside the country.

The regime has also made more serious efforts to accommodate the needs of private business for foreign currency. The mixed results of this effort can be seen in the way policy has zigzagged between the tightening and loosening of controls in the 1980s. On the one hand, the government has sought to secure state control over scarce foreign exchange and protect the value of the Syrian pound. The public sector was generally given priority in access to government-held foreign exchange. Yet the government has also wanted to give investors the access to foreign currency crucial to doing business and to encourage exporters to earn and repatriate it. At first, the state insisted that all foreign currency should be sold to state banks; but foreign exchange became steadily scarcer, such that the private sector could not readily gain access to it. This stimulated the foreign currency black market, and in the mid-1980s the regime cracked down on currency manipulators, but supposedly not on genuine local investors. Most business can not proceed without foreign currency, and since everyone engages in such speculation, to observe the law puts a businessman at a competitive disadvantage; thus, currency crackdowns generally chill the business climate. So, in the late 1980s, the government relaxed restrictions on private sector access to foreign currency and businessmen were allowed to keep 75 per cent of the foreign currency they earned, provided they sold the rest to the state at a rate close to the free market rate (Lawson, 1988: 590–4; US Embassy, 1989).

Revitalized bourgeoisie?
The bourgeoisie has, to some degree, responded to this new environment. When the easy pickings from petrodollars dried up in the late 1980s, the bourgeoisie had more incentive for productive investment. The regime, moreover, succeeded in convincing important elements of the business sector of the seriousness of the reform programme.[2] The result has been a palpable expansion of the private sector. The number of private businesses grew from 220,000 in 1981 to about 370,000 in 1988, and industries employing more than 10 workers

doubled from 890 to almost 1,800 (Perthes, 1990: 5–8, 15–16). Since, at the same time, the public sector was stagnating, private sector investment and value added increased at a much greater rate (Meyer, 1987: 53–6). In late 1991, the government was reporting that more than 150 projects had been approved in a mere few months under its new investment law, although most were small light consumer goods projects.

Several examples indicate the wide range of the different forms of enterprise which have popped up. A trio of favoured 'new rich' business giants, Sa'ib Nahas, Abd al-Rahman Attar and Uthman Aidi, have had high visibility in many fields, particularly tourism and transport. Nahas combines Euro-Arab banking and investment interests with tourism and agricultural interests in Syria. Aidi, imprisoned under the radical Ba'th for taking commissions on an aircraft deal between France and Syrian Arab Airlines, now runs the Sham hotel chain throughout Syria. Attar, who stems from a middle merchant family, now heads the Chamber of Commerce and is engaged in a foreign joint venture in electronics. The Shallah family represents old merchant capital, with diversified interests in manufacturing and agriculture. Badr ad-Din ash-Shallah, head of the Damascus Chamber of Commerce, won Asad's gratitude by keeping the Damascus *suq* open during the Islamic uprisings. A handful of large-scale private industries have reappeared: a large textile factory, founded by an entrepreneurial artisan and employing 800 persons is in operation, exporting to the (former) Soviet Union and selling luxury clothing (which is not price controlled) on the local market. Consumer industries manufacturing under European licence, being able to recoup their investments quickly, have proven attractive to capital (Perthes, 1990: 19). Generally, the private sector share of foreign trade, both imports and exports, has widened rapidly. Finally, there exists a large thriving underground economy, outside of official statistics, which keeps the country afloat in hard times. Low-cost goods are traded on an informal market, allowing low-income people to survive (Kuroda, 1992: chapter in this volume). A wide variety of smuggled goods, from luxuries to consumer necessities and materials and parts, are available on the black market. Peace and economic revival in a Lebanon integrated with the Syrian economy could give further impetus to this trade, especially if it were legitimized.

But it is also clear that the potential of business remains constrained. The very precarious sense of business confidence is manifest in the record of the agricultural investment companies which are supposed to be the cutting edge of a new state-business partnership. Of the eleven originally founded, four failed to raise enough capital. Those that have done so combine the most influential public and private sector figures. Others rely chiefly on expatriates wanting to gain a foothold in the country. But even those which are going operations have spearheaded no great breakthroughs in production, and are said to be making a good bit of their returns on import–export operations and from funds deposited abroad. They may be diversifying their risk, or simply using the new arrangements to give cover to traditional speculative ventures (Hopfinger, 1990).

Another story is told by the constraints on expansion of purely private ventures. In certain rural areas, such as Yabroud, family-owned light industries have developed from a pre-existing artisanal tradition, outside of state influence. There, a tradition of emigration has fostered the import of technology and the accumulation of capital, closeness to Lebanon has permitted smuggling to overcome raw material constraints, and product lines are chosen from those outside of state price controls. Yet, the habit of hiding assets from potential nationalization, the fear of competition from state industries, and the constantly changing import–export regulations deter the natural expansion of these industries into larger-scale fully legitimate firms (Escher, 1990).

In general, private sector industrial growth has taken the form of a further proliferation of small enterprises, sometimes relying on secret partners who prefer to invest in other firms rather than enlarge their own (Perthes, 1990: 13). Firms remain small because of the risks of large-scale investment. To become too big is to invite trouble from the government. Growth requires involvement in currency and import smuggling, making investors vulnerable to crackdowns. As business-men see it, the labour law gives workers so many rights that a union can ruin a business; hence they are loath to hire many workers. There is also no strong tradition of joint stock companies or a legalized stock market. In this climate capital has generally gravitated into commerce, where risks are less and profits quicker. As such, the private sector will not replace state dominance of the economy any time soon.

Obstacles to liberalization

The fact is that the state has yet to foster an economic climate in which investors can take full advantage of the liberalization of official policy. Many of the regime's own practices deter investment. Elite corruption creates a climate of uncertainty and opportunities for riches from illicit or non-productive activities, which deters the productive investment needed to develop national capitalism. But eradicating the parasitic activities of regime insiders could threaten the regime itself. Private business wants 'legislative stability' – permanent and clear laws – but the government's hit and miss attempt to control the economic crisis translates into a plethora of often contradictory and transitory decrees. Government intervention continually alters the condition. of business. For example, private manufacturers are dependent on public sector imports, but the foreign exchange crisis of the 1980s cut off their supplies, forcing them to rely on highly priced smuggled imports. When price controls did not permit a rise in prices of their products, many manufacturers had to cut back production (Perthes, 1990: 15). High taxes (although much evaded in practice) until recently taxed all income over 100,000 Syrian pounds at a 92 per cent rate, which, as the pound has fallen, has recently amounted to less than $5,000. The absence of private banks and a free financial market has frustrated capital concentration and investment flows. The regime has perhaps unwittingly diverted private enterprise into commercial, speculative and parasitic channels by favouring the public sector in industry and through the state–business alliances which make middleman operations so lucrative. Even when policy changes, no overnight transformation of the bureaucracy, from one used to viewing the private sector as the enemy into one which seeks to facilitate business, is likely.

The bourgeoisie proved strong enough to derail the Ba'th's original socialist project but, despite acquiring new scope, it lacks the cohesion, motivation and strength to force a major liberal transformation. It is still relatively small and lacking in strong links with other classes. Liberal ideology has really not recovered from its pre-Ba'th discrediting. So long as private control of the means of production remains so limited and fragmented, the bourgeoisie is likely to lack the social power to force liberalization. Moreover, divided, the bourgeoisie presents no common front to the regime in favour of it. Some sectors, largely the new bourgeoisie which rose in the shadow of the regime and certain sectors of the old commercial bourgeoisie which have found the climate for import–export operations favourable, have co-operated with the regime. Some, benefiting from the monopolies their connections permit in an over-regulated economy, have little to gain from liberalization. Other segments of the old bourgeoisie, particularly industrialists who lost their assets to nationalization or new would-be ones who resent state constraints on their opportunities, favour liberalization but often continue to reject accommodation with the regime and thus have no influence over it (Perthes, 1990: 21–3).

Economically, it is questionable to what extent a productive national bourgeoisie can be reconstructed in Syria. There is, first of all, the fact that the Ba'thist state seized much of the bourgeoisie's assets and limited its ability to extract a surplus for nearly three decades, retarding its ability to compete on the international market. Without a stock market or private banks, it is handicapped in mobilizing and concentrating capital. The international wing of the high bourgeoisie has enormous wealth but has so far only a limited stake in Syria, and has much better and more secure opportunities for profit elsewhere. Syria has a long entrepreneurial tradition, but the indigenous private sector may be too fragmented or engrossed in comprador activities, in which risks are less and profits high, to take the lead in national capitalist development. Moreover, most business families generally have branches abroad where the bulk of their investment is channelled. The export of capital from the Arab oil states is testimony to how much more attractive core markets are for indigenous capital. Incentives to invest in national industry and agriculture are limited in a part of the world where great opportunities to skim off petro-rent exist.

Business confidence will remain limited as long as the state is seen as arbitrary and unpredictable, and this can only be overcome if the bourgeoisie acquires some political power. The pre-Ba'th capitalist experience suggests that the bourgeoisie will not lead the deepening of capital unless it has secure control of the state. The regime has begun a very limited political liberalization to appease the bourgeoisie, as an escape valve for pent up economic frustrations, and to co-opt a wider coalition into supporting unpopular decisions. The bourgeoisie has won increasing access to decision-makers. The departure of Prime Minister Kasm, who was committed to public sector dominance, favoured them. In the person of the Economy Minister, Muhammad Imadi, the bourgeoisie has access to a sympathetic and influential figure who has promoted economic reforms favourable to business. The establishment of the Committee for the Rationalization of Imports, Exports and Consumption, which meets regularly under Prime Minister Zoubi and on which the heads of the chambers of commerce and of industry are represented and influential, gives unprecedented institutional access. This, combined with growing personal security and business freedom may be enough to satisfy the bourgeoisie.

There is little likelihood of substantial political liberalization, despite the yearning for democracy stimulated by events in Eastern Europe and Middle Eastern countries such as Algeria and neighbouring Jordan, whose television broadcasts many Syrians watch. Asad argues that his 1970 rise to power initiated a Syrian *perestroika* – political relaxation, opening to the private sector – long before Gorbachev, and that 'the phase through which [Syria] is passing is not suitable for implementing [competitive elections].' The Ba'th Party would have a hard time surviving free elections, and its leaders, if swept from office, would be vulnerable to the settling of many old scores. Even a limited opening could, as the rapid collapse of East Europe's single-party states suggests, unleash uncontrollable forces. Asad has reputedly tried to foster a 'moderate' Islamic party willing to co-operate with the regime and lend an Islamic legitimation to economic liberalization and the growing social inequalities accompanying it. But the ideological gap between a secular minoritarian regime and political Islam appears too wide for this to succeed. As long as a powerful Islamic-oriented wing of the bourgeoisie rejects the legitimacy of Ba'thist rule, political liberalization carries with it the risk that Islam will become a vehicle of anti-regime mobilization. Although various independent businessmen and even Ikhwan-associated figures have been co-opted into parliament, their role is to gain access to the state, not to organize as a social force to check it. The bottom line is that the military seems unprepared to withdraw from the centre of politics. The Alawis who dominate the state would be threatened by any return of power to the Sunni-dominated business establishment, and the security forces have the firepower and personal stake in regime survival to contain popular demands for democratization (Drysdale and Hinnebusch, 1991: 36–43).

As for integration into the world capitalist market (which tends to accompany the deepening of economic liberalization), this is unlikely to have unambiguously positive consequences for Syrian development. Foreign investment will probably be limited to areas where Syria has advantages: petroleum, tourism, and certain light industries. The heavy industrial or high-tech investment necessary to transform the Syrian economy will not be forthcoming from that quarter. A world capital shortage is developing. Eastern Europe and the states of the former Soviet Union will draw off much Western investment, while the instability inherent in the Middle East is likely to deter significant long-term investment there. Moreover, a favourable investment climate would require driving down wages, depriving workers of labour rights, and giving tax concessions. Liberalization may even threaten what industrialization the country has attained, since most Syrian industries, state or private, could not survive unregulated foreign competition. If the artisanal petite bourgeoisie which has benefited from protection were to be victimized by liberalization, it could adopt Islam as an ideology of protest.

Finally, the regime's preoccupation with the struggle against Israel makes continued control over society and its resources indispensable. The imperatives of the national security state take precedence over all else, and the confrontation with Israel continues to block a radical departure from étatism. For one thing, the military absorbs a large portion of public revenues which might otherwise stimulate capitalist development. For another, the conflict discourages private investment in long-term productive fields, channels it into short-term speculative ventures, and makes Syria ineligible for foreign private investment on a serious scale. Ultimately, liberalization in the Third World involves internationalization of the economy, but this is unacceptable to the regime so long as it perceives the West as being hostile to Syria's national aspirations. The perception that Egypt's more advanced liberalization experiment led to an abandonment of national honour (and dependency on the West rather than prosperity), discourages more liberal voices in Syria. The 'triple alliance' of state, domestic and international capital, which is the engine of capitalist development elsewhere, is stunted in Syria.

If the international state system has been an obstacle to capitalist development in Syria, its transformation may unblock the road. Statism was partly a function of bi-polarity, of the possibility of aid and protection from the Soviet Union. The fracture and dissipation of the old Soviet state has radically altered the conditions in which Syrian *raison d'état* must operate. Asad is apparently convinced that Syria's national goals can no longer be pursued in opposition to the only remaining superpower, the United States. If a settlement of the Arab–Israeli conflict were to result, it would give major impetus to internal liberalization, the gradual dismantling of the national security state, and the emergence of a dominant bourgeoisie. In the end, the international context and the logic of *raison d'état*, may be decisive for internal developments.

Conclusion

The nature of the state is decisive in determining the course of liberalization. In the 1960s, a still unconsolidated Ba'th state had to change course under pressures from external threat and internal resistance. But as, under Asad, the Syrian state achieved autonomy, its policies were shaped above all by its own conception of *raison d'état*. As the Marxist theory of the Bonapartist state explains, such autonomy was partly the product of a period of transition – from 'feudalism to capitalism' – when old ruling classes were in decline and no new dominant class capable of capturing the state had emerged, allowing the state to rise above and balance between societal groups.

But state autonomy was also the outcome of efforts to respond to international threats. This is the missing variable in most discussions of the effect of the international arena. The liberal model sees the global economy as a benign world of opportunity, but the environment most immediately perceived by Syrian decision-makers is an intensely threatening regional state system. Survival in this environment has its own special logic, its *raison d'état*, just as valid as that necessary to survival in a competitive economic market. If decision-makers reject the recommendations of liberal economists to free the market, and the state extracts resources that could go into economic development (or deploys patronage to satisfy key constituents), this may not be explicable solely as some neo-patrimonial capture of the state. It also expresses *raison d'état*.

So far, neither economic constraints nor the recapture of the state by a new bourgeoisie has dictated in any mechanical way a liberal transformation in Syria. Does this mean that the state is the enemy of capitalist development, as the neo-patrimonialists would have it? The Ba'th has indeed institutionalized a whole set of barriers to liberalization: the legacy of class animosity, the politicized military, sectarian conflict (particularly Alawi–Sunni communal cleavages), the huge bureaucracy, and the interminable struggle with Israel. The patrimonial features of the regime constrain liberalization. But none of this has prevented an incremental adaptation of state policy to the demands of economic rationality. While a neo-mercantilist regime subordinates economics to politics, it recognizes that national power requires a healthy economic base. Moreover, in such a regime, foreign policy shapes economics and, just as external threat forced limited liberalization in 1970, the end of bi-polarity could deepen it in the 1990s.

Liberalization in Syria has, in fact, responded both to economic constraints and to opportunities. The state's limited ability to foster capital accumulation, its own 'over-development', and its consequent dependency on external aid have made it continually vulnerable to resource crises. Twice, in the 1960s and again in the 1970s, import-substitute industrialization led to crisis: as elsewhere, it resulted in dependency on the import of parts and materials with little export revenue to pay for them, put strains on the balance of trade and payments, generated foreign exchange problems, and forced the state to look for private sector safety valves. Constraints, when added to perceived opportunities to attract external resources – notably after the 1974 oil boom – resulted in liberalizing adjustments. Liberalization was a state concession to the Syrian and Arab bourgeoisies, whose capital and cooperation the state sought. But the state's relative autonomy allowed it to adapt at its own pace. The interests incorporated into the state opposed any radical abandonment of statism, while the bourgeoisie was not strong enough to force greater liberalization than the state wanted. The regime weathered a full decade of economic stagnation and hardship in the 1980s and evaded international (IMF) pressures by adopting its own austerity measures. Now higher oil revenues and renewed Arab aid may again buttress its autonomy. Controlled liberalization, stopping short of full scale *infitah*, is the result.

The extent of liberalization depends on the political process. Policy-makers must respond to environmental exigencies, but since it is seldom obvious how to do so, policy change typically emerges from intra-élite conflict over how best to adapt at least political cost. Amid economic crisis, patrimonial practices may be needed so as to placate key constituencies and protect short-run stability. Resource crises and opportunities to foster investment, however, may also help liberalizers gain an incremental momentum which may be irreversible. Competing élite factions are not isolated from society, and often speak for shifting coalitions reaching into the state apparatus or the private sector. The former line-up, in which the bourgeoisie favoured and the state apparatus opposed liberalization, has broken down. While entrepreneurial sectors of the bourgeoisie want more liberalization and bureaucrats with a strong stake in the public sector want less, the state as a whole no longer sees an interest in resisting controlled liberalization, while parts of the bourgeoisie favour no more than that. The incorporation of elements of the bourgeoisie, old and new, into the regime coalition has greatly diluted its populist character, but the salaried middle class and the peasantry have not been excluded. Unless a conservative anti-populist coalition is constructed, Syrian economic policy is likely to pursue incremental but eschew full-scale liberalization.

The cumulative outcomes of state policy – the Ba'thist legacy – have, even if unintentionally, fostered some of the conditions for renewed capitalist development. The Ba'th, as the state-capitalist model would have it, 'cleared the way' of feudal debris, that is, of the archaic agrarian structure which obstructed Syria's initial capitalist expansion. Syria has, today, a more open class system, a more diversified infrastructure, more developed human capital, and a wider market than when the Ba'th took power. The private sector has benefited from linkages to the public sector and has siphoned off capital and skilled labour from it. The regime has, moreover, fostered a petty capitalism which could give renewed capitalist development a wider base than before 1963. In general, the state has created forces and conditions which could relaunch captalist development but has so far retarded their maturation.

The Syrian bourgeoisie is as crucial as is state policy in determining the outcome of liberalization. It has a long commercial tradition, and in the post-independence years seemed to be turning its talents and capital to industrialization. In Syria, today, a bourgeoisie has re-emerged. Much of the bigger bourgeoisie appears to be 'comprador' or 'parasitic', rather than constituting productive investors operating in a competitive market. It must be recognized, however, that these labels express ideal types, that real capitalists are likely to mix these various features, and that such businessmen may be prepared to invest the capital accumulated in 'non-productive' activities in productive entrepreneurial activities if profit is legitimized and its pursuit protected from arbitrary state actions. Continuing incremental liberalization is likely, over time, to encourage confidence and foster a stronger bourgeoisie. Moreover, the base of the bourgeoisie may be broadening as the old and state-generated fractions are joined by upwardly-mobile segments of other classes: Syria's age-old entrepreneurial culture may be spreading from the bourgeoisie into the heart of state and village.

The Syrian case manifests something distinctive about the Middle East, which explains resistance to capitalist development. On the one hand, the authoritarian state is obsessed with national security, retains a huge stake in the economy, enjoys periodic rent windfalls which buttress its autonomy, and controls a politically disorganized society incapable of forcing liberalization but with the negative power to hold the state to a populist social contract. On the other hand, a trade and rent-based society can evade the state, thrive on the informal, black market economy, on remittances and parasitic activities and fall back on its Islamic ethos. Given the limits of dependent development in the world capitalist system, state and middleman capitalism have so far appeared to many Syrians to define the limits of the possible. Time will tell whether in future the two can join hands in more productive enterprise.

Notes

1 *Tishrin*, 4–5/12/89.
2 Economist Intelligence Unit, 1990, *Syria*, no. 2, p. 4.

11· ECONOMIC LIBERALIZATION AND THE *SUQ* IN SYRIA

Miyoko Kuroda

The first section of this chapter analyses the trend and nature of 'liberalization', with particular reference to the implications which follow from the transnational activities of multinational companies. It emphasizes the handicaps which Third World countries (including Syria) face as they liberalize their economies. The handicaps arise from these countries being relative late starters in the world capitalist economy. The section suggests that unlimited liberalization may not provide Third World countries with the solutions to their current economic problems which they seek.

The second section suggests an alternative approach to development, based not on existing theories but on a re-examination of the nature and role of the traditional economy. The approach is specifically geared towards overcoming the problems of handicapped liberalization, through positively utilizing and reorganizing the non-capitalist traditional market sector. A brief examination of the role of this traditional sector in Japan is provided to demonstrate how it can contribute to the development of an economy by drawing on the historical and cultural attributes of the people of a country.

The third section outlines the shape of the traditional sector in Middle Eastern countries, and in Syria in particular. It considers the undertaking of socialist principles in Syria and the subsequent Syrian experience of liberalization. The case study indicates that the prospects for an orthodox mixed economy in Syria are not bright, but that the potential exists for development of the Syrian traditional sector; the *suq* economy.

The trend towards liberalization: its rationale and its values

Since the early 1980s, the developed countries have generally been moving towards expanding the market, through reducing the role of the public sector in the economy and through introducing greater competition or 'marketization'. During the 1980s, the established mixed economy system was destined to undergo large-scale revision: the prevailing economic orthodoxy demanded drastic changes to be made in the relationship between government and the market. This tendency was also evident in many developing countries.

In principle, as J. Burnham has written (Burnham, 1941: 106), in capitalist society the role of the government in economic activities is secondary. For the half-century which followed the 1930s, however, the trend in favour of a mixed economic system was strong. The trend was encouraged by Keynesian theory, and it aimed at the wise management of capitalism by means of the effective functioning of social institutions and organizations. Governments increased the degree of their intervention in economic affairs, such that 'big government' was prevalent in capitalist countries until the 1970s. Keynesian theory asserted the importance of macro-level factors affecting the national economy. This theory was closely linked with the coherence of nation states and assumed that nation states could and should solve their own problems.

The move away from 'big government' solutions to economic problems is in part an effect of the growth of economic interdependence, the increasing activities of multinational corporations, and new aspects of international monetary and financial transactions expanding beyond the control of a nation state. These developments have started to threaten the independent character of national economies based on the nation state. The aggravation of the South–North divide has impinged on the ability of developing countries to pursue independent policies.

The role of multinational corporations in the new structure of international economic relations is crucial. Until now, the countries of origin of multinational corporations, as well as the host countries accepting their activities, have generally assumed a positive attitude towards them. Many developing countries try hard to attract multinational corporations on the assumption that they represent foreign investment, which is vital for their own development. In many cases, host countries offer conditions which are beneficial to investors, such as exemption from various taxes and the bearing by the host country of infrastructural expenses. In some cases, the assistance offered to multinational corporations surpasses that given to local or national investors. Paradoxically, the countries of origin of these corporations have also given them protection, on the pretext that their strengthening is essential if the country's economy is to remain internationally competitive. Thus they have encouraged the development of big industrial enterprises, through offering vast financial support in the form of subsidies, loans, tax exemptions and so forth.[1]

Multinational corporations can be said to possess double identities, derived from both their country of origin and their activities outside of it. Their range of activities surpasses that of a national economy, reducing the significance of national borders. Economic activity is no longer confined to the parameters of the nation state. This internationalization of capital means that capital itself no longer depends simply on the support of the nation state, but is active beyond the realm of regulations and restrictions created by the nation for its economic administration.

Multinational corporations developed through the amalgamation of foreign capital with enterprises in the host country. This caused the large-scale internationalization of capital circulation and production. The policies of economic liberalization pursued by so many of the developed countries during the 1980s were an imperative for the continuation of this process. It appears, then, that liberalization is incumbent on every country to a greater or lesser extent. For countries striving to maintain their national economic integrity, however, liberalization poses serious dilemmas. A weak private sector and too many restrictions creates stagnation; a strong private sector and considerable freedom of manoeuvre tend to invite political subjugation and dependency in decision-making. Thus the question arises: liberalization for whom and what kind of liberalization?

Clearly, development in the Third World should be aimed at the betterment of social life, the fulfilment of the basic needs of ordinary people, and the protection of their economic and social welfare. Development should strengthen the ability to produce and distribute wealth. In reality, however, experience shows that total commitment to the free market makes it impossible to attain these objectives. The liberalization which is helpful and meaningful for developing countries is a limited form of liberalization, which can protect them from the systematic exploitation of differentials by multinationals. Successful liberalization can only be achieved in developing countries when it is limited as part of a planned economy. Limiting liberalization, and maintaining an interventionary role for the state, can help to offset the disadvantages of a late start in the world capitalist economy.

One of the areas in which the state can most usefully participate is in the encouragement of the 'traditional' sector.

Utilizing the traditional sector

Throughout history, every country or region has accumulated an enormous amount of economic know-how, institutions and capacity, specific to its own particular and individual survival and development. It can be argued that it is time for the Third World to pay greater attention to the utilization of these traditional values in order to achieve development.

The reason for seeking to utilize traditional approaches lies in the difficulties of developing from a position of dependence within the capitalist system. Economic liberalization under capitalism involves free competition; and under free competition the late starter has almost no chance of winning. Evidence for this is found in the growing gap between the strong and the weak (Amin, 1983: 54), and in the failure of any Middle Eastern state to achieve genuine modernization. This argument corresponds closely to the views expressed by concerned intellectuals in the Third World, who equate liberalization with neo-colonialism. If weak (developing) countries can only play the capitalist games of the developed world at a disadvantage, then it is vital for the the developing world to seek alternative paths to development, one of which may be to pay more positive attention to the traditional aspects of their economies.

It is worthwhile, therefore, reassessing the firmly-established line of analysis which focuses solely on the formal sectors of the economy, totally neglecting the informal or 'traditional' sector. The established line of analysis makes the simplistic assumption that the continuing existence of the traditional sector is a sign of economic underdevelopment and that there is no need, therefore, to take notice of it. A developed industrial economy must, no doubt, be the final goal, but in order to achieve this, more serious attention should be paid to the existing reality. While the traditional sectors may not be considered particularly useful in the march towards development, the very fact of their continued existence suggests that they fulfil some useful function for the society itself and that modernist notions of development alone can not satisfy the immediate needs of the people. Third World countries are not yet fully transformed into capitalist economies.

Traditional methods of exchange, such as bargaining and commercial second-hand or inferior goods markets not only survive but frequently prosper. Bearing in mind that people in the Third World are living on extremely low incomes, we should not underestimate their resourcefulness or ingenuity in developing indigenously-derived answers to their economic problems.

The positive reactivation of the traditional sector offers the possibility of encouraging free competition without being burdened by the handicap of a late start. Offering legitimacy to the traditional sector as part of the market economy should not involve using the planning institutions of the central government to bring about the sector's integration into the national economy. The government must, rather, offer some means to let all the participants in the market economy possess the feeling of equality and fairplay which will encourage them to develop their activities. To do this, it is incumbent upon the government of the developing country to re-evaluate the functions of traditional economic activities.

Encouraging the traditional sector to assume a greater role in the production and distribution of wealth may initially appear to indicate that the government has set a lower target level of economic development, inconsistent with modernist ideals of economic development. In the long term, however, the traditional sector may provide economic growth based not on international competition (in which the weak developing countries are inevitably handicapped by their late start) but on domestic activities and small-scale business, at which these countries excel. The traditional sector may thus constitute the strongest basis on which the economy can develop.

Although there are examples in the Middle East of governments displaying an ingenious ability to utilize aspects of the traditional sector to counter changing economic situations, before turning to that area it is worth first briefly examining the example of Japan, for comparative purposes.

The case of Japan

Effective economic development was visible in Japan in the Edo era (1600–1868). There existed substantial internal trade, mediated by a developed banking system which connected savings with investment. Well-established rules for commercial transactions provided participants in this market economy with confidence in the safety of those transactions, as well as a sense of equality which provided an incentive for participation and extended economic activity. This feeling of equality, which has been the driving force behind development since World War II, has left Japan with a classless society – more than 80 per cent of the population considering themselves to be middle class. Although Japanese society was traditionally divided vertically into four groups – samurai (warriors), peasants, artisans and merchants – socio-economic status did not hamper a person's entry into economic activities. When mass production technology developed in Japan, this occurred on the basis of enterprises rather than industries. Rather than mass production leading to the emergence of very large industrial units, then, the units of production remained small and 'organic' (Odaka, 1984). The structures of 'whole-life employment' and the seniority-wage system which have functioned so successfully in Japan in recent years have their origins in this system.

Foreign academics have criticized the system as being inefficient and underdeveloped, for it encourages the proliferation of medium- and small-scale enterprises, rather than large-scale industry. Nevertheless, it possesses a certain strength. Rather than being goal-oriented, as in the West, Japanese enterprises may be said to be organic. They are able to multiply and adapt themselves to new circumstances, changing the goals themselves. The proliferation of strong organic cells throughout Japan is at the heart of Japan's current industrial strength. Yet the development of such a system has been the result of a reliance on traditional market values and practices, rather than of any Western model.

From the beginning of the Meiji era (1868), Japanese government institutions have developed simultaneously to overcome friction between the government and market, playing a decisive intermediary role in the formation of the Japanese market system and emphasizing the essential role played in the economy by medium- and small-scale enterprises, as well as regional industries[2] Government policies in education, for example, were shaped to benefit the country's economy. A well-balanced educational system was developed, where university courses catered for the needs of the future administration of large-scale enterprises while appropriate vocational education was provided for the future employees of small- and medium-sized enterprises.

The traditional sector in the Middle East
Middle East economic activities were based largely on Islamic concepts and practices for more than ten centuries (Kuroda, 1991). Only

since the eighteenth and nineteenth centuries has the capitalist system been in operation (initially mainly through physical imposition) in this region. Yet researchers and students of the Middle East tend to examine the region through the use of analytical tools and methodologies appropriate only to the capitalist phase. The tools are developed from the analysis of Western history and embody West-oriented modernist developmental concepts. But can we grasp the reality of historical aspects of this region with such an approach? Is the total neglect of traditional factors helpful in planning this region's future development?

Scholars have tended to over-emphasize the spiritual aspects of Islam at the expense of analysis of its socio-cultural functions.[3] Originally in the Middle East, economic activities were regulated within the framework of an aggregate network system. One might say that the people pursued a liberal system of their own. For commercial transactions some basic rules existed. Theoretically, justice was maintained by means of the Islamic law, which contained detailed regulations forbidding various kinds of fraud, cheating, selling of inferior goods, unreasonable profit-making and so forth. This Islamic, or 'traditional' economy had a set of regulations which provided for some freedom of economic activity (Kuroda, 1988), but which restricted it in other ways.[4] This system functioned throughout the Middle East for more than ten centuries. Although the system became somewhat distorted (by the degeneration of the Ottoman economic system, the intrusion of colonial capitalism and so forth) it continued and continues to function at some levels, unrestricted by the framework of the nation state (Kuroda, 1991). Originally it acted as a unifying element within the region, forming the basis on which markets in the area were linked together.

The collapse of the Ottoman Empire after the First World War, and the subsequent colonization of the region by Western powers, combined with the implications of the struggle for independence, meant that the people of the Middle East were forced to accept the artificial framework of the nation state. The organic integrity of the region was destroyed. The strong trading networks and sophisticated monetary systems of the Middle East were subordinated to the demands and mechanisms of capitalism, and were unable to continue to dominate economic activities as were the traditional structures of the Japanese economy.

A role for the traditional economy in Syria

Syria was a prominent victim of this tragedy. Traditionally, Syria included several regions presently belonging to other nation states, including Lebanon and parts of Israel (Palestine). As part of the Ottoman Empire, Syria enjoyed the political and economic fruits of this territorial integrity, being one of the wealthiest provinces of the empire. The destruction of this integrity, with artificial borders being established on the basis of new born nation states, carried with it a high price for the people of the area.[5]

When Syria became independent, it had only a narrow range of choice in determining its path towards economic development, under the given political circumstances. Syrian governments adopted the planned economy approach in order to achieve effective capital accumulation and to make preparations for industrialization. At such a stage, the strong centralization of economic activities, through coercive measures taken by the government, was deemed not only effective but essential. The alternative option would have been to seek large-scale foreign aid, which could easily have endangered political independence. Moreover, centralization reduced the initial outlay required for undertaking infrastructural and industrial development.

The Syrian banking system was nationalized in the 1950s, soon after independence. Most of the largest industrial firms were nationalized in 1965. Between 1966 and 1969 the main part of foreign trade was also nationalized, and state companies were established in most economic sectors. Government participation in the different economic sectors increased year by year, and the public sector came to occupy a leading position in the Syrian economy.

However, even in the most statist phases of Syria's economic development, the private sector continued to play an important role in the economy. The nationalizations of the 1960s focused on the industrial sector, the rest being left for private activities. This situation allowed the private sector sufficient room to manoeuvre to sustain its vigour for survival and later revival. The country which had once thrived on vivid commercial activities did not lose its roots, and the private sector began to expand again after 1970, in response to the various measures taken by the government to liberalize the economy. The private sector became dominant in such fields as retailing, tourism, trucking and real estate. The gradual liberalization aided the reconstruction of the Syrian economy, which had experienced a low growth rate for more than ten years. Although the October 1973 war caused serious damage to the economy (estimated at $180 million), for several years after the war Syria experienced marked economic expansion. Due to the prevailing advantageous conditions – ample financial assistance from the oil-producing countries of the Gulf, and increases in oil income and agricultural products – Syria rapidly recovered from the setbacks of the war. The years between 1977 and 1981 saw the consolidation of this economic growth, but the growth of Gross Domestic Product dropped to a half that of previous years, due to poor weather (and harvests) and internal and external financial problems (Lawson, 1982: 24–8). The decrease in the price of oil was a critical element in these 'financial problems', as also was the large proportion of Syria's budget which was devoted to military expenditure (amounting to 56 per cent in 1986). Since 1987, however, military expenditure has been reduced[6] and the priority of policy has been shifted to economic restoration based on the development of agriculture, the utilization of oil and gas income, and increased electricity generating capacity (Meyer, 1987: 61). Although the sum of remittances from Syrian workers in the Gulf countries was reduced as a result of the recent Gulf war (Mansfield, 1980: 467–8), increases in oil income from the Thayyem oil field are expected to relieve many financial problems.

The Syrian government, then, has pursued a policy of 'limited liberalization', planned to take account of specific Syrian capacities and difficulties. While these developments have been occurring, the traditional *suqs* have been of some importance in meeting the needs of ordinary people. According to rough estimates, the *suq* economy in Aleppo accounts for nearly 50 per cent of all economic activity in the town.[7] In Aleppo, one can identify four different types of *suq*, each of which has a clearly defined role. They are:

i   *suq al-hal* (the official market, managed by the government);
ii ordinary *suq* (market in the old quarters);
iii *suq al-jum'ah* (periodic market);
iv one season *suq* (market for specific seasonal items).

Besides these *suqs*, there are many shops in the new quarters, run in a manner similar to those in the old quarters.

The commercial activities in these shops and markets can be divided into two categories: formal (operating within a framework of government controls and regulations), and informal (operating outside of that framework). The latter category includes a sub-category of traditional *suq*s – ones which employ the techniques and practices of the traditional economy. In this categorization, *suq al-hal* and a one-season *suq* (together with ordinary shops) fit into the formal category; a *suq al-jum'ah* fits into the general informal category, and an ordinary *suq* into the traditional sub-category. Of particular importance to the theme of this chapter is the role of those *suq*s which are not in the formal category.

The significance of the *suq*s will be described here with particular reference to the *suq al-jum'ah*. This *suq* opens every Friday and is the untaxed open market, selling mainly second-rate goods and second-hand items at cheap prices. Merchants and amateur vendors sell a great variety of daily goods, starting from rusty bicycles, second-hand watches and radios, to cattle, eggs and seasonal vegetables. A throng of people visit the market. Often illegal articles are also for sale, but it is well known that the police are not seriously interested in controlling such minor illegal activities: the inflow of some illegal items is vital for the stability of the economy. The existence of the market for second-rate and/or second-hand goods is important, enabling people both to provide and to purchase cheaper goods. The market operates according to informal rules, the relationship between vendor and purchaser being well understood by both parties but not necessarily conforming to the fixed-price system of exchange which is associated with the modern capitalist economy.

While the scope of this paper does not allow for a full explanation of the character of traditional markets, it should be noted that some of the commercial transactions in these markets have been modernized. Many shops do make deals according to the fixed-price system. Even here, however, there are traces of traditional factors in the relationship between sellers and buyers. In the selection of which merchant to approach and in obtaining goods on credit, commercial behaviour is not regulated totally by the symmetry between price and value. The characteristic of bargaining transactions – the asymmetry between price and value – prevails even though the market is greatly influenced by modern capitalistic behaviour. In bargaining, every price of merchandise has its unique feature, corresponding to the real demand of every purchase. It is this characteristic which causes modernist planners not to treat the informal sector in a serious manner.

Conclusion

In the flourishing *suq*s of Syria, we can see an example of the traditional sector at work, providing for production and distribution of wealth outside of the formal sectors which the government utilizes for development of the national economy. This chapter seeks to suggest that in this traditional sector there lies the potential for sustainable economic development, just as can be found in the formal, modern sectors of the economy. If Third World governments can be persuaded to show a greater interest in protecting and encouraging these markets (but not in restraining them by trying to introduce new forms of regulation), then they may provide an alternative path to development; one which does not automatically penalise late starters.

If liberalization is taken to mean a simple transition from a socialist planned economy to a capitalist market economy, then Third World countries like Syria will inevitably be unable to compete in international terms. However, liberalization can also involve the encouragement of traditional markets. This could link the past economic glories of the Middle East (and the associated forms of social organization) to activities which continue to play an important role in social and economic life. Through the encouragement of the traditional markets, the countries of the region may be able to acquire a higher degree of self-reliance, which is essential if they are to escape from their present relative weakness.

Notes

1 See Michalet (1987); also Mathias and Salama (1983), pp. 32–5.
2 See Hara (1991).
3 See Kaneko (1990); also Ziadeh (1970).
4 See Masters (1988), chapter 5.
5 See Rafeq (1983), also Tarabayn (1986).
6 See Sadowsky (1986), pp. 3–8.
7 This figure is based on field research conducted by the writer in Aleppo. Information provided by the Aleppo Chamber of Commerce was utilized in making this estimate.

12· IRAN

Anoushiravan Ehteshami

Economic liberalization and deregulation has spread rapidly in the Middle East, afflicting the radical/revolutionary and conservative/pro-Western states alike. The case of the Islamic Republic of Iran is of particular interest, not only because the Islamic Republic has claimed to be revolutionary in North–South terms, but also because its revolution was meant to be unique in its blend of Islamic political and economic development. The revolutionary Islamic Republic aspired to surpass the capitalist/socialist models of development. The pragmatic Islamic Republic, however, has in fact ended up as a mixed economy, albeit one where the strong arm of the state is very much in evidence.

Sympathetic political and ideological circles rejoiced at the prospects of a new and 'authentic' (that is, non-Western) alternative model of development arising from the Third World. This chapter contends that if indeed there ever existed an 'Islamic' model of development in revolutionary Iran, it has been shelved with the emergence of the Rafsanjani leadership. As will be shown later, the government of Rafsanjani has tried to put behind it the rhetoric and practice of populism in favour of a tighter integration into the world capitalist system. It has aimed to reconstruct the shattered economy in the context of greater private domestic and foreign participation. The new policies are deepening the capitalist enterprise, and fuelling the profit-making spirit of private entrepreneurs. This has, of course, had a significant impact on the balance of power among the social classes comprising the Iranian community, seen here as comprising Iranians living in and outside of Iran.

This chapter examines the new economic strategies which Iranian governments have pursued in recent years, the impact which these

Table 12.1: *Share of Investment by Public and Private Sectors in Iran, 1959–78* (%)

Year	Public Sector	Private Sector
1959	33.7	66.3
1961	32.3	67.7
1963	32.4	67.6
1965	42.7	57.3
1967	49.0	51.0
1968–72	54.7	45.3
1973–78	66.1	33.9

Source: *Iran Shows the Way* (1976).

strategies have had on society, and the significance which economic policy has had for the form of the state.

State and economy before the Islamic revolution

The early 1960s saw the rise of intensive capitalist development in Iran. The Pahlavi regime's ambitious plans for the future made necessary an expanded role for the state in the economy, one which was to be interventionist and orchestrating. The government fostered private accumulation through expanding the market, and facilitated capitalist reproduction through institutional control of labour and through investments in infrastructure and those industries which, for one reason or another, were not attractive to the private sector. As the source of much national wealth and being external to the society's structure, oil revenues helped to give the state some autonomy of domestic social forces (Najmabadi, 1987) and to reinforce the supremacy of the Pahlavi court and of comprador bourgeois fractions.[1] The internationally-linked capitalist strata thrived on the state sector, which in turn legitimized the values and interests of the private sector as a whole.

The Second Development Plan (1956–62) had envisaged that public sector investment would be limited to a few basic industries,[2] but as the private sector proved unable to fulfil the obligations assigned to it by the planners, the state became a more active investor. Table 12.1 shows that by the late–1960s, public sector investment was beginning to outstrip private sector investment. The investment ratio between the public and private sectors in the late 1970s was almost the reverse of what it had been in the early 1960s; the public sector being expected to account for approximately two-thirds of total investment in the economy. This may have been intended to be a

Table 12.2: *Gross Fixed Capital Formation and Consumption Expenditures, 1967–76 (billion rials)*

	1967/8	1972/3	1974/5	1975/6
Gross Fixed C.F.	151	287	564	1,100
Public sector	74	146	364	647
Private sector	77	141	200	453
Consumption Expen.	540	898	1,820	2,277
Public sector	98	253	581	769
Private sector	442	645	1,239	1,508

Note: Figures have been rounded up for convenience.
Source: Amuzegar (1977).

temporary reversal of roles, but public sector dominance was to prevail until the end of the Pahlavi system.

Table 12.2 provides evidence of the changing relationship between the public and private sectors at the macro-economic level. It is interesting to note that, while the public sector's share in gross fixed capital formation had overtaken the private sector's contribution by the early 1970s, the private sector continued to dominate in consumption expenditure.

Iran's increasing dependence on oil exports in the 1970s, compounded by an acceleration in the direct penetration of the Iranian market by foreign capital, led many analysts of the Iranian scene to refer to the Pahlavi state as 'dependent capitalist'. The locus of power was declared to lie with the capitalist metropolis. In the evolving international division of labour, it was contended, Iran would serve as a stable source of relatively cheap oil and a consumer of Western-supplied goods and services. As a semi-peripheral country, however, it would also be active in the production and export of some industrial products. Within this arrangement the Iranian bourgeoisie could participate in investment as a partner of foreign capital or of the state, or both. What remained ambiguous in the dependentistas' analytical framework, however, was whether the above-mentioned relationship with the international capitalist system would weaken or strengthen the state in relation to domestic and foreign forces. It is now clear that monopoly control of the country's hydrocarbon resources did give the Pahlavi state of the 1970s the edge over the capitalist class fractions, even though at the same time it deepened the state's exposure to external forces and international market processes. Having the edge at home at the same time strengthened the state's position *vis-à-vis* foreign capital and the supra-national capitalist structures.

The oil revenues, which rose from $2.8 billion in 1972/73 to $17.8 billion in 1974/75, provided for levels of capital accumulation hitherto unimagined by the Iranian bourgeoisie. Owners of private capital, however, tended to focus on only a few (highly profitable) economic activities, such as construction, some intensive investment in light industry, commerce and real estate speculation, rather than becoming a substantial and active class of industrialists engaged in large-scale production. As a result, entrepreneurs became even more dependent on the state for their economic well-being.

While the bourgeoisie as a whole was enjoying the economic boom, the Pahlavi court took advantage of the new situation to extend its influence even further and to consolidate its alliance with the comprador bourgeoisie as its senior partner. Senior bureaucrats also benefitted from the opportunity to amass capital and private fortunes. The Pahlavi-linked state élite thus became an important economic partner of the bourgeoisie.

Conscious of the implications of the expanding role of the state, the regime and its defenders were always careful to draw attention to the distinction between state intervention in a capitalist economy (Iran) and in a centrally-planned one.[3] Development planning, a major function of the state, was not be confused with socialist planning. The rapidity of the industrialization process necessitated an enlarged public sector participation in the economy. An economist's explanation goes as follows:

> The pattern of the economy is such that ... if the government does not continue expanding means of communication, electric power capacity, areas under irrigation, water supplies, and other utilites, private investment, particularly outside Tehran, cannot prosper. Far from conflicting with public investment, private investment is dependent on it (Looney, 1973: 20)

Under the tutelage of the Pahlavi élite, and largely through its control of oil revenues, the state was increasingly becoming an accumulator in its own right, all the while that it was serving the specific interests of the large domestic bourgeoisie. By the late 1970s, the state was employing 10 per cent or more of the adult workforce of the country and provided some 70 per cent of the total investment funds in the economy. So even though the ownership of Iranian industry and trade was predominantly private prior to the revolution, with about 45 families controlling approximately 85 per cent of the larger privately-owned firms, the state and the state sector provided the capital basis of the capitalist economy.[4]

Thus, when the revolution occurred, it had a profound impact on both the political and economic structures of power. The revolutionary process brought to an end the Pahlavi regime, but it also 'scattered the ranks of the comprador and Pahlavi/state segments of Iran's bourgeoisie', as one observer has put it (Cockcroft, 1980: 151). The power of the dominant fraction of the ruling class, in short, was broken. The vacuum created at the top of the hierarchy by the fall of the Shah, was in part filled by the expansion of the 'new' state machinery, through its acquisition and control of the assets of the court and its state and comprador associates. While the revolution failed to turn the social pyramid upside-down, it did achieve its more immediate goal of removing the pinnacle of the dependent capitalist structure. With the court-linked fraction of the bourgeoisie liquidated or exiled, ideal opportunities for growth and accumulation presented themselves to the smaller traditional and modern bourgeois forces.

State and economy in the aftermath of the revolution, 1979-81
The fall of the Pahlavi regime was followed by intense competition for power amongst the various bourgeois fractions and petit-bourgeois factions, but the overthrow of the dominant fraction of the bourgeoisie gave the emerging (Islamic) state the opportunity to reshape the structure of economic and political power to fit the new Iran. Article 44 of the 1979 Constitution envisaged there being three sectors in the economy: the state, co-operative and private sectors. Reflecting the revolution's spirit, the constitution gave pride of place to the state sector, bringing under its jurisdiction all strategic, large-scale and parent industries, foreign trade, major minerals, banking, insurance, the broadcasting media, post, telegraph and telephone services, avia-tion, shipping, roads and railways, power generation, dams and large-scale irrigation networks. The constitution thus envisaged that the private sector would play a secondary role: 'The private sector consists of those activities concerned with agriculture, animal husbandry, industry, trade and services that supplement the economic activities of the state and the cooperative sectors'.[5] In theory, then, the private

sector was not to lead the economy but to be led in the Islamic Republic.

The three years which followed the revolution saw a substantial expansion of the state sector. It should be stressed, however, that ideological factors played little part in this expansion of state control. It was, largely, pragmatic reasons which led the state to take over industries and enterprises which had previously been in private hands. To prevent the economy's collapse, and at the insistence of Ayatollah Khomeini, the abandoned factories, workshops and other productive units of the exiled comprador class and the substantial assets of the court élite were nationalized, bringing under government control the industrial complexes of the 51 major industrialists (see Table 12.3). This gave the state direct control of between 80–85 per cent of the country's major productive units. In a parallel development, the Pahlavi Foundation, the court's holding company, gave way to the Foundation of the Deprived.[6] The latter embraced some 600 companies (including 150 factories, 200 trading houses, and 80 per cent of the country's cinemas), a number of 'five star' hotels, hundreds of agribusinesses and mechanized farms, private properties and dwellings, and real estate in New York.[7] In due course other foundations and Islamic organizations were formed to act as holding companies for the huge abandoned wealth, or to channel resources to the regime's most ardent supporters.[8] The initial nationalizations, then, should be understood not as a deliberate move to transform the economy to the advantage of the deprived, but as a stop-gap measure motivated by the urgent need to bring back productivity as well as order and management to a large and abandoned section of the economy.

The policy of confiscation was soon formalized with government directives covering the nationalization of:

  i those properties owned by the court and its close associates;
 ii those properties whose owners had fled;
iii any firm which owed in excess of one half of its assets to the banks.

The last measure was clearly an attempt at providing a rescue package for those firms in deep financial difficulties. Assumption of ownership by the state, therefore, was again a pragmatic rather than an ideologically-motivated move.

Table 12.3 *Nationalization of Assets of Major Industrialists*

Name of Industrialist	Main Business Activities Nationalized
Abunasr-Azad	Ahvaz sugarbeet works; writing paper-making and paper products factory.
Akhavan	Majority share-holding in Darioush Bank; General Motors, Iran; car assembly plants and agency; substantial shareholding in other banks.
Akhavan-Kashani	Great Iran superstore; Sa'di tiles and ceramics factory; Kashan textiles; Shilat supermarket.
Alam	Tehran Siman; Kermanshah sugarbeet processing factory.
Alikhani	Isfahan Navard metal works; Isfahan brick-making factory.
Arieh	Ariana industrial group; shareholdings in financial houses and mines.
Assadi	Iran industrial group; Leyland Motors.
Barkhordar	Pars Electric industries; Kerman Siman; Iran Metal Industries; Iran Batri (vehicle battery manufacturing); Iran Kompresorsazi (compressors manufacturing); agency for Toshiba; mechanized carpet-weaving factory.
Behbahani	General household appliances manufacturing: motor bikes and bicycle works.
Boushehri	Pak dairy products; proprietor of the Organization of International Gatherings (Societies) and the Iran and Sweden Association; four small factories.
Daneshvar	Proprietor of Ekbatan new town; shareholdings in Iran National vehicle assembly group.
Ebtehaj family	Shareholdings in Shomal Siman; shareholdings in many banks, industrial groups and large construction contractors; sub-contracting businesses.
Farmanfarmayan	Pars oil company, Tehran Siman (cement), Soufian Siman, Pars paper-making and paper products factory; substantial shareholding in Iran National vehicle assembly group, and in one or two banks and construction companies.
Fouladi brothers	B. F. Goodrich agency, Iran; Kiyan Tyres.
Hajtourkhani	Shahid sugarbeet processing factory.
Harandi	Barak garment-making plants.
Harati	Isfahan brick works; Shomal Siman.
Hedayat	Naqsh-e Jahan sugarbeet processing factory; Ahvaz metal tube foundry.
Irvani-Motaqi	Melli industrial group (36 productive units).
Isfahani	Major shareholdings in a number of industries.
Javaheri	Major shareholdings in a number of industries.
Khayami (two brothers)	Koroush superstores; Asia Insurance Co.; Jamco, Iran Mobl and Belerian furniture-making factories and stores; Iran National vehicle assembly group; Reza industrial complex (Mashad); financial institutions shareholdings.
Khosrowshahi (two brothers)	Pars factories; Alborz Investment Co.; Tidi industrial units; Mino biscuits and food-processing factories.
Lajevardian	Kashan textile factory; Isfahan textile and nylon yarn factory; mechanized carpet-weaving factory; shareholdings in Ama industries.

Lajevardi family	Kashan textile and silk yarn factory; Behshahr industrial group; packaging factory.
Mahdavi	Khorasan food-processing units and industrial factories; shareholdings in some major banks.
Mazinrad	Major shareholdings in a number of large industrial units.
Mirashrafi	Tehran Taj textile and weaving factory.
Namazi	Buick, Iran, assembly plants and agency; textiles and fibres manufacturing; shareholdings in some large industries.
Omidhuzoor bros.	Bells shoes factories (12 industrial units); shareholdings in banks.
Panahpour	Many factories making intermediate industrial goods; construction companies.
Payravi	Chromite mines.
Qadimy-e Navayi (two brothers)	Neyshabour sugarbeet processing; Naqsh-e Jahan sugarbeet processing.
Rahimzad-e Khoi	Soufian Siman; Tabriz Industries; industrial cables manufacturing.
Rashidian	Ta'avouni & Touz'i Bank; shareholdings in many industries.
Rezai (two brothers)	Shahriar industrial group (five major factories); Ama industries; Skol brewery; a number of mineral mines; Arak heavy agricultural machineries and road construction equipment manufacturing.
Sabet	Representitive of Audi–VW group agency, Iran; RCA audio–visual consumer goods factory; Mina bottle and sheet glass-making factories; manufacturing of soft drinks.
Shekarchian (two brothers)	Zeeba thread and weaving factory.
Vahabzadeh	Pakdis distillers; BMW and Caterpillar agencies, Iran; shareholdings in major banks.
Yasini	Abgineh sheet glass-making factory; Momtaz textile and yarn factory.
Ziyaii	Fars and Khouzestan Siman; other shareholdings.

Sources: Atiqpour (1979). Also *Kayhan* and *Ettala't* (various issues, March–July 1979). Also personal interviews.

The banking sector and insurance companies were also brought under state ownership. Some 37 private banks (14 of which had foreign partners) and 10 insurance companies were nationalized as a result of an order issued by the Revolutionary Council.[9] The clerical establishment was seeking, by this means, to remove the remaining influence of the former élites in the financial sector, while at the same time providing the state with mechanisms for aiding Iran's troubled industrial sector. During the last years of the Shah's rule, industrialists had been removing an average of $2–3 billion a year from the country, draining Iran of industrial investment and private savings. Data is sketchy, but some sources suggested that more than $15 billion may have left the country during the revolution alone.[10] It was imperative, therefore, for the new regime to take charge of the abandoned assets and to find a way of injecting funds into an industrial sector which was not immediately profitable or attractive to private investment.

The net result of these nationalizations, and the extension of state control over all mines and mining activities (and the country's natural resources), was to give the Iranian state a tight control over the Iranian economy. That this state control did not reflect a strategy of deep-seated economic transformation is indicated by the government's failure to deal with three issues, all of which arose from the revolutionary process itself: the redistribution of wealth in favour of the 'deprived', land reform, and the control of foreign trade. Prolonged disputes over these issues pointed towards the lack of direction in the Islamic Republic. What was as yet undetermined was which forces would have ultimate control of the state, and to what specific end. Political instability and economic uncertainties during this period merely postponed the resolution of this question.

State and economy, 1982–8

The elimination of the liberal faction from the ruling coalition, post-1981, extended the power of the clergy and its allies. The Moussavi government, which took power in February 1982, was in reality the first authoritative government which Iran had had since the revolution. It was, therefore, the first government which was in a position to pursue a coherent economic programme, to re-define Iran's relationship with foreign capital, and to re-examine its trading links.

The new government promised to introduce substantial economic reforms, indicating its preference for a populist ('radical' in the Islamic Republican political context) socioeconomic programme. It was committed to re-orienting the economy, in a manner which promoted economic self-sufficiency and self-reliance, redistributed income and wealth in favour of the deprived, and reduced the country's dependency on international capitalism. The line of policy adopted brought about some important changes in the country's economy: the revolutionary foundations became significant economic actors, and the government allocated economic resources and capital for large-scale industrial activity at the same time as encouraging small-scale manufacturing.

Nonetheless, the extent and nature of the changes which occurred were less than might have been expected. There were three reasons for this. First, ad hoc decisions and haphazard policies which the previous governments had pursued had already given some character to the

Islamic Republic. Second, bearing in mind the Western-imposed embargo and the pressures associated with running a war economy, the new government's policy had to be based on securing the flow of oil revenues and on expanding industrial and agricultural output. The fulfilment of these objectives required that the Islamic Republic continue to be bound into the international capitalist system. Policies stemming from ideological principle did not cohere with that context. Even measures which appeared to emanate from radical and egalitarian motivations often had other objectives. The rationing of essential goods, control of imports and food subsidies, for example, owed little to populism. The measures constituted, rather, a pragmatic set of policies aimed at minimizing the impact of the war and of the embargo on society as a whole. Third, there were conservative elements within the regime (strongly represented on the Council of Guardians) which sought to restrain the government's more radical inclinations.[11]

The Council of Guardians' interventions against the direction which government policies were taking (specifically opposition to further nationalizations, to other basic economic reforms such as land reform and sequestration of property, to high taxes and to further limitations on the activities of the private sector on religious grounds) had important implications. As the Guardian Council was largely representative of the bazaar and land-owning classes, its opposition to government legislation represented the resistance of these classes to further encroachments by the state. The Islamic basis of its opposition, moreover, was indicative of the problematic nature of the constitution itself, which rather eclectically recognized the sanctity of private property while simultaneously endeavouring to impose limitations on the extent of its activities. As far as the Guardian Council was concerned, new government legislation was questioning the very basis of private ownership in the Islamic Republic, going far beyond the premises of the constitution.

Two prominent trends of thought regarding the direction which the economy should take were now clearly visible. One, the Hojatieh faction, was composed of passionate free-marketeers who opposed radical socio-economic legislation, high taxation and statist policies, advocating instead a more cautious and traditional 'Islamic' approach. Particularly effective was their protest that high taxation and efficient collection of taxes by the government might in fact undermine the authority of the religious establishment and reduce the flow of annual revenues to the mosque. One government official, opposed to this line of thinking was to say: 'those who argue against taxes are the same people who believe we should privatize oil pipelines and mines'.[12] Above all else, therefore, the debate focused on the control of the economy and the nature of the system under the Islamic Republic.

The second trend, the Maktabis (also known as the Followers of Imam's Line), believed equally strongly in the politics and economics of the 'dispossessed', advocating centralized economic planning, higher taxation, substantial material support for the poor and confiscation of land without compensation and its redistribution in favour of the peasantry. Although the Hojatieh's power in the government was effectively on the wane in the mid–1980s, the radical agenda of the Maktabis was continually stymied by the pragmatic elements in the regime and the intervention of the Guardian Council. Despite the official demise of the Hojatieh Society, many in the regime continued to express the need for a strengthening of the private sector. Even Ayatollah Khomeini (the holder of the Line so to speak), spoke on more than one occasion in favour of the bazaar and the private sector: 'we promise that as long as there is Islam there will be free enterprise also'.[13]

It is perhaps not surprising, in view of the influences impinging on the government, that the overall impact of government economic policy between 1982 and 1988 was far from what government rhetoric might have suggested. In the state-controlled industrial sector, primary attention was given to continuing or re-starting projects which had been initiated under the *ancien régime*. All necessary intermediate goods were to be imported to supply the old assembly plants, although the government did embark upon the construction of intermediate industries in Iran to supply the plants. Such major new industries as the state sector was instructed to undertake were to be based on petrochemicals and mineral resources, and were intended to reduce the country's overall dependency at some point in the future. In all of this, the thrust of practical policy-making was, as Rafsanjani was to put it, that 'the Islamic government has to lead the private sector' rather than necessarily to replace it.[14] As for the privately-owned industrial sector, the revolution sparked off an unprecedented development of small-scale private industry, largely financed in the initial stages by soft government loans. According to official statistics, the number of new factories and workshops employing over 30 people during the period 1979 to 1985 may have been as many as 14,000.[15] Government encouragement was reflected in approximately $2.5

billion worth of industrial investment commitments by the private
sector in 1983 alone, involving 6,804 proposals and licences.[16]

Despite this apparent demonstration of economic activity, however,
the economy as a whole became increasingly crisis-ridden through the
Moussavi premiership (1982–9). Rising food imports (compounded
by the needs of the rapidly growing population; some 3 per cent per
annum on average) testified to the continuing stagnation of agriculture.
Industry was said to be running at 50–60 per cent of capacity and
many of the state-owned establishments running at a loss. Significantly, the Industrial Development and Renovation Organization's
losses in 1983 were estimated at $3.5 billion.[17] This organization,
which had held a stake in over 100 companies in the late 1970s,
including a majority interest in 55 of them, had ballooned after the
revolution. The losses represented, therefore, a substantial blow to
the economy as a whole. Nearly 70 per cent of the foreign exchange
allocated to heavy industry was being consumed by only 10 major
owners.[18] In effect, the Islamic government had become the subsidizer
of the Shah's white elephant projects. A clear indication of the
regime's economic failures was that, during the 1979–87 period, the
Gross Domestic Product of Iran averaged a growth rate of −0.7 per
cent, or a 15.7 per cent decline of GDP compared to the average
annual GDP for the 1976–78 period (Amirahmadi, 1990: 134–6).

The combined effects of mismanagement, lack of clear direction
(even the republic's Five Year Development Plan formulated by the
first Moussavi government had to be shelved indefinitely), war and its
associated physical destruction, absence of expertise, inefficiency and
sheer neglect, coming at the same time as a relative decline in oil
revenues, meant that by the second half of the 1980s the government
had little choice but to turn to the private sector, international capital
and the nationalized banks for assistance in embarking on a programme of national economic recovery. The manifestation of this
trend had to wait, however, until the cessation of hostilities with Iraq.

Post-war reconstruction, economic liberalization and the retraction of the state

The end to hostilities with Iraq in August 1988 promised the
commencement of an era of economic reconstruction and industrial
rejuvenation in Iran. The developments in this period can be divided
into two phases: the twilight of the Moussavi premiership and the rise
of the Rafsanjani presidency.

Economic liberalization under the Moussavi government

Moussavi's re-election as prime minister in May 1988 was to be short-lived. By August 1989, the constitutional reforms had swept both him and his office away. Unable to reduce or limit private ownership in land and capital, and faced with an inefficient and overblown bureaucracy, the Moussavi government had ultimately become resigned to an expanded role for the private sector. After a decade of state intervention, the radical government of the previous eight years indicated its preparedness to reduce the state's economic exposure.[19] This was signalled by the prime minister's 1989/90 budget speech, delivered in January 1989. In this, Moussavi stressed that the aim of the government's economic policy was not to destroy the private sector.[20] Soon after, the heavy industries' minister indicated that, as part of the reconstruction policy, there was a 'strong' tendency in the government to give the private sector a greater share of the economy.[21]

The first concerted move towards economic liberalization and deregulation came, not surprisingly (in view of the importance of the bazaar to the Islamic Republic), by way of the government lifting restrictions on the importation of many essential and luxury items by the private sector. This was to be followed by a comprehensive privatization policy, announced in April 1989, based on the transfer of ownership of all 'non-essential and non-strategic' profit and loss-making companies to the private sector.[22]

On the major issue of foreign borrowing, Moussavi's government continued to hold out, for a time.[23] As the pace of reconstruction accelerated, however, and the demands on the government's resources multiplied, the government began to reassess the value of upholding even this sacred cow. The economics and finance minister, Mohammad Iravani, boldly stated in July 1989 that the Islamic Republic should borrow from abroad for investment purposes.[24] This initiative seemed destined to change Iran's international position, for up to this point Iran had been one of the few developing countries with no long term foreign debt. The debt crisis of the 1980s had largely passed Iran by, and the proposed change of attitude towards foreign borrowing meant that it would be entering the world's capital markets as a worthy customer.

The Moussavi government, however, was ill-suited to leading the trend towards a liberalized economy. Its indecisiveness throughout its eight years at the helm had reflected the same tensions within the élite as existed in society as a whole. Lack of direction in economic planning had left a large public sector in charge of the country's productive activities, while confusing the private sector with contradictory policies. As was shown above, its lack of commitment either to full central planning or a dominant and unhindered private sector meant that the resulting mixed economic system tended to bring out the worst in both sectors.

Economic liberalization under the Rafsanjani presidency
The continued presence of a strong private sector meant that, when the need for reconstruction was recognized in the late 1980s, a radical change in élite thinking could develop. The private sector could be utilized as an instrument of recovery, provided economic policy clearly favoured the free market alternative. As Rafsanjani said, in late December 1988, and while the Moussavi government was still attempting to resolve the economic crisis:

> To face these difficulties, we have to take certain measures. First, to increase the country's production and in order to implement this we should inject the capital which is at present accumulated in the private sector. However, these people have no confidence; most of them are afraid to show their wealth.[25]

A combination of factors, including the death of the patriarch, the institutional weakness of radical factions and the emergence of a united leadership around the Rafsanjani–Khamenei axis (one as the new executive president and the other as the *faqih*), allowed the adoption and implementation of new economic policies. The spasmodic economic liberalisms of the previous decade were replaced by a concerted policy of economic liberalization, privatization and deregulation. The strategy was to include private and public bilateral and multilateral foreign participation as sources to be tapped for Iran's economic recovery (as embodied in the new Five Year Development Plan). The potential for redirected economic policy which emerged in the postwar period was recognized, again by Rafsanjani, as early as December 1988. He said then: 'The concentration of affairs within the state was a necessity during the war, a necessity which does not exist any more'.[26] Rafsanjani's rise to executive power in August 1989 was to provide the opportunity for him to adjust economic policy to suit the new circumstances. This necessitated a greater role for the private sector. The choice of ministers indicated his administration's

Table 12.4: *Continuity in Government: A Comparison of Personnel, 1984 and 1989*

	Moussavi's 1984 Government	*Rafsanjani's 1989 Government*
G. Aqazadeh	Supervisor, PM's Office	Oil Minister
H. Habibi	Justice Minister	Vice-President
M. Khatami	Islamic Guidance Minister	Islamic Guidance Minister
B. Namdar-Zanganeh	Construction Crusade Minister	Energy Minister
M. Nezhad-Hosseinian	Roads & Transport Minister	Heavy Industries Minister
M. Reyshahri	Information Minister	Prosecutor-General
A. Velayati	Foreign Minister	Foreign Minister

Sources: MERI Report (1985), *Iran*, London: Croom Helm, p. 133; Ehteshami and Nonneman (1991) ch. 1.

strong tendency towards technocracy; but it also highlighted a measure of continuity with the past. Many of the individuals chosen to serve in the 'reconstruction cabinet' of Rafsanjani had held ministerial or similar posts under Premier Moussavi. The point is illustrated in Table 12.4

The president's strategy was a complex one. It aimed, first and foremost, at economic reconstruction and expansion in output. His government was aware, however, that in order to achieve this goal it would need to release the private sector's energies and resources. Economic liberalization and the retraction of the state were now regarded as the keys to releasing Iranian private sector resources (estimated at billions of dollars in 'hoarded' capital), allowing capital to flow into activities which so far had been forbidden to it. The share of the private sector in the country's economy was projected to rise from 25–30 per cent at the end of the 1980s to 75–80 per cent in the course of the 1990s, thus reversing the trend prevalent in Iran since the first oil boom of 1973. Under a plan drawn up by the new government, some 800 publicly-owned enterprises were earmarked for privatization.

The revival of the Tehran stock exchange was one of the main components of the liberalization strategy. The government aimed to use the stock exchange to raise investment capital and to encourage private sector participation in the country's reconstruction efforts. Public organizations were directed to offer more shares on the exchange. At the same time, consideration was given to reforms to the taxation system, and to commercial accounting and legal procedures and regulations to ease the increased transactions taking place in the stock exchange.[27] The number of transactions in the stock exchange had already begun to rise in 1984, reaching a value of 10 billion rials in 1988. In 1989–90, 11.13 billion rials worth of stock was transacted. This was substantial, although still only a fraction of the highest recorded amount of transactions, totalling 44 billion rials in 1977.[28] The number of companies which offered their shares rose from 39 in 1988 to 54 a year later.[29] To encourage further trading, the Central Bank offered 100,000 of its shares in the National Iranian Investment Company on the exchange in December 1989. It was announced in November 1990 that 49 per cent of the shares in the industries affiliated to the National Iranian Industries Organization (NIIO) were to be sold off in the form of securities and bonds. 365,000 shares in 13 industries, worth 1,128 billion rials, were by then already de-nationalized.[30] The speed of de-nationalizations accelerated in 1991. It was announced in May 1991 that NIIO would sell 100 billion rials worth of shares in state-owned companies to the private sector.[31] This was revised upwards in August 1991, when it was stated that 120 billion rials worth of shares in firms and factories controlled by NIIO would be put on sale through the stock exchange by the end of March 1992.[32] By the same date, the stock exchange was expected to handle 200 billion rials worth of shares, including 120 billion rials worth previously owned by NIIO.

The net result of these developments was that total stock exchange transactions for the year March 1990–March 1991 reached a value of 65 billion rials, the highest recorded since its operations began in 1967.[33] Preliminary figures for 1991 show that by October some 150 billion rials worth of shares had changed hands, 102.1 billion rials of which were from public sector companies and government organizations (a total of 16.2 million shares).[34] So far, 50 per cent of all shares made available on the stock exchange belong to companies formerly controlled by NIIO. By the end of March 1991, 77 factories had been sold to the private sector.[35]

Sales of other government assets have included the privatization of all mines except those regarded as holding strategic reserves. To encourage the private sector, the Supreme Council of Mines extended the time limit on private sector mine extraction from 6 to 15 years. In addition, Iran's National Steel Company announced that it was willing and prepared to give financial assistance to the private sector with regard to the exploitation of mines. Thus, the state was subsidizing the re-entry of the private sector into large-scale mining and mining-related operations. Within the first 17 months of this policy, over 150 mines extracting coal and various minerals were transferred to the private sector.[36] All disused copper mines and identified copper seams were to be likewise transferred, and all coal, industrial dolomite and chalk mines to be privatized. In total, more than one billion rials were invested in the field of mining by the private sector by the end of August 1991.[37] By May 1991, 4.4 billion rials had been raised by the Ministry of Mines and Metals through transferring a large number of mines to the private sector.[38]

A similar policy was adopted for transferring heavy and other industries to the private sector. Vice-President Zanjani announced in December 1989 that the government should handle only big and strategic industries, thus indicating that the rest of the industrial sector was to be made open to private investment and control. The status of some 800 manufacturing and industrial companies was being studied by the Economics and Finance Ministry in late 1990, with a view to offering them to the private sector.[39] A major development in this process was the cabinet decision of 30 January 1992 to privatize Iran's main car industries and a number of other heavy industries which had been nationalized in 1979. The pre-revolution shareholders of these concerns were to receive compensation from the government.[40] The car makers are Iran Kaveh, Iran Khodrow, Iran Vanet, Khavar, Khodrowsazan, Moratab, Pars Khodrow, SAIPA, Shahab Khodrow and Zamyad. The four heavy industries were named as Ahvaz Rolling Mill, Arak Aluminium Rolling Mill, Arak Steel Company and Iran Marine Industries. In addition, the private sector was encouraged to make investments in new construction and industrial plants. According to the minister of industries, Nematzadeh, 38,000 agreements in principle had been reached with the private sector by mid-1990.[41] In 1990 private sector investments in heavy industry reached a value of 300 billion rials, indicating the rapid response of the private sector to these opportunities and the sheer scale of private capital which had previously laid unutilized.[42] A number of large industrial projects initiated by the public sector were also to be handed over to the private sector upon completion.

In conjunction with the privatization of state assets, the government sought to improve its international competitiveness, as well as to ease foreign trade by the private sector. The latter objective was reached through the formulation of a three-tier flexible foreign exchange rate policy and the eventual abandonment of government subsidies (estimated at $4 billion in 1990).[43] This was to ease restrictions on imports, thereby developing domestic competition and providing the raw materials and intermediate goods necessary for expansion of Iranian manufacturing and industry. In addition, private sector involvement in importing essential and consumer goods was seen as an efficient means of alleviating shortages in the economy. To this end, some $1.6 billion worth of permits to import basic goods was given to the private sector in 1990 alone.[44] Exporters were also offered direct and indirect incentives. As well as emphasizing Iran's traditional exports, the government sought to encourage private sector participation in new areas of exports. Incentives included the return of up to 11 per cent of foreign exchange designated for exports to the exporter. The Minister of Heavy Industries encouraged Iranian private sector contractors, producers and contract engineers to take part in international tenders, both at home and abroad. They were also encouraged to participate in joint ventures with foreign firms engaged in projects under the Five Year Development Plan.

The international competitiveness strategy envisaged direct foreign investment in the economy. The government planned to raise $20 billion in foreign capital investment in the course of the Five Year Plan. The figure was later readjusted to $27 billion in foreign finance and investment, including $3 billion of foreign investments in heavy industries during the Five Year Plan. To facilitate this, the country's Foreign Investment Law was reformulated to allow up to 49 per cent equity holding by the foreign partner, an historically unprecedented level, later to be amended indirectly to allow 100 per cent foreign ownership rights in certain sectors. Despite Article 81 of the Constitution banning the establishment of companies and institutions by foreign interests in Iran, the government's policy was to bring Iran's foreign investment law and its attitude towards foreign capital into line with those of other medium-sized industrializing economies (especially those wishing to maintain good relations with foreign interests without a complete loss of central government control).

The internationalization of the Iranian industry and economy received another boost through the establishment of the three free trade zones (FTZ) in the Persian Gulf. President Rafsanjani reflected the views of his administration in saying that the FTZs 'can serve as a bridge between domestic and foreign industries'.[45] The Kish island FTZ is Iran's first experiment with control-free offshore economic activities. Like FTZs elsewhere in the world, the Kish and two other FTZs are designed to attract Iranian and foreign investment for both industrial and non-industrial activities. Besides the clear financial and commercial advantages of such FTZs in Iran, the development of sites far away from the seat of political power and on territories detached from the mainland will have clear advantages for the government whose radical opponents within the regime continue to oppose many of the government's integrationist strategies. One further element in the integrationist trend pursued by the Iranian government was the boosting of Iran's IMF quota to 360 million SDRs ($850 million). The Governor of the Central Bank, Adeli, described this as having the advantage of improving Iranian voting rights in the IMF. Until then, the IMF had been regarded as the bastion of the 'satanic' powers.

Two aspects of the economic liberalization drive in Iran need further comment. First, unlike economic liberalization attempts in the West and elsewhere in the developing world, tax cuts have not been considered an essential part of the package in Iranian policy reforms. On the contrary, the government has emphasized the importance of taxes as a source of revenue for its activities (estimated at 11 billion rials in the Five Year Development Plan), and is keen to bring a more efficient tax collection system into being. In planning to raise taxes, the government is no doubt risking both its friendship with the Islamic free-marketeers and some alienation from business and private taxpayers. The government's objective in retaining a high rate of taxation, however, is important to its overall strategy in maximizing the use of domestic resources for reconstruction.

Second, the state seems reluctant to de-nationalize the financial sector. The reason for this seems to be because the government can use the banking, insurance and other financial institutions to exercize some control over the activities of the expanding private sector. As the banks are heavy investors in industry, state control of the banking system gives the government a backdoor influence over the direction of private sector investment and other economic activities in the country. In the absence of other mechanisms (as deregulation proceeds), control of the economy through finance capital constitutes a useful instrument for government policy. Nonetheless, significant deregulation in the operation of banks has already been introduced. From October 23 1991, banks were authorized to open foreign currency accounts in both their national and overseas branches, and to pay interest (called 'profit' locally) on all such accounts. The rate of interest is set on a daily basis by the Central Bank, according to the deputy director of the Bank.[46] Customers can switch money between their rial and foreign currency accounts without prior permission, and will not risk forfeiting the interest due during such transactions.

Far from displaying an ideological commitment to de-nationaliza-tion across the board and at all costs, therefore, the government has been pursuing a sectoral economic liberalization strategy. The future direction of this policy is likely to depend on the impact of the process already under way, rather than on the fulfilment of an abstract economic ideal.

The drive towards attracting private resources has led the Iranian government to encourage the return to Iran of capital-rich and technocratic exiles. In effect, the return of the former comprador bourgeoisie and its technocratic facilitators is envisaged. Promises have been given that much of the former owners' assets and properties will be returned to them when they undertake to invest in economic reconstruction. What impact this would have on the nature of political power in Iran and on its class structure remains uncertain. The return of capital-laden exiles and a large section of the Western-oriented middle class, however, would have a direct impact on the economy. Greater emphasis would have to be given to the satisfaction of luxury and consumer demand, as opposed to that for essential goods. After a decade of active state intervention in the economy, then, the govern-ment policy of privatization and deregulation is shifting the balance of power in the economy decisively away from the deprived, and towards the bourgeoisie and its middle class allies. This trend is reinforced through the deregulation of prices of foodstuffs and other goods and services.

Conclusion: state, class and the implications of liberalization

Quite clearly the post-Khomeini government is seeking a new position for Iran in the international division of labour.[47] Throughout the post-revolutionary period, Iran has remained bound to the world capitalist market through the export of its hydrocarbons, import of industrial and consumer goods, and affiliation to various capitalist multilateral institutions. The Rafsanjani government is now attempting to turn Iran into another successful newly-industrialized country (NIC) (on the patttern of South Korea, Brazil and Malaysia). This was one of the objectives of the *ancien régime*: the Shah's plan was to have borne fruit by the early 1980s. But while the international environment in the 1970s was conducive to such a transformation, it is not clear that this is still the case. The market for NICs may already have been saturated, and the Islamic Republic may not have sufficient to offer which is unique and marketable in terms of the international division of labour. In addition, the Iranian government seems to have remained committed to the traditional strategy of import-substitution industrialization (ISI), and it is hard to envisage a complete state withdrawal from active participation in production or direction of resources. The role of a market-oriented private sector, in an economy where the state continues to pursue a pre-ordained economic goal, remains unclear.

The same pragmatism that led the previous governments to intervene in the economy has led Iran's postwar governments to free the country's owners of private wealth. As the market was never extinguished in revolutionary Iran, the steps towards economic liberalization will not entail a transformation of the class structure. They will, rather, reinforce the position of the bourgeoisie.

Economic liberalization and deregulation has often been accompanied by the rationalization of the bureaucracy: a reduction in state activity entails a reduction in the size of the bureaucracy, the streamlining of procedures, and the elimination of red tape. But in Iran, the bureacracy is very much a symbol of the revolution. Its expansion owed much to the corporatist pull of the regime, and to tinker with it would be politically suicidal for the Rafsanjani leadership. First, because the leadership can not afford to risk losing its institutional power base; and second, because without the bureaucracy's blessing the new government policies would not reach fruition. Hence, the government has chosen not to risk civil service reform. The political price to be paid for such reforms outweighs its economic rationale.

Within weeks of the passing of the December 1988 political parties legislation, 29 groups and societies had applied for registration and had expressed their willingness to comply with the guidelines laid down by the interior ministry. None were associated with the militant and armed opponents of the Islamic Republic. The new government, however, has been reluctant to implement the law: opening up the political system would carry risks, without necessarily ensuring support for the instigators of political reform. The Rafsanjani government appears to believe that it can rely on the support of the middle classes only for as long as the hardline Maktabis remain the sole available political alternative. Hence the ruling alliance's intolerance of opponents – leftist, Monarchist, liberal, nationalist and others – acting as alternatives to the regime. Whether such opponents maintain a presence in Iran, or operate from beyond the domestic political arena, their mere existence has the potential to undermine the legitimacy of the current rulers. Political reform, thus, has not gone hand in hand with economic liberalization and market-oriented policies, because it poses a threat to the survival of the entire system.

The economic metamorphosis of the Islamic Republic outlined in this chapter, coupled with the anticipated return of the exiled bourgeoisie, indicate that the class structure of Iranian society is fast changing. In due course it may revert to the pyramid pattern which existed under the Pahlavis. This raises the question as to whether the Islamic economy is in reality little more than a mythical concept, advanced more as an alternative to revolutionary economic policy than as its result.

Notes

1 The term 'comprador' here refers to that fraction of the Iranian bourgeoisie whose interests compel it to cooperate with foreign interests in the national economy in production, provision of services and exchange.
2 Quoted in *Iran Shows the Way* (1976), p. 84.
3 [Our economy] is not, repeat not, a socialist economy. Ours is a mixed economy, with a very profound social conscience' (Premier Hoveyda's speech, delivered at the Iran–United Kingdom Financial Conference in Tehran), 12/10/75.
4 See Ehteshami (1987).
5 See *Constitution of the Islamic Republic of Iran* (1980).
6 Even this foundation, springing out of the revolutionary process, was said to be ready, as early as 1983, to return some of the companies under its control to their former owners. *Financial Times*, 6/5/83.
7 'Iran', *Financial Times Survey*, 1/4/85.
8 These include the Martyr Foundation, 15 Khordad Foundation, Foundation of Life Sacrifices and Foundation for the Imposed War Refugees. Many of these foundations have been active in industry, engaging in various aspects of low-level and non-technologically intensive production.
9 Economist Intelligence Unit (1979). *Quarterly Economic Review of Iran*, No. 3, pp. 12–17.
10 See Ehteshami (1990).
11 The Guardian Council functions as an upper parliamentary chamber, empowered to veto legislation passed by the Majlis which does not stand up to scrutiny in terms of its own interpretation of Islamic law.
12 Minister for Heavy Industry, Behzad Nabavi, quoted in Ehteshami (1987).
13 Quoted in *The Sunday Times*, 10/1/83.
14 *The Middle East*, April 1985, p. 52. The corollary of this approach was, as

Nabavi said, 'We are not communists and ideologically we believe in private ownership. On the other hand we don't believe in the total dominance of the private sector. We are not going to allow entrepreneurs to run our government'. Quoted in 'Iran', *Financial Times Survey*, 1/4/85.

15 *The Middle East*, March 1986, p. 8.

16 'Iran', *MEED Special Report*, November 1984, pp. 26–8.

17 *Ibid.*

18 'Iran', *MEED Special Report*, November 1984, p. 26.

19 As early as 1985 the government had prepared a denationalization plan geared towards transferring non-basic industries to the private sector.

20 *The Echo of Iran*, 12/1/89 and 19/1/89.

21 *Summary of World Broadcasts*, ME/W0077 A1/1, 16/5/89. 'There's high temperature to privatize', he was to say.

22 *Resalat*, 26/4/89.

23 'Foreign loans,' the Deputy Prime Minister (Hamid Mirzadeh) was to state, 'would in the long run make the country dependent.' *Summary of World Broadcasts*, ME/W0074 A1/1, 25/4/89.

24 *Eqtesad*, July 1989.

25 *The Echo of Iran*, 5/1/89, p. 15.

26 *Summary of World Broadcasts*, ME/0341 A/2, 22/12/88.

27 *Summary of World Broadcasts*, ME/W0106 A1/2, 5/12/89. Any company with more than a hundred shares was allowed to register on the stock exchange according to an Economics and Finance Ministry directive in 1988.

28 *Summary of World Broadcasts*, ME/W0106 A1/2, 5/12/89.

29 *Summary of World Broadcasts*, ME/W0124 A1/3, 17/4/90.

30 *Summary of World Broadcasts*, ME/W0153 A1/3, 6/11/90. Shares of 14 other units were to be sold off in the same fashion.

31 *Summary of World Broadcasts*, ME/W0180 A1/2, 21/5/91.

32 *Summary of World Broadcasts*, ME/W0193 A1/3, 20/8/91.

33 *Summary of World Broadcasts*, ME/W0193 A1/3, 20/8/91.

34 *Summary of World Broadcasts*, ME/W0199 A1/3, 1/10/91.

35 *Summary of World Broadcasts*, ME/W0195 A1/1, 3/9/91.

36 *Summary of World Broadcasts*, ME/W0161 A1/4, 8/1/91.

37 *Summary of World Broadcasts*, ME/W0193 A1/4, 20/8/91.

38 *Summary of World Broadcasts*, ME/W0181 A1/3, 28/5/91.

39 *Summary of World Broadcasts*, ME/W0149 A1/1, 9/10/90.

40 *MEED*, 14/2/92.

41 *Summary of World Broadcasts*, ME/W0134 A1/2, 26/6/90.

42 *Summary of World Broadcasts*, ME/W0173 A1/1, 2/5/91.

43 *MEED*, 2/8/91.

44 *Summary of World Broadcasts*, ME/W0159 A1/5, 18/12/90.

45 *Summary of World Broadcasts*, ME/W0149 A1/1, 9/10/90.

46 *Kayhan Havai*, 30/10/91.

47 As the heavy industries minister commented in January 1992: 'we must find our own place in industry and in the international market place', *Kayhan Havai*, 29/1/92.

13· ISRAEL

Emma Murphy

Although Israel remains largely isolated and unintegrated with the rest of the Middle East, it has not been left untouched by the wave of liberalization-oriented policies which has swept through the region. The new orthodoxy of the international lending agencies and the post-industrialist economic powers which control them, has been profoundly visible in Israeli economic policy since the early 1980s. It is possible, however, to examine the case of Israel as being somewhat unique, certainly in terms of comparison with neighbouring Arab states.

Ideologically, similarities exist. The concept of economic independence is of great importance for the Israeli political agenda, representing some degree of security for a nation which perceives itself as being surrounded by hostile parties, eagerly seeking an opportunity to exploit Israeli weaknesses. Economic liberalization, especially when it is in part the result of pressure from the United States and the international lending agencies, is considered to be a process of increasing the economic vulnerability of the country. The resistance to liberalization which this engenders is not so different from that found in some other Middle Eastern countries, where the population feel that the West is once again imposing strategies of its own devising upon the region for the advancement of Western, not Middle Eastern, interests.

The impact of economic liberalization upon society and politics does differ, however, for two specific reasons. First, the standard of living in Israel is in general considerably higher than in many neighbouring states.[1] The population is therefore less vulnerable to the social costs of economic liberalization than in poorer societies. The social reaction to the negative redistributive effects of liberalization is consequently likely to be less dramatic. Second, Israel has an

237

essentially democratic political framework. Popular discontent can therefore be largely contained within the existing political system. Thus, economic liberalization as a set of government policies may lead to the rise or fall in the fortunes of the party in government, but is not likely to either require or lead to transformation of the existing political system.

This chapter discusses the origins of policies of economic liberalization in Israel, the extent to which (and the manner in which) they have been implemented, and the factors which have inhibited their effectiveness.

Economic liberalization in Israel has, from its outset, been a very sensitive issue. The combination of the socialist ideology which guided the country's early years, and the priority given to immigration in policy-making, has ensured that the state has traditionally taken an active and interventionist role in the economy. It seemed that this role might change following the 1977 elections, when the Likud, championing free-market policies, was brought to power. The ascendance of the political right-wing, however, did not after all lead to a far-reaching change in economic policy. Nonetheless, by the early 1980s, the economic crisis in Israel had made a radical shift of policy increasingly urgent. The shift which then occurred was designed to strengthen and liberalize the private sector in an attempt to solve the chronic difficulties which the country was facing in its balance of trade, rate of inflation and production capacity, and to rationalize the vastly overblown and bureaucratic public sector. The Israeli governments which have held power since 1984 have subsequently consistently maintained that the need to privatize and liberalize is paramount.

Despite a broad political consensus that the Israeli economy was in urgent need of substantial liberalization (a consensus reinforced by considerable US and international pressure), the policy has in practice proved to be extremely difficult to implement. In July of 1991, a major report on the Israeli economy was published by the Jerusalem-based thinktank, the Institute for Advanced Strategic and Political Studies.[2] The report reviewed the government's progress on privatization and liberalization plans, introduced as early as 1985, and concluded that far from the role of the state having been reduced in the intervening period, it had in fact been expanded.

The failure to reduce the role of the state stems from a combination of three interconnected features of the Israeli state. First, the legacy of socialist Zionism (albeit ideologically largely discarded since the

1970s), has left a particular institutional formation which is highly resistant to economic liberalization. Second, the structure of elite power-holding, and the organic linkage between the owners and controllers of capital, has created a class with conflicting interests and political priorities. Third, the very basis of the Zionist state, the precedence of immigration in economic organization, means that attempts to reduce the scope of the public sector are continually frustrated by the centrality of the state's role in immigrant absorption. This latter point is particularly well illustrated by the response to the recent wave of Jewish immigration to Israel from the former Soviet Union.

The stimulus to liberalize

The government of national unity created after the 1984 elections was united on one issue at least; that the economy was in urgent need of radical reform. The year 1984 had seen inflation rise to 444.9 per cent.[3] Foreign debt amounted to nearly $24 billion, requiring a third of GNP to be spent every year on interest payments and debt repayment. Foreign currency reserves were falling; there was a massive balance of trade deficit (imports of $15.7 billion as opposed to exports of $10.5 billion); budget expenditure appeared out of control (with annual budget deficits of over $1 billion – equal to over 5 per cent of the total budget expenditure); and Israeli exports were suffering as a result of their uncompetitiveness on foreign markets. The economy had suffered a dramatic slowdown, dating back to the 1983 stockmarket crisis, and indeed the virtual stagnation of the economy after the impressive growth rates of previous years. Worst of all, for a state which attracted immigrants on the basis of guaranteed state support and jobs, unemployment was also rising.

Israel's economic problems stemmed ultimately from five factors. First, the economy was burdened by the upkeep of an extensive bureaucracy. The latter was made necessary by the primary role of the Zionist state, which had always been the encouragement and facilitation of immigration, requiring an expanded bureaucracy and large-scale budget expenditures on housing, welfare and provision of employment. When Israel came into being in 1948, and despite the priority given to the import of private Zionist capital prior to that, the private sector was not capable of fulfilling this task. The socialist orientation of Zionist ideology at the time made the state the obvious candidate for shouldering the burden of immigration costs.

Although the heavy pressure on government expenditure resulting from the state's role in facilitating immigration might appear to have made such a role an unattractive prospect in the long term, this was not the case, at least while Labour-led governments held power over the first 30 years of Israel's existence.[4] The Labour-led governments assumed that the immigrants would be grateful to the state and would allocate their political loyalties to the Labour party, reinforcing the structures which had made their absorption possible. The power and influence of the Zionist labour bureaucracy would be strengthened. The latter grouping was made up of the leaders of the Zionist struggles of the Mandate era (and their *protégés*), who shared a European, socialist-oriented background, and who went on after the establishment of the state to head the various parties of the Labour alignment, the senior echelons of the public sector, the Histadrut and even the private sector. The extended role of the state in economic affairs (made necessary by the facilitation of immigration), was thus seen as a means whereby the Zionist labour bureaucracy could maintain political control. The activities of the General Federation of Hebrew Workers in Israel, the Histadrut, were crucial to this strategy. The Histadrut was formed in 1920 as the primary socialist Zionist colonizatory body; establishing settlements, organizing Hebrew labour and maintaining Jewish exclusivism in Hebrew enterprises. After the establishment of the state, the Histadrut became the primary trade union, representing workers' interests and providing welfare aid, employment and subsidization to immigrants.

Second, the symbiotic relationship between the Histadrut and the Labour party had created an inefficient and unproductive form of economic organization. Special government financial assistance had enabled the Histadrut to establish a business empire that was eventually to account for 25 per cent of economic enterprises in the country. The holding company, Hevrat Ha'ovdim, which administered the Histadrut's industrial and economic holdings, alone grew to account for almost 15 per cent of GNP.[5] Moreover, as a trade union, the Histadrut represented (and indeed still does represent) over 80 per cent of the Israeli workforce, giving it unique bargaining power in wage negotiations with the government and the employers' organization, the Manufacturers Association.

The Histadrut was not, therefore, in essence a trade union. It was, and is, together with the state sector, the largest employer in the country and has generally been run on a profit-making basis. Operating as a highly centralized and hierarchical agency, it has permitted minimal worker participation in decision-making, running the election of officials on an effectively closed-shop basis. It has acted (although decreasingly so) as both a political powerbase for the Labour party and as a conduit for the replenishment of the latter's personnel. Thus it has generally supported the Labour Party's political line in return for having its interests afforded some protection in the Knesset. Given the Histadrut's economic and labour power, Likud governments have also had a strong incentive to work with it, rather than against it. For many years Likud has fought hard to improve the standing of its own officials inside the Histadrut.[6] The paradox of the Histadrut has been that, while it remains the largest single workers' representative body in Israel, it is at the same time a capitalist organization. The two functions have inevitably come into conflict with each other, the end result being a highly inefficient and over-manned 'firm'.

Third, there existed considerable over-employment in the economy as a whole, making industry uncompetitive internationally, and generally allowing a higher standard of living than was merited by the Israeli national product. In order to attract and keep immigrants, the government had virtually to guarantee employment, providing jobs both directly in an expanded state sector,[7] and indirectly through subsidies to both the Histadrut and the private sector. Histadrut pressure on the government made it virtually impossible to reduce state subsidization of employment without risking general strikes.[8] Consequently, the unemployment rate stayed low (averaging about 3.3 per cent of the workforce) until the early 1980s. It was unaffected either by the period of world recession in the 1970s or by Israel's severe economic problems following the 1973 war (caused by oil price shocks and the need to buy new weaponry).

Fourth, the high living standards required to attract immigrants were achieved through the subsidization of the economy by foreign aid, diaspora revenues and international loans rather than through high productivity. The enormous size of US aid carries with it 'the disadvantage of a generous but temporary gift of nature, such as oil, gas, etc., which, despite its benefits during a limited period, impairs a country's competitiveness in the international market'.[9] The aid has traditionally been used to help the government to achieve a budgetary balance without a substantial reduction in the size of the public sector. By virtue of having to distribute this income, the disporportionate size of the public sector has remained assured, while national income has been unrepresentative of national product.

The combined result of these factors was the economic crisis of 1984. The situation was exacerbated by the bank scandals of 1983 and the Tel Aviv stock market crash. The government of national unity which took over in 1984 needed to act urgently and decisively.

The 1983 bank scandals

In 1983 the four major commercial banks were threatened with financial disaster, after it came to light that they had been artificially inflating their share values on the stock exchange in order to stem the effects of rampant inflation. The scam was revealed after a currency scare had led investors to start unloading their shares, in a rush to convert savings into dollars. In order to prevent economic disaster, the government stepped in to lend the banks $7 billion (over three times the capital value of the holdings) with instructions that the banks should buy back the shares from the shareholders. The shares were to be placed in *batuchot* trust companies. After an initial period of five years, later extended by two two-year periods, the banks were to repay the loans to the government or, failing that, to pass ownership of the shares to the government. Since the banks were clearly not going to be in a position to repay the loans after the initial period, the government would need to facilitate the resale of the majority of shares to the private sector so as to recoup the loan, and to reverse this inadvertent nationalization. The government was unable, however, to make the shares attractive to private investors. While the shares did represent majority holdings in the banks, they did not carry with them a majority of voting rights, this was held by the original owners of the banks who controlled the 'founding shares'. The Jewish Colonial Trust, for example, still held 75 per cent of Bank Leumi's voting shares (and therefore effective control of the company) but only 2 per cent of ordinary shares. Hevrat Ha'ovdim, the Histadrut holding company, held 50 per cent of Bank Hapoalim's voting shares; the World Mizrahi Association held the majority of voting shares in United Mizrahi Bank; and the Recanti family were the largest voting shareholders of the Israeli Discount Bank. Thus the government, although having the majority holdings of ordinary shares in all four banks, was unable either to sell the shares or to use them to control the banks. This raised in a central manner the issue of the relationship between the state and the private sector, and emphasized the need to seek new means whereby ownership of the banking system could be redistributed on a wider basis. The sale of the banks has since been at the centre of government privatization plans and their failures.

The new economic policy: the consensus for reform

The Peres years, 1984–6

The new economic policy of the government of national unity which took office in September 1984 was based on a series of 'package deals' (commencing in November 1984) between the government, the Histadrut and the Manufacturers Association, designed to restrict wage increases and freeze prices. When the plan achieved only partial success, with inflation stabilizing at around 350 per cent in the summer of 1985, the policy was stiffened with a package of austerity measures (known as the Emergency Stabilization Plan – or ESP – and introduced in July 1985).[10] These measures were intended to make realistic cuts in government expenditure, to reduce over-consumption and to contain the budget deficit. It was acknowledged, however, that austerity was not enough to overcome the basic problems of the economy; it could only alleviate the symptoms. The ESP included a compulsory wage and price freeze, a 20 per cent devaluation of the shekel and a $500 million budget expenditure cut. Public services and subsidized basic commodities were set to rise in price by as much as 75 per cent, while the real erosion in wages was to be around 30 per cent.

Both the Labour and Likud parties deemed it vital to increase competition in the economy in general and to reduce the size of the public sector. The privatization of government-owned companies would also enable the government to raise revenues so as to ease the budget deficit. Capital markets would need to be deregulated, as would the utility sectors and the currency and exchange markets. In 1985 a list was prepared of 192 state-owned companies which were to be encouraged to seek foreign investment as a means of halting their decline.

The government's determination to pursue its newly-proclaimed policies, however, soon started to waver. The wage-price agreements began to fall to pieces in early March and the government, reluctant to allow unemployment to exceed 7 per cent, failed to reduce expenditure. Such determination as the government did have was strengthened by pressure from the United States, which tied the $1.3

billion aid planned for 1985 to Israeli commitments to devaluation, a halt to injections of government money into the economy, and an erosion of the index-linked wage system. Further aid of $1.5 billion, to be spread over two years was likewise made conditional upon a set of plans drafted jointly by the United States and Israeli economists. This became known as 'Herb's ten points'.[11]

The stabilization programme was reinforced by similar measures in the 1986 budget. Under pressure from the Histadrut, however, the Labour government abandoned austerity prior to its handing over the reins of government to the Likud. Financial help was promised for public sector industries in difficulty, in return for a return to a wage limitation agreement. Most notable were the commitments to the two giant Histadrut-owned companies, Solel Boneh (construction) and Kupat Holim (medical health insurance), which were requesting a total of $2 billion (or 9 per cent of GDP), just to cover their debts.

The government under Shamir, 1986–90

The government was by now facing renewed calls for drastic economic reform, this time from the governor of the Bank of Israel, Moshe Mandelbaum.[12] The response of Shamir when he took office was to launch a radical economic reform programme, slashing personal taxes, opening up domestic capital markets, instituting a 12-month wage and price freeze and promising across the board government spending cuts. There was to be a 20 per cent cut in welfare benefits and allowances, a cut in the top tax rates from 80 per cent to 45 per cent and significant reductions in government health, defence, education and social welfare budgets. The reintroduction of austerity was to be the preliminary step in the larger reform intentions, which were geared towards general economic liberalization and privatization.

Having handed over the reins of government to Shamir, the Labour Party adopted a position of fierce opposition to these measures. The Labour alignment was supported by the Histadrut, which desired neither an erosion of workers' living standards nor cuts in subsidies. It continued to seek bail-outs for its enterprises. Shamir's policies were the greatest challenge so far to Israel's socialist-oriented structures, and the groups which derived the greater part of their political and economic power and influence from those structures were inevitably most resistant to change. The Histadrut was not hostile to the growth of the private sector per se, but was opposed to any reduction in the government's commitment to the public sector. It therefore exerted its not inconsiderable influence on both the Labour and Likud sides of the coalition, ultimately convincing the cabinet to reduce planned spending cuts by half. When the governent introduced stage II of the reform package in January 1987, it was only able to gain Histadrut participation in a new tripartite agreement (government/Histadrut/Manufacturers Association) by making considerable concessions to the Histadrut. A rescue package was provided for the debt-ridden kibbutzim (amounting to over $200 million)[13], and later pressuring the banks into a debt-rescheduling package for Solel Boneh.

Shamir's desire to press ahead with the privatization plans which had been floated since 1984 met with mixed results. In trying to revitalize the privatization process (which had barely advanced under Peres' government), in 1987, Shamir faced a setback when an agreement which was to have facilitated the sale of Bet Shemesh Engines, the debt-ridden aero-engine manufacturer, collapsed. The prospective buyer backed out on the grounds that transfer had been held up for too long by bureaucratic red tape – the result of an inherent resistance to privatization.[14] On the more technical side, the company still had $100 million worth of debts and the cancellation of the Lavi project made it a less attractive proposition. The bureaucratic and political manouevrings against privatization resurfaced in December 1987, when the sale of PAZ (the leading fuel distributor), was prevented by the opposition of the country's powerful oil cartel. Reforms intended to liberalize the energy market had been postponed three times in the face of the oil cartel's resistance to the introduction of competition to the market.[15] In February 1988, the government's stake in PAZ fuel group was finally sold to Jack Liebeman, an Australian businessman, for $5 million. This was the largest single foreign investment ever made in Israel and was approved by the Knesset Finance Committee largely because Liebeman had a substantial and proven commitment to the Zionist state.

The proposed sale of Egged, the Israeli public bus company, further illustrated the difficulties of privatization for Israel. Egged had near monopoly control of urban and inter-urban bus routes and was reluctant to agree to competition within those markets. When government pressure forced the company to agree to salary cuts, the sale of assets and a reduction in the $390 million pension fund deficit, the Histadrut responded with threats of a general strike. Since the Histadrut could call on at least 80 per cent of the workforce to participate in a general strike, the result would have inevitably been a general shutting down of shop for the Israeli economy, plunging it still further into crisis. The government was forced to give in, signing an agreement with the trade unions and the employers' organization on cost of living pay awards.

Government plans to sell off the public stakes in the commercial banks also ran into difficulties. In July 1988, Peres, then finance minister, announced that Bank Igud, a profitable subsidiary of Bank Leumi, was to be sold off separately from Leumi. However, the government held only 37 per cent of Bank Igud's shares, compared to over 40 per cent in the hands of Bank Leumi itself. Since the goverment did not have voting control over Bank Leumi, it was unable to enforce the sale against Bank Leumi's opposition. All that the government could do, therefore, was to sell off its own shares in Bank Igud by tender.

The only significant sale of state assets which occurred during 1989 was the sell-off, approved by the Knesset in September 1989, of the government-held 82.4 per cent stake in the Jerusalem Economic Corporation (a property company). The sale was managed through closed tender, and went finally to a group of US investors headed by Bear Stearns, the New York investment bank, for a total of $54.5 million. The government had by now clarified that it hoped to raise a total of over $5 billion from the sale of nearly 170 public assets. The next in line was scheduled to be a 50 per cent share in Israel Chemicals, a prospectus for which was circulated to just 25 potential buyers.

The Histadrut's industrial holdings had also figured on the Shamir government's list of potential sell-offs. Likud was eager to end the role of the Histadrut as both employer and trade union, and wanted to use the sale of assets to prop up the underfunded Histadrut pension scheme. Histadrut companies accounted for 30 per cent of Israeli industrial production, and Likud believed that it was vital to transfer this share into the private sector. This would open the companies to competition and thereby encourage efficiency and competitiveness instead of the existing and pervasive overmanning and resort to debt. In challenging Labour for control of the Histadrut in the latter's internal elections, Likud proposed that assets should be sold on the basis of 30 per cent to employees, 30 per cent to the public and 40 per cent to private investors. The Histadrut would retain 'golden shares' to protect workers' rights. The project, however, held little appeal for Histadrut members, as proved by the Labour victory in the internal elections. It would inevitably have resulted in manpower streamlining and consequent unemployment for many members. Moreover, Israeli workers felt that a reduction in the economic power of the Histadrut, and consequently in its influence upon the government, would lead to them losing any remaining wage-price indexation bargaining power. The entrenched tradition of state-ownership in industry, which had for so long been a mainstay of Zionist ideals, would not easily be abandoned. While privatization was generally accepted as a necessary evil, Histadrut members were reluctant to abandon the security of an expanded state sector in return for the long-term promise of economic stability. The Shamir government's plans to privatize Histadrut companies, therefore, had to be shelved.

Thus, despite the bureaucratic restrictions and rigidities which governed the Histadrut and state sectors, making them poor economic performers and detracting from the effectiveness of the state at the leading edge of the Israeli economy, the Zionist labour bureaucracy was able to resist privatization with a large degree of public support.

By October 1989, five years after privatization had first been seriously placed on the agenda, only PAZ, JEC and three small-scale floatations on the Tel Aviv stock exchange had taken place. It was little wonder that Ze'ev Refua, who had headed the Government Corporations Authority since 1985 and whose job it had been to reverse the tradition of state ownership, was to describe his job as 'mission impossible.'[16]

Privatization accelerates

Plans for privatization were revitalized with commitments to sell government stakes in Oil Refineries (the monopoly supplier of refined oil products), Bezeq, the Israel Electric Corporation, El Al and Israel Chemicals. The last was the most attractive state-owned asset to be sold, with an annual group turnover exceeding $1 billion and a strong export and profit record. The government hoped to raise $400 million from the sale of a 50 per cent stake, to be sold privately to a corporate investor. This was preferred to a floatation because it was assumed that the company would need strong corporate backing to enable it to stand up to international competition. It was envisaged, however, that at a later stage minority stakes would be sold to the public and employees. The same process was to be followed in the sales of Oil Refineries and Eita, a successful subsidiary of Israel Aircraft Industries. Bezeq and El Al were to be sold through public offerings, while smaller companies (with values of less than $20 million) would be sold directly to private investors.

There were substantial technical obstacles to these privatizations. Some of the companies were in substantial debt and few were actually profit-making. El Al, for example, although back in profit after a succession of disastrous years (caused by the fall in tourism associated with the *intifada*) was still in receivership. In the case of Bezeq, the telecommunications monopoly, the initial proposed 10 per cent floatation was dependent upon tariff increases which alone could put the company in profit and make its shares appealing.[17]

In the case of Oil Refineries, the sale was complicated by the rigid monopoly structure of energy distribution in Israel. Market reform was required, although this would inevitably lead to an initial decline in revenues for the company.

The issue of 'strategic importance' was also a major factor inhibiting progress towards privatization. In the case of companies judged to have strategic importance, the government would have to convince the Knesset Finance Committee, who could veto any sale, that Israel would suffer no strategic loss by sale of the company. In most instances the government intended to keep the ultimate veto in the companies' affairs through use of 'golden shares', but objections were still raised to the sale of such strategic assets to foreign investors. Since the Israeli financial market had only a limited capacity to absorb privatization sales (whether private or through public floatations), it was inevitable that foreign investors should make up the majority of potential buyers.[18] They had, therefore, to be carefully vetted for pro-Zionist credentials.[19] The sale of Israel Chemicals Limited, initially scheduled for completion by April 1990, was vetoed by the Knesset Finance Committee (22 votes to 4) on the basis that 'the state should not relinquish control of ICL because of its role as exploiter of Israel's chief natural resource, potash, and its importance to the economy as a whole'.[20] A 'golden share' solution was specifically rejected. Moreover, when the Knesset limited the stake allowable for sale to 49 per cent, to block foreign control, foreign bidders backed away.

The privatization of the commercial banks presented its own problems. By early 1990 the government had sent a bill for the equalization of share voting rights in the banks to the Knesset. This was geared towards transferring actual control of the banks to the government (in line with the government's existing majority shareholdings) and clearing the way for the sale of shares. Legislation had been deemed necessary after the failure of prolonged negotiation with the controlling shareholders. As the former finance minister, Moshe Nissim, said at the time (November 1989), 'they just want to stay in control with no money, no capital and no economic responsibility'.[21] Although some changes in management had taken place within the banks after the 1983 collapse, the same people still held control of the bank decisions, acting as a cartel and monopolizing the financial system. It was deemed necessary, therefore, by a broad consensus in the Knesset, to remove such power from the limited few to a much wider base of shareholders.

In the light of the proposed legislation, and in the desire to gain as much as possible in the face of the by now inevitable demise of its own controlling influence, the Recanti family made an agreement with the government in January 1990 on how the government majority holding in the Israel Discount Bank was to be sold off. It was agreed that the sale should take place through a competitive bid. The Recanti family agreed to concede one-share, one-vote and a competitive tender for a stake of between 26 and 51 per cent in the group, in return for compensation in the form of a 3 per cent equity portion and guaranteed pre-qualification in the auction.[22] Moreover, the IDB would not be broken up into its various component groups for sale, as was planned for the assets of the other banks. The Bank of Israel refused, however, to pre-qualify the family to buy back the shares, since the more prominent members of the family were still on trial for their parts in the 1983 scandals. The final decision as to whether the family will pre-qualify or not will depend upon the outcome of the trial.

Hevrat Ha'ovdim also declared its intention to buy back control of the Bank Hapoalim from the government, thereby seeking to ensure that the Histadrut's financial mainstay should remain under the Histadrut's own control. Even with compensation, however, the Hevrat Ha'ovdim started with an equity base of just 4 per cent in Bank Hapoalim, compared to the Recanti stake of 12 per cent in IDB. This meant that its bid was less favourably positioned. Nonetheless, the Labour Party was committed to maintaining the bank within the orbit of Histadrut control, so the Hevrat's negotiating position was strengthened by political pressures against the government. In November 1991, a shareholders' meeting abolished existing voting rights and accepted external directors appointed by the government. In return, the government committed itself to strict conditions to preserve the rights of Hapoalim workers and the ethos of the bank. These conditions mean that only Hapoalim itself is likely to consider bidding for the bank shares.

There has been more success with privatization and liberalization measures in other sectors. The absorption of Soviet immigrants has placed new urgency on the plan to privatize. The public sector would clearly be unable to provide jobs for the massive numbers of immigrants expected from Eastern Europe, who in 1990 were expected to total 500,000 over two years or an increase of 20 per cent in the size of the population.[23] In September 1990, it was estimated that GDP would have to increase by 8.5 per cent a year if the economy was to accommodate the immigrants and the business sector alone by 10 per cent. Over half a million new jobs would have to be created over the following five years just to keep unemployment at 10 per cent, while exports would have to increase by 13 per cent a year.[24] Economic growth was held to be dependent upon liberalization and privatization, making the latter of utmost and immediate importance. In March 1990, the IMF urged Israel to liberalize capital and labour markets and to speed up the process of privatization if it was to be able to provide useful employment for the immigrants and to avoid the need for excessive government subsidization of their settlement.

In the first half of 1990, a series of measures aimed at liberalizing the general functioning of the economy were successfully implemented. In May, the government relaxed foreign currency controls so as to allow for increased integration into world markets, especially that of the European Community. Israeli companies were now allowed to invest up to 20 per cent of their equity abroad. The investment could be in any venture with the exception of those in the financial and real estate sectors. Previously permits had been limited to investment which could be proved to be promoting Israeli exports or industrial development. New regulations meant that up to 50 per cent of profits earned abroad could now be reinvested abroad, rather than having to be repatriated. This move was completed despite considerable opposition from the Histadrut, which argued that such measures would create jobs outside of Israel rather than inside. The percentage of funds which savings institutions had to invest in government instruments was reduced from 65 to 50 per cent, and restrictions on foreign borrowing were reduced. Increased freedom was given for banks and corporations to operate in foreign currency, and import licences for areas outside those covered by free-trade agreements were scrapped in favour of levying duties. The latter were to be scaled down over a period of five years. This combination of measures was designed to encourage investment in the private sector and to improve Israel's trading position, by releasing it from the structural rigidities which had originally been intended to preserve its economic independence. Israeli banks were for the first time allowed to guarantee corporate loans raised overseas and to make loans to Israeli corporations from overseas branches. Companies were given greater freedom to borrow short-term funds from abroad, and ceilings and taxes were lifted on such loans. It was argued that by exposing domestic producers to greater competition the short-term problems of uncompetitiveness would ultimately be replaced by sustained growth. To ease the way, direct incentives were given in the form of employment subsidies.

Despite the problems over privatization in certain sectors, some privatization schemes did go ahead in 1990. In the first half of the year, several small floatations were completed, including a 49 per cent stake in Maman, an air cargo holding company. Privatization received a further boost when a slice of Bezeq totalling 6 per cent of shares was successfully floated in September 1990. The offer was over-subscribed by four times, suggesting a very different pattern from that evident in previous privatization offers. In October 1990 tenders were invited for the government share in the Israel Electric Corporation, and in July 1991 the ministry of finance finally began preparations for the sale of Israel Chemicals. The latter involved a public offering of 25 per cent of shares and a private block of 15 per cent to be sold by tender to a private investor. On 29 January 1992, the Knesset Finance Committee approved the public floatation of the 25 per cent share in Israel Chemicals Ltd, after intense US criticism of the Israeli economy, linked to Israel's request for $10 billion in loan guarantees from America. It is now intended that a total of 72 per cent of the company will eventually be sold, with a 15 per cent block being privately placed.[25] Also, in July 1991, the government announced that nine other companies were to be privatized by the end of the year, in a scaled-down privatization programme which was designed to fulfil US and IMF requirements that aid in absorbing East European Jews be tied to a reduction in the state's role and size. Between 30 and 40 further companies, out of the more than 150 still owned by the state, were to be privatized over the next three years, raising an estimated total of up to NIS7 billion. The main vehicle for this programme was to be the Tel Aviv stock exchange, with a lesser role for foreign investment. It was hoped that this would reduce domestic resistance. Most of the companies targeted were therefore quite small, with the exception of the Zim Navigation shipping company and the remaining part of Bezeq.[26]

Obstacles to privatization
The above account of the government's efforts to privatize many of its assets points to several leading characteristics of the Israeli economy which have hindered the process.

The structure of capital ownership and management clearly mitigates against the reduction of the public sector. The sheer size of the Histadrut (and the bargaining power which it derives from its close links with political élites), gives it the ability to resist government attempts to enforce the sale of assets or the liberalization of markets. To some extent this is indicative of the continuing existence of the Zionist labour bureaucracy which developed during and after the Mandate and which controlled the Israeli state for 30 or more years. As a socioeconomic class, the Zionist labour bureaucracy has co-opted those private capitalists who have become used to having their businesses subsidized and their domestic markets protected. Economic liberalization for the Zionist labour bureaucracy and these associated private capitalists means, in the short term, exposure to competition at a level which will certainly lead to redundancies and business failures. The result has been that while the government has liberalized certain aspects of investment in the private sector and currency dealings for international trade, it has had constantly to reassure both public and private sectors that it will continue to bolster the economy with extensive government funding and subsidies so as to minimize the more painful effects of the liberalization.

While it is to be expected that national bureaucracies and the public sector will be most resistant to liberalization, on the grounds that this will reduce their role and influence in the economy, Israel is perhaps unique in terms of the alliance between the public sector, a large part of the political élite and the trade union movement. The latter, far from advancing worker interests at the expense of capital, acts directly to suppress them by itself taking on the role of capitalist employer. Thus the Histadrut has developed interests of its own, separate from those which arise from its function as a trade union. At times these interests conflict with the interests of its members. It juggles the interests by extracting funds from the state and distributing them to the workforce as compensation for its own capitalist exploitation of that same workforce. This may be done directly, as when it holds the state to ransom with threats of general strikes until Histadrut or public sector firms are provided with government financial support. Alternatively, it can be done indirectly. In the latter case, the ties with the Labour political élites can be utilized to ensure a softening of government policies on welfare, employment, housing and so forth. Any government strategy of liberalization, aimed at reducing government intervention in the market, will be frustrated or distorted: the Histadrut will continue to demand (and has the political power to win) government compensation and subsidization for the Histadrut and public sectors in return for apparent compliance with the strategy.

Other factors also render it unlikely that the Israeli government would reduce the size of the public sector, at least for the foreseeable future. The current wave of Soviet Jewish immigration must be absorbed for ideological, strategic and demographic reasons. This means raising revenue from still more loans and foreign aid, and distributing those revenues. While the lenders and donors may be trying to impose conditions on the funds, relating to economic liberalization, the mere fact of the state having to act as distributor mitigates against a reduction in the size of public agencies. Ironically, if liberalization had been more successful earlier, foreign investment in the private sector might have been in a position to provide the jobs, the construction and the facilities which are now required. The reality, however, is that the state has had to engage in massive building, education and welfare programmes.

While a decrease in the size of the public sector, and a reduction of government intervention in the economy, are not likely to be achieved in the foreseeable future, liberalization (and specifically privatization) still remains a central theme of government policy. It will continue to be argued that immigration can only result in long-term economic growth if the private sector is large enough, and healthy enough, to absorb the new labour. Privatization in this view, both restores competitiveness to industry and raises vital revenues for the government. For this, market liberalization and the opening of the economy to foreign investment are essential. Structural impediments, therefore, are unlikely to lead to economic liberalization being abandoned. It remains for Israel to find some way of squaring the implications of liberalization and the free market with the state-interventionism and public support of immigration which are a necessary aspect of the Zionist state.

Note: The author wishes to acknowledge Amnon Barger and Rafi Melnick for their help in understanding the intricacies of the Israeli banking system.

Notes

1 The proviso here being that the chapter is discussing the Jewish majority in Israel and not the Arab minority.
2 *Financial Times*, 10/7/91.
3 See 'Israel's economic crisis', *Merip Reports*, October–December 1985, pp. 20–23.
4 It should be noted that the term 'Labour' is used here to refer to the coalition of parties making up the Labour Alignment at the particular time referred to.
5 *Financial Times*, 31/5/91.
6 In the 1989 Histadrut elections, Labour took 55.5 per cent of the vote, despite an aggressive campaign by Shamir's Likud. Although this was still a slip in Labour's position overall, it left Labour with effective control of the union. See *Financial Times*, 15/11/89.
7 In 1989, the public sector accounted for 12 per cent of all business activity, employing 65,000 workers with an annual production of $6 bn and exports of $1.6 bn. See *The Middle East*, October 1989. This was after the government had cut the public sector from 71,000 employees in 1986. Despite the cuts, wage costs increased from $2.2 bn to $3.1 bn between 1986 and 1988. Furthermore, during that period, the government established two new ministries: environment, and economics and planning.
8 *Time* Magazine, 8/4/91. Ze'ev Refuah, former director of Israel Corporations Authority and prime mover in the government privatization programme since 1985, said, 'The goverment fears losing power and control over jobs'. *Time* continued: 'The real stumbling block is politics: no one in government wants to be responsible for the mass layoffs privatization will bring'.
9 Gafny, A. (1991), former governor of the Bank of Israel, quoted in *The Christian Science Monitor*, 5–11/7/91.
10 See *The Middle East*, October 1989, p. 33.
11 The name derives from the American economist, Herbert Stein, who worked with Stanley Fisher, Michael Bruno, Eitan Berglass, Ephraim Ben-Shahar, Moshe Zanbar, Adi Amorai and others on the plan and who eventually was to formulate it in a document leaked to the Israeli press. See *Merip Reports*, October–December, 1985, pp. 20–3.
12 *Financial Times*, 2/6/86.
13 See 'Business versus ideology', *Financial Times*, 6/11/89.
14 *Financial Times*, 24/11/87.

15 See Ayallon, A. and Shahed, H. (eds) (1988).
16 *Financial Times*, 27/10/89.
17 See *Financial Times*, 26/9/90.
18 This view was not universally held. Sam Bronfield, the Stock Exchange deputy manager, argued in 1989 that the public should come before foreign investors and that at least 50 per cent of any company's shares should be offered to the public. See *The Middle East*, October 1989, p. 34.
19 In early 1987, for example, the government sold its share in Haifa Chemicals to an American-based investors group headed by former Israeli Aye Genger (a good friend of Ariel Sharon) and billionaire Meshulam Riklis. In 1989, the Australian Jewish millionaire, Jack Liebeman was allowed to purchase the government's portion of Paz Oil Company. See *The Middle East*, March 1990.
20 Committee statement, *Financial Times*, 20/12/89.
21 *Financial Times*, 25/11/89.
22 See 'Israeli banks under starter's orders', *Financial Times*, 20/2/90.
23 *Financial Times*, 29/5/90.
24 *Financial Times*, 14/9/90.
25 *Financial Times*, 30/1/92.
26 *Financial Times*, 10/7/91.

14· OMAN AND YEMEN

Gerd Nonneman

Both Oman and Yemen have participated in the worldwide phenomenon of economic liberalization, encouraged by advocates of the free market, such as the IMF, and mindful of the gradual collapse of centrally-planned systems around the world.

In both cases, there has been a link between economic and political liberalization, at least in recent years. Oman, until lately, had no formal political participation worth mentioning; at the same time, while there was no real state control over private enterprise, the economy was effectively state-run because of the preponderance of oil. In recent years, liberal economic principles have been more widely pushed, while at the same time, a new, largely elected, National Assembly is being given shape, supplanting the existing Consultative Assembly. While this is a fairly minor move compared with developments in Yemen and worldwide, it does have some significance when placed in the context of Oman being a fairly small oil rentier state.

In North Yemen, the economy was always relatively unregulated; this went hand in hand with a lack of political control by the centre over considerable parts of the territory. Politically, traditional tribal leaders retained much influence, both within and outside the central governmental apparatus, and the countrywide election in 1985 of representatives for the Local Councils for Co-operative Development proved an important democratic exercise (the LCCDs were responsible for the administration of village development projects and for nominating the electors who in turn chose the delegates to the General People's Congress). Yet political parties were prohibited until the unification with South Yemen. In development planning, a significant role was always foreseen for the private sector. The general economic laissez-faire attitude was limited by two main factors: some control had to be exerted on commerce so as to combat smuggling (a policy which was both an economic and a political imperative); and the severe balance of payments crisis in 1986 forced a tightening of currency controls and import restrictions. The late 1980s saw a return to a more relaxed regime, as oil revenues began to flow in, but efforts to bring the unofficial economy under official control continued. The unification with the south also heralded a political liberalization, with most restrictions on the press and political parties lifted.

In South Yemen, the economic framework was one of heavy and intrusive central control, reflected politically in a one-party system on old-style Soviet lines. Modest steps towards giving the private sector a role were of equally modest effect until the late 1980s. The upheavals of early 1986, when an attempt by the moderate President Ali Nasser to oust his radical challengers resulted in his own exile but also the death of the main radicals, opened the way to eventual reforms and unification with the North. The glaring political and economic bankruptcy of the existing system, the disappearance of the key hardliners from the stage, and the new wind blowing in the Kremlin, allowed the increasingly pragmatic new leadership to institute a number of reforms. Especially from 1988 onwards, a strong policy of political and economic liberalization was pursued. The reforms in turn made possible the unification with the North in 1990. Conversely, the need which the South Yemeni leaders felt for unification (on political and economic grounds), pushed them further in a reformist direction.

In Oman as well as both Yemens, hydrocarbons have played a major role in private sector activity and/or the opening up to foreign private capital. The chief oil company in Oman, Petroleum Development Oman (PDO), is 40 per cent owned by Shell and two other Western firms. In North Yemen, the discovery and development of the Marib/Jawf oil fields by the US firm Hunt during the 1980s spurred further interest by other companies; all operate on the basis of production-sharing concessions. Perhaps the most striking example is again South Yemen. In the early stages of the reform process, the potential for oil finds in the disputed border zone with North Yemen (adjacent to the latter's main oil fields), led to the establishment of a joint exploration and development zone in 1988. The operation of the latter was awarded to a four-nation consortium which included Hunt as well as the Soviet concern then dominating exploration and development in the South. In fact, the government in Aden had already in 1984 begun to make active attempts to attract foreign oil companies, and increasing frustration with the slow progress of the Soviet group (especially in building the pipeline to the coast) helped heighten the propensity for looking West in oil affairs. The oil strikes in North Yemen increased openness and encouraged companies' interest in the South. Since 1987 a whole string of concessions has been awarded. The Soviet bloc was reduced and renegotiated in February 1990, leaving them with only two parts of it, but now as a production sharing concession. The government kept the producing areas (which the Soviet firm continued to service); the remainder has since been awarded to other oil firms, leaving everything outside of the government's bloc to be run by foreign private capital. It can be argued that oil, through the joint development zone with the north, helped strengthen the trend towards unification, which in turn brought about further economic reform. (The oil sector will not be addressed further in the remainder of this chapter).

Before moving on to the specific data on liberalization in the individual countries, attention should be drawn to the complexities which surround the term 'economic liberalization'. It can mean a variety of things which may, moreover, be contradictory. In the widest sense it means allowing the full operation of the market, both domestically and internationally. But support of the domestic private sector in many cases implies protection against the market forces outside the borders: foreign competition. Conversely, opening up the country for foreign investment and trade may hurt the interests of many domestic private sector producers. In approaching the evidence below, therefore, it is as well to keep in mind that privatization programmes and measures to boost the private sector may in fact involve increased subsidies and protection.

Oman: the overall economic context

Oman is in many respects an oil rentier state, where the economy is based more on distribution than production. Even non-oil sectors of the economy are to a considerable extent dependent on the oil sector and revenues derived (and redistributed) from it. The characteristics which affect the economic liberalization process in Oman, therefore, are not dissimilar from those which affect the process in other Gulf states. First, there is the problem of finding enough genuine entre-preneurs (rather than just merchants or speculators) to take up the developmental challenge after the completion by the state of the basic infrastructure. Second, the network of subsidies and protection to an extent undermines the building of an efficient free enterprise system. Third, it is frequently the case that much of the equity in privatized companies its taken up by the royal family or by those closely linked in with the ruling group. The supposed buttressing of the private sector in those instances is artificial, inadvertently enriching a few well-connected individuals rather than establishing a general free enterprise philosophy. It may be the case that, while Sultan Qaboos genuinely believes that the expansion of the private sector is the key to Oman's future development, he is unable to control the acquisitive drive of some of those who have prospered at the higher echelons of this allocation economy. As Qaboos still, at least in part, depends on this group for the political, security, economic and managerial buttressing of his regime, they are able to take advantage of privatizations such that the ownership of capital is transferred from the state to a minority élite rather than being more widely distributed. It should be stressed, however, that while this tendency exists, privatization programmes have still had a certain success. A fourth point which Oman by definition shares with the other Gulf states has been summed up as follows:

> one major obstacle to establishing a private sector climate in the Gulf is the persistent fragmentation of the market. The GCC is committed to creating a free trade area, but national interests continue to slow down implementation of the process. While markets continue to be, for all intent and purpose, protected, there is little room for the competition on which free trade is supposed to thrive.[1]

As Paul Stevens argues elsewhere in this volume, there is often no point in pursuing privatization when the market is so small that 'natural monopolies' will remain, whether state-owned or privatized, and when the desired greater competitiveness and efficiency do not ensue. Thus, when trying to focus on domestic liberalization, one comes face-to-face with the need for regional integration and a general opening up.

Where Oman has differed from the other Gulf states has been first, in the cautious and often common-sensical way in which economic decisions have been taken; and second, in the large and both economically and socially important traditional private sector in agriculture, fisheries, traditional industries and trade. This has received genuine support (other than merely benefitting from protectionist measures), and as a result continues to flourish. The policy of support has much to do with Sultan Qaboos's conviction that the traditional culture and society of Oman must be preserved and kept vibrant. Another important consideration may be that by avoiding major social transformations and dislocations (for instance, those stemming from a rural-urban drift), the political status quo can be more easily maintained.

The private sector in Oman and the economic liberalization process

Under the first development plan (1976–80), the state took responsibility for the construction of all the basic infrastructure. While private sector activity was encouraged, the plan did not depend greatly on such activity. The emphasis placed on the private sector's role in national development has since been more heavily stressed, but the share of private capital formation in total capital formation remained around 30 per cent in the first two periods (1976–80 and 1981–5), and was planned to remain at about the same level for 1986–90.[2] Support for the private sector (initiated in a concerted manner under the second five-year plan) reached OR157 million under the third plan. In the fourth five-year plan (1991–5), a figure of OR129 million has been foreseen.[3] The overall pro-business attitude in recent plans is exemplified in the repeated extension of the exemption for Omani companies from paying tax. The latest extension, dubbed 'final', is until the end of 1992. Nonetheless, the private sector has not been left without controls and restrictions. In order to attract young Omanis to the private sector, a decree was issued in 1989 giving the government powers to fix a minimum wage for employees in the sector, committing entrepreneurs to stricter conditions than before. In February 1991, Sultan Qaboos announced plans for guaranteeing the rights of private sector employees. Private sector representatives reacted by demanding that in return a clause be inserted requiring these employees to remain in private sector employment for at least six months. At the time of writing it had not become known whether the government would accept this demand.

Under the third plan, part of the budgeted deficit was meant to be financed by the sale of government assets, or privatization. OR25 million worth of such sales were planned for 1988 and 1989, and double that amount in 1990 (to a total of OR100 million). In an October 1989 interview, Deputy Prime Minister Qays al-Zawawi stressed that these plans would go ahead, starting with the sale of state-owned hotels. He indicated that the government also considered selling shares in the Rusail plant of the Oman Cement Company, and later perhaps privatizing utilites in the water, electricity and communications sectors.[4] It appears that the targeted OR100 million figure for the third plan was not reached. Under the fourth plan the sum of OR429 million is expected to accrue to the government through the sale of government bonds and through privatization. The size of this sum provides evidence that the government wants to keep external debt to a minimum.[5] During the preparation of the plan, a team of British consultants recommended by the British government was inivited to Oman to look at issues of diversification and privatization there.[6]

In agriculture, traditional private farming is still very important; the number of new, modern farms is still relatively small, but growing. As part of the privatization plans, the profit-making government-owned dairy company, Oman Sun Farms, was sold to the public. Twenty-five per cent of the shares went to the people of Sohar (where the firm is located), and the remainder to 21 prominent businessmen (several of them linked with the political élite).[7] Although the government has on the whole pursued a liberal policy on food imports (which may be deemed prejudicial to domestic agricultural production), the sector has been helped by research and extension programmes run by the Ministry of Agriculture and Fisheries, as well as the Oman Bank for Agriculture and Fisheries, and by initiatives such as the Year of Agriculture (1988). In another development quite typical of much private activity in Oman today, a firm called the Oman Agricultural Development Company was established in 1989 with a OR2 million capital, of which OR480,000 worth of shares were offered to the public. The initiative was taken by a number of very prominent individuals and firms (the latter themselves often at least partly controlled by equally prominent individuals). The founders included two members of the royal family, as well as the chairman of the Water Resources Authority (established in 1988), Muhammad bin Zubair.[8]

The government has also financed the building of workshops and ice factories for the private fisheries sector, and the purchase of equipment. Fish and fish products are Oman's largest non-oil export (worth some $75 mn in 1990). The major part of the catch (85 per cent in 1990) is still brought in by the 18,500 traditional fishermen. However, a commercial large-scale company, the Oman Fisheries Company, was set up in 1989, on public subscription. OFC's share issue was widely oversubscribed; the new firm merged later that year with the Oman National Fisheries Company, and is now no more than 24 per cent government-owned. The new 10-year master plan for the fisheries sector, intended to double the sector's share in the economy, forsees huge public investment in infrastructure as well as training, aiming to encourage subsequent private investment in the sector.[9]

In manufacturing industry, the government has encouraged small enterprises through offering soft loans, cheap land and electricity, feasiblity studies, and import duty exemptions. In the course of distributing these benefits, the government has promoted the spread of investment outside the capital area by offering special incentives. As of 1987, a total of 2,990 industrial establishments were registeres, almost exclusively private. The government-funded infrastructure of the Rusail industrial estate has been put at the dispositon of the private sector, and a further four such estates are being developed in Raysut, Sohar, Sur and Nizwa (again geographically spread). A number of protective measures also cushion Omani industry. In May 1988 a new committee was set up, chaired by the Deputy Prime Minister for Economic Affairs, Qays al-Zawawi, with the specific brief to encourage the private sector to play a bigger role in the national economy.[10]

Under the pressure of reduced oil revenues in the second half of 1988, however, the government has also been exhorting local industrialists to wean themselves from subsidies and improve competitiveness. This remains problematic. During 1991 there were increasing calls for greater protection of domestic industries, despite demands from the Commerce and Industry Minister that firms should reduce costs and improve efficiency.[11] It is likely that the government will try to alleviate some of private industrialists' greatest fears with minor concessions, while sticking to the long-term aim of encouraging competitiveness. It is by no means certain that the sector will be up to the challenge.

The third plan gave emphasis to attracting foreign investment. Such investment must, however, adhere to some clearly-specified conditions. Foreign participation in an Omani company can not exceed 65 per cent; and there must be majority Omani shareholding in companies holding commercial agencies, travel and shipping agencies, advertising, insurance and press agencies. As incentives, companies enjoy a five-year tax holiday if the enterprise is deemed to be a development project. Integration plans with the GCC have resulted in GCC citizens being allowed, since 1990, to engage in business in the Sultanate on the same terms as Omanis in supply contracts, marketing services (but not buying and selling), and cleaning services.[12]

In the banking sector, the role of foreign banks and foreign capital has been of considerable importance. Thirteen of the twenty-three commercial banks licensed in Oman as of 1990 were foreign. Foreign capital has also participated in a major way in two of the three development banks. The capital of the Oman Development Bank is subscribed 53 per cent by the government, 40 per cent by a number of international institutions, and 7 per cent by Omani private investors. Its remit was originally to lend for industrial, agricultural, mining and oil projects, in addition to running schemes for small industries, vocational entrepreneurs, and craftsmen. In May 1991, the bank was allowed to expand into the service sector; to finance hotels, tourist restaurants, clinics and schools. During that year, the bank announced a scheme aimed at encouraging young Omanis to set up small businesses, which involved the offer of soft loans (even interest-free if all employees are Omani).[13] The Oman Housing Bank is owned 51 per cent by the government, with the remaining share ownership held by the British Bank of the Middle East and Kuwaiti interests. It has provided soft loans for subsidized homes to Omanis earning less than OR150 per month. The Oman Bank for Agriculture and Fisheries aims to assist farms and fisheries with loans. In the insurance business, 17 of the 20 companies present are foreign, although since 1987 they have been obliged to leave 30 per cent of the market to local firms.

An important landmark for the expansion of private sector activities was the establishment of an Omani stock market, which opened for business in May 1989. Sultan Qaboos began the trading with OR50,000 worth of share purchases. In the first year of operation, trading totalled OR16.3 million, distributed over 48 listed companies (in addition to 23 companies not listed on the exchange but whose shares were traded over the counter). Among the rules governing the market were the stipulations that the value of shares was not allowed to change more than 10 per cent in one day; that there should be no trading in margins or futures; and that shares must be delivered in full immediately after the transaction. Settlement was to be in cash. At the end of 1989, it was estimated that there were 18,000 shareholders in the country. Initially, trading on the stockmarket was limited to Omani citizens, but after June 1989, any GCC citizen was able to do so. At the time of writing, the government is considering allowing other foreign investors (including expatriates living in Oman) to buy shares in local companies. The emergence of the stock market made necessary the introduction of regulations for joint stock companies. These were announced shortly before the stock market was opened. The minimum capital was set at OR50,000 for quoted firms and three times that for unquoted firms. Companies with a capital of more than OR500,000 were obliged to offer at least 40 per cent of their shares to the public, while founders had to subscribe to at least 30 per cent (any individual founder to a maximum of 20 per cent).[14]

Despite the apparent success of the stock market, some parts of the Omani private sector appear to have been reluctant to become involved. Local Omani trust funds and even the Oman Chambers of Commerce and Industry have not participated actively in stock market investments and trading, to the extent that the exchange's director-general felt compelled to admonish them publicly in September 1989. It was believed that this reluctance stemmed from these funds (run by PDO, the Royal Oman Police, OCCI, and Ports Services Corporation) being managed by expatriates.[15]

The political corollaries of Oman's economic evolution are worth stressing. In the past, top local merchants have acquired fortunes in part through association with the government; now the balance of influence and power is in danger of being reversed. Some sections of the Omani population suggest that Sultan Qaboos's role in economic decision-making is effectively being replaced by people such as the Zawawi brothers, Qays (the Deputy Prime Minister for Finanacial and Economic Affairs) and Omar (the head of a business empire). A limited number of names have been acquiring increasing dominance in both business and governmental decision-making. If this trend is consolidated, a higher level of political disaffection may be inevitable. While Qaboos has earned a fair degree of legitimacy by his association with the creation of the Omani welfare state, and with a number of well-considered policies (on water, ecology, small farmers, and the geographical spreading of development), this could cause political disruption, especially in the absence of effective channels for wider political participation.

Yemen: the overall economic context

North and South Yemen merged in May 1990 to form the Yemen Republic. The new state adopted a basically liberal economic philosophy as far as the participation of the private sector and the role of foreign investment were concerned. This was not, however, as far-going as the laissez-faire environment of the North before the mid-1980s. Political reform was introduced, with the new state becoming a functioning multi-party system.

Prior to unification, the main economic problems in both North and South Yemen stemmed from a dearth of resources and the lack of a central control over parts of both territory and economy. In the South, the second point was manifest in dirigiste pretensions clashing with an inability to implement decisions down the line. This inability was caused by a lack of personnel and expertise, as well as by popular political apathy. In the North, the character of the economy was such that the government's options in economic policy were severely limited. To maintain its balance of payments, North Yemen was, until the late 1980s, overwhelmingly dependent on foreign aid (the bulk of which came from the Gulf states) and on the remittances of migrant Yemeni workers. The development of oil production in the 1980s, moreover, required foreign capital and expertise. There was never, therefore, an alternative to openness. As indicated earlier, in the South also the prospect of oil production performed a catalytic role in advancing reform, unification, and openness to foreign capital.

The private sector in the Yemen and the economic liberalization process

The North

Much of the North Yemeni private sector is in fact an informal sector which, despite major efforts by the government, remains outside of governmental regulation. Large parts of this sector have been concerned with smuggling and the unofficial repatriation of migrants' earnings. Over 1 million North Yemenis were working abroad (mainly in the Gulf) in 1986. Consequently, official development policy and planning has been limited in its reach. This has been accentuated by the absence of firm central control over parts of the territory, and limitations in expertise and personnel. The data provided below should be considered in that context.

Under the first two five-year plans (1977–86) little specific attention was given to encouraging the private sector; the attitude was one of laissez-faire. The government concentrated on basic infrastructural development. The country's investment law, in the revised form adopted in 1975, did however guarantee freedom of investment for foreign capital, repatriation of capital and profits, and a number of incentives in the form of exemptions from customs duties and tax. The second plan emphasized import substitution industries, especially food processing, textiles, and building materials, but this was mainly in the public sector.

The third plan (1987–91) projected a more refined role for the private sector, within the framework of a more 'guided' (though by no means dirigiste) development strategy. Agriculture was given particular emphasis in this regard. Farming in North Yemen has been organized mainly in smallholdings, with 55 per cent of the farmers owning less than 1 hectare.[16] The government established five regional agricultural authorities, to coordinate the provision of irrigation, power, and other local development needs which would allow the rural population a better environment within which to live and produce. The Co-operative and Agricultural Credit Bank was established to provide loans for rural enterprises. The country's first private agricultural marketing company (Bilqis) was being established at the time of unification. In the late 1980s increased interest was also reported in agro-business development. A United States Embassy (Sana'a) report stated that some large agro-business companies were receiving development acreage from the government and that these tracts sometimes amount to several thousand hectares and are the focus of considerable economic and political interest.[17]

While the third plan did give more encouragement than before to private sector manufacturing, developments in this field (as also in currency and banking) are best described in the context of a steady liberalization starting from the mid-1980s. As regards foreign involvement in manufacturing, the government began to actively encourage such investment, seeing Yemeni–foreign joint ventures as a means for productively mobilizing domestic private capital as well as foreign. Nevertheless, foreign investors often found they had to struggle through complex bureaucratic tangles. In practice, they usually had to restrict their activities to a minority stake in a partnership or to a joint venture.[18] Through the Industrial Bank of Yemen, domestic private participation in industry was also actively encouraged. The bank has, for example, supported feasibility studies for projects using local raw materials and/or creating import substitution, and has provided half the investment cost of such projects in soft loans (as well as providing hard currency).[19] In addition, the government has improved facilities for manufacturers through the creation of three industrial estates, in Sana'a, Hodeida and Taiz. Local industry has benefited from a 25 per cent reduction in import duties for raw materials, and has been exempted from tax for five years. The temporary import restrictions on consumer goods imposed in response to the 1986 balance of payments crisis, moreover, led to an expansion in some industrial sectors. Partly as a consequence of these policies, some major private Yemeni firms (usually run as family operations) have since the mid-1980s been shifting from their traditional import business to small-scale manufacturing.[20] A UNIDO report stated in July 1989 that 'the driving force of industrialization has been private sector investment.'[21] In a move to help bring expatriate Yemeni earnings into the official economy, the pre-unification recovery programme of 1990 contained an offer to allocate a plot of land to any returnee who wanted to begin a business with his savings. With this in mind, a priority list of export-oriented ventures was drawn up.[22]

Policy on the control of foreign exchange has been mixed, with several changes in regulations. As part of the austerity clampdown and to avoid a slide in the value of the currency, strict foreign exchange controls were introduced in 1986. Private local money changers were closed down and the Central Bank took sole control. Imports were at the same time made more expensive by only offering importers rates of exchange close to the official one. Since 1987, all goods have required import licenses (whereas before, food, pharmaceuticals and raw materials were exempt). Some relaxation in controls, however, was introduced in 1990. The 1990 recovery programme, which brought about the devaluation of the rial by nearly 23 per cent (intended to make imports yet more expensive on the local market) was followed by a measure allowing expatriate Yemenis again to hold higher rate foreign exchange accounts with their own bank (as one way of attracting their remittances). Nonetheless, an import licence was still required before such funds could be used for imports. Import duties currently vary between 5 and 50 per cent (although tobacco, a local product, attracts 70 per cent). The import of luxury goods remains officially suspended.[23]

In the banking sector, government regulation has been (and remains) strong. Following the withdrawal of BBME and Citibank from the country, there are now 11 commercial banks in the north. A specialist report in 1987 noted that:

> the banking and financial sectors are ... subject to the most noticeable government intervention and regulation, with the foreign bank branches being subject to an intrusive scrutiny ... A general atmosphere of mistrust between the government and [these] sectors can be attributed to a slight feeling of government inferiority vis a vis [their] financial strength and expertise, to the foreign involvement ... [and to] sensitivities concerning the interest paying principles employed by the banking sector.[24]

The South

In the course of 1989 and 1990, after some two to three years in which a trend towards economic and political reform-mindedness had become apparent, Marxism was for all intents and purposes dropped, the political system liberalized, and investment and private ownership matters reconsidered. These reform plans were given explicit form in a programme published by the official weekly publication, *Al-Thawri*, in July 1989.[25] In political terms, South Yemen was, by the time of unification, considerably more liberal than the North. Amnesty International confirmed that all political prisoners had been released by the time of unification, while in the North the fate of 26 remained unsure.[26] Economically, the country was a special case both in history and resources. Of the latter it had hardly any until the discovery of oil in 1987; most development had only been possible with foreign, particulary Soviet, assistance. With the exception of the oil refinery in Aden, the area had, and has, little by way of modern industry. Until the advent of oil, the best potential lay in the fisheries sector. South Yemen was the only Arab economy to be planned ostensibly along scientific socialist lines, but theory succumbed to practice when the state came up against a severe lack of national integration, the difficult accessibility of some regions, political instability, limited planning capacity, and the need to leave some room for traditional private initiatives which might attract migrant remittances.

The country's dependence on foreign aid was evident from the second development plan (1981–5). This assumed that some 70 per cent of development expenditures would be covered by outside aid. The third plan, which was delayed by the domestic political strife of January 1986 and finally became operative in 1988, assumed that, of the planned $1.7 billion in development, half would be covered by foreign resources. The plan, still rooted in the system's pre-reform roots, foresaw a fall of the private sector's share of Gross Domestic Product to 27 per cent, limited to agriculture and fisheries. However, this projection was rendered irrelevant by the subsequent consolidation of the reformist line and the unification with the North. Due to the great need for reconstruction following the 1986 fighting, the plan's main emphasis was on reconstruction and rehabilitation, with very little in the way of new industrial projects.

The reform plans published in *Al-Thawri* in July 1989 focused on boosting agricultural and industrial production, encouraging fishing co-operatives, attracting local and foreign investment, repatriating and recycling expatriates' savings, and introducing competition for the state monopolies in order to cut government expenditures. The critical foreign exchange situation in the country was blamed for the need to maintain tight monetary and currency controls. In September 1989, the YSP Political Bureau decided to encourage tourism, and to try to spur the free market through developing a free zone in Aden. The following month, Prime Minister Yasin Said Nu'man stressed that legislative reforms should be introduced to allow the private sector to play 'a true role in economic development'. In February 1990, the Prime Minister announced that private ownership of homes would be allowed, and that some categories of people would even be enabled to acquire their own land on which to build.[27]

In agriculture, traditional share-cropping had been abolished by the Agrarian Reform Law of 1970, which limited private holdings to 8 hectares of irrigated land or 16 hectares of non-irrigated land. In the 1980s, agriculture had been organized into state farms (10 per cent), co-operatives (70 per cent), and peasant freeholdings (20 per cent). Most livestock remained under private ownership. The performance of this system was poor: from 1980 to 1988, both agricultural production and the index of production of crops per head fell by about 15 per cent (compared to a rise of about 5 per cent in North Yemen).[28] In the potentially rich fisheries sector, while the government made concerted efforts to modernize the fishing fleet, the 8 per cent increase in catches from 1980 to 1987 (to some 90,000 tonnes) was largely due to the activities of a foreign (Eastern bloc) fleet. Private fishermen kept up their level of 15,000 tonnes, but the catches of the public, mixed (Yemeni–Soviet) and co-operative sectors actually declined, with the public sector's catch falling by 42 per cent.[29] As part of the reform programme of the late 1980s, fishermen and farmers were allowed to sell more of their produce directly on the markets, instead of through state organizations or co-operatives. This, together with the government raising the prices at which it purchased agricultural produce and lowering agricultural taxes, led to more vegetables and fish becoming available already in 1989. In September of that year the YSP Political Bureau decided to liberalize imports in order to boost agricultural production, by allowing private imports of machinery and spares.[30]

As indicated above, South Yemen had little modern industry. The only large-scale industrial operation was the Aden oil refinery (originally a BP venture) which, ever since the closure of the Suez Canal, had operated at a fraction of its capacity of 170,000 barrels per day. With the implementation of modernization programmes, this government-run establishment has appeared to have improved prospects. The 1981 investment law provided incentives (such as freedom to remit hard currency) for foreign companies or investors to become junior partners in joint ventures. This succeeded in attracting mainly expatriate Yemeni capital. By 1990, 16 (generally small-scale) schemes had been established this way, largely for the production of basic consumer goods. The general political and economic environment deterred potential investors (especially foreign), a situation which was compounded by the 1986 events. This notwithstanding, the private sector did retain a legitimate place. In the last year for which general statistics are available (1987), 19 private industrial establishments were counted, against 38 in the public, 10 in the mixed, and five in the co-operative sectors (the mixed sector being the vehicle for private equity participation in larger-scale industrial activity). The share of production value contributed by the private industrial establishments was nearly 18 per cent. According to overall statistics, productivity appears to have been about six times as high in the private sector as in the mixed sector, while the public sector was the least productive.[31] Considerable excess liquidity in the domestic economy remained untapped, even leaving aside expatriate savings. Given the government's own shortage of resources, the importance of giving more concerted encouragement to the private sector became increasingly apparent, especially after the destruction of 1986.[32]

Part of the reforms of the late 1980s was an explicit call for the participation of domestic and foreign private capital in economic investment in the country. President Attas himself, in October 1988, pleaded the case for foreign investment. Early in 1989, both the minister and deputy minister of trade and industry stressed the role private investment had to play in the economy, calling on both local and foreign investors to apply for permits. The deputy minister announced a campaign to attract expatriates' funds, including a plan to offer shares in ventures to migrant workers.[33] The 1981 investment law was amended in 1990, to simplify application procedures. Under the new law, investment in all sectors was to be encouraged, and tax and customs exemptions were to be given on the necessary imports. Once established, ventures would enjoy a three-year exemption from tax on income and property. Foreign investors were allowed to repatriate net annual profits made on the capital invested, but (apart from some projects of national importance) only up to the value of export earnings. Nationalization was normally excluded, but if national interest absolutely required it, then equitable compensation would be paid.[34]

The eight foreign banks formerly operating in South Yemen had been nationalized and amalgamated in the National Bank of Yemen, the only bank in the country other than the Bank of Yemen (Central Bank). However, as part of the reforms, the former shareholders began to receive repayments in early 1990.

The Yemen Republic

On the day of the merger of North and South Yemen, 22 May 1990, a statement on economic policy by the leadership laid stress on freedom of economic action and the attraction of local as well as foreign private investment. The intention was to make Aden into a free economic zone. Subsequently, it was announced that the private sector would be encouraged to invest in agriculture (the top priority productive sector), fisheries and industry. A policy statement on 16 June stated that, while the government would 'work to limit the prices of basic commodities and services', it would leave other prices to market forces.[35]

The immediate impact of the merger on southern Yemen's economy was to increase prices. Although the government tried to ensure sufficient supplies of staple foods such as rice, sugar and flour at fixed prices, many other prices increased substantially, both because of the liberal economic framework and because goods brought south from the north were sold with transport costs added. This soon caused major labour and social unrest in the south, with calls for strikes and work stoppages, and the demand (later acceded to) that the rights and wage grades acquired by southerners before unification would be maintained. In July 1990 the government standardized the price of some oil products, lowering them comparatively in the south.[36]

On the anniversary of unification, Aden was duly declared a free zone. It was hoped that this would enable the port to recapture its erstwhile glory. The ministry of industry had by then already identified about 50 industrial projects for inclusion in the zone. Some local and foreign interest had been expressed, and in July 1991 an official Yemeni delegation visited the UK for talks with British firms about investment in Aden free zone.[37] However, foreign investors were deterred by the difficulties following the Kuwait crisis which caused the return of about a million migrant workers from Saudi Arabia and Kuwait, creating a potential for social and political upheavals;[38] and also by dissension over the process of unification between northerners and southerners, modernists and conservatives. A more settled political and social situation in Yemen is necessary before the free zone's chances can be properly assessed.

The dismantling of the remnants of the marxist system in the South proceeded steadily. The minister of agriculture and water resources announced in July 1991 that 60 per cent of disputed land cases in Wadi Hadhramaut had been solved, including the return of nationalized property to over 50 landowners in Tarim and Al-Qatn. This followed the decision in March of that year to establish a committee, chaired by the prime minister, to oversee the resolution of such disputes: an official statement said that the 'mistakes' of the 1970 nationalization law would be corrected, on the basis of agreement between the original owners and the current beneficiaries of nationalization. The housing and urban planning minister had already confirmed that all those affected by the nationalization of private houses under the socialist regime would receive compensation. Also in March, those intending to build private homes in the south were told that they would be invited to meet representatives of the housing ministry in Sana'a to arrange the details and obtain allocations of land.[39]

In another move, a small enterprise support unit was opened by the Industrial Bank of Yemen in November 1990. It aimed to provide technical assistance to entrepreneurs, as well as foreign currency for the necessary imports of machinery and equipment. Some $5.1 million has been budgeted for its funding, to be drawn both from the government and from international sources.[40]

The key stone of the new liberal edifice was the publication of the new unified investment law, valid as of July 1991. The law applies to domestic as well as foreign investment, and covers the sectors of industry (except hydrocarbons and minerals extraction), agriculture and fisheries, tourism, health, training and education, transport, and construction and housing. Any other field which the Council of Ministers might accept (at the recommendation of the new General Investment Authority) can also be included subsequently. Apart from certain areas of economic activity where foreign investment may be restricted or banned at the prime minister's discretion, foreign and local capital are to have the same status. Investors can buy or rent land to establish commercial premises. The law rules out the nationalization or sequestration of private assets, the impounding of goods without due legal process, and the requisitioning of property without compensation.

The investment law provides investors with substantial tax incentives. Imports of fixed assets for an investment project are exempt from all customs duties and taxes. Profits are exempt from taxes for five years, which the Council of Ministers can extend by a maximum further ten years. In a measure aimed at spreading investment across the country, the republic's territory was divided into two zones, 'A' and 'B', for investment purposes. If the project is in zone B, it is given an immediate seven-year profit tax exemption, while in zone A it is granted a five-year exemption. A similar rule also applies to projects owned by a company at least 25 per cent of whose capital was raised by public subscription (a stipulation which the government hoped would mobilize local private capital further).

The law specifies that there will normally be no compulsory pricing for products of projects licensed under the law, provided monopolies are not created. In 'extraordinary' circumstances, the Council of Ministers may fix the price of staple foods (flour, bread, milk), baby foods and medicines. Once a licence is issued, a company can open a foreign currency account with a bank registered with the Central Bank, and net profits made as a result of foreign capital invested can be transferred abroad; provided that the company remains within the limits of the credit balance of the foreign exchange account (in accordance with specific executive regulations). The investment law is explicit in requiring investment projects to employ as many locals as possible. Expatriates can, however, be employed under a licence, in which case they will receive a renewable working permit for three years. Expatriates working in administrative and technical jobs are allowed to transfer 60 per cent of their net earnings abroad, also within the limits of the credit balance mentioned above.[41]

It is too early to say what effect the new law will have. As remarked earlier with regard to the Aden free zone, there are preconditions for any substantial success including a stabilization of the internal political situation, and the country's reintegration into the regional and international community as regards trade, aid and other benefits (which were lost in the wake of the Iraqi invasion of Kuwait). Yemen's financial situation is critical and this affects both the general economic environment and the government's ability to build up the services and basic infrastructure required by investors.

Conclusion

It is clear that the impetus for economic liberalization in Oman and the two Yemens has varied, although the three cases do exhibit some common features. The divergence must be sought, in part, in the pre-existing background: not merely in the decade or so preceding current reforms, but in the more distant past and in the nature of the state. Oman is characterized by a long tradition of small-scale private enterprise. Traditional manufacture, agriculture and fisheries have retained their vitality while, at the same time, the nature of the Omani rentier state and 'circulation economy' since the 1970s has implied prominent government involvement in the development process. In North Yemen, the present status of private enterprise has its roots also in the centuries-old tradition of private economic activity in agriculture, manufacturing and trade. In what used to be South Yemen, a somewhat less vibrant and more 'patchy' traditional economy (significant elements of which nevertheless survived and continued to influence developments) was suppressed by the Arab world's only avowedly Marxist–Leninist framework (this helps to explain both the difficulties encountered and the eventual reaction).

There were also more immediate factors which helped to induce the present mood of liberalization. In the case of South Yemen, these were the country's economic collapse and the evident failure of the existing political and economic system (now deprived of Soviet support). In North Yemen, debt, and the need and/or willingness to satisfy the IMF and the international banking and donor community on their conditions for more aid or debt reduction, form the major explanatory factor. In Oman, the role of pro-market expatriate advisers appears to have been important; but so was the Sultan's own committment to economic diversification, an aim towards which the encouragement of private investors could contribute.

In each of these countries, the hydrocarbons factor was important as an instance of, or a stimulus for, private sector activity and economic opening-up even though, paradoxically, it also ends up reinforcing the role of the state. Another key shared motivation for the liberalization/ privatization measures encountered, has been the need and/or intention to tap the available domestic liquidity, in order to channel it into productive directions rather than hoarding or consumption.

In the all-important field of foreign investment, the results of the economic liberalization have been mixed. Oman's record in this respect has been strongest, because of the country's perceived stable environment and good services. In contrast, the explicit efforts by the Adeni government, and subsequently the Yemeni Republic, to present their country as a favourable option for foreign investors has met with a patchy response at best, the hydrocarbon sector apart. This is due, firstly, to the perceived lack of social, political, and institutional stability, and secondly, to a deficient 'investment climate' in terms of available skills, services, communications, and infrastructure.

As regards the linkage between economic and political liberalization, the difference in the experiences of Oman and the Yemen(s) is instructive. The hypothesis that economic liberalization measures, by imposing economic hardship on large sections of the population, create a potential for social unrest and political upheaval which governments may need to defuse or preempt by liberalizing politically, seems to have been borne out by events in Yemen. In Oman, however, the state's resources have allowed the government to avoid creating economic hardship, in turn obviating (at least in the short term) the need for more than small adjustments to the mechanisms of political participation.

Notes

1 *The Middle East*, April 1989, p.8.
2 Sultanate of Oman, Development Council (1987), *The Third Five-Year Development Plan, 1986–1990*, p. 65.
3 Sultanate of Oman, Development Council (1991), *The Fourth Five-Year Development Plan, 1991–1995*.
4 *Ibid.*
5 Sultanate of Oman, Development Council, *The Fourth Five-Year Development Plan, 1991–1995*; see also *MEED*, 19/7/91.
6 *MEED*, 'Oman: a MEED sponsored report', December 1989.

7 Economist Intelligence Unit, (1989), *Bahrain, Qatar, Oman, the Yemens: Country Report*, No 1, p. 30.
8 Economist Intelligence Unit, (1989), *Bahrain, Qatar, Oman, the Yemens: Country Report*, No 3, p. 35.
9 *MEED*,23/8/91.
10 Economist Intelligence Unit, (1988), *Bahrain, Qatar, Oman, the Yemens: Country Report*, No 3, p. 23.
11 See for instance *MEED*, 1/3/91.
12 Ministry of Commerce and Industry, Ministerial Decree 33/90.
13 *MEED*, 22/3/91, and 31/5/91.
14 Economist Intelligence Unit, (1989), *Bahrain, Qatar, Oman, the Yemens: Country Report*, No 2, pp. 23–24; and Economist Intelligence Unit, (1989), *Bahrain, Qatar, Oman, the Yemens: Country Report*, No 3 p. 32.
15 *Times of Oman*, 7/9/89.
16 Economist Intelligence Unit, (1991), *Oman, Yemen: Country Profile, 1990–91*, p. 42.
17 US Embassy, Sana'a, 'Foreign Economic Trends Report', 15/6/88.
18 Business International, (1988), *Critical Issues for the American Investor in the Yemen Arab Republic*, Geneva; and UNIDO, (1989), *Yemen Arab Republic: Diversifying the Industrial Base*, Industrial Development Review Series.
19 United States Embassy, Sana'a, 'Yemen Arab Republic: Investment Climate Statement, March 1988'; Economist Intelligence Unit, (1989), *Bahrain, Qatar, Oman, the Yemens: Country Report*, No 1, p. 3; and Paul Barker Associates, (1988), 'Yemen Bank Study', Section II, (mimeographed).
20 US Embassy, Sana'a, 'Foreign Economic Trends Report', 15/6/88; and Economist Intelligence Unit, (1990), *Bahrain, Qatar, Oman, the Yemens: Country Report*, No. 2, p. 45.
21 UNIDO, (1989), *Yemen Arab Republic: Diversifying the Industrial Base*, Industrial Development Review Series, p. 5.
22 Economist Intelligence Unit, (1990), *Bahrain, Qatar, Oman, the Yemens: Country Report*, No. 2, p. 45.
23 Economist Intelligence Unit, (1990), *Oman, Yemen: Country Profile 1990–91* pp. 49, 54; and (1990), *Bahrain, Qatar, Oman, the Yemens: Country Report*, No 2, pp. 44–45.
24 Paul Barker Associates, (1988), 'Yemen bank study', Section II.
25 *Al-Thawri*, 30/7/89.
26 The Amnesty International 1991 report; see *MEED*, 19/7/91.
27 *The Middle East*, January 1990, p. 21; and Economist Intelligence Unit, (1990), *Bahrain, Qatar, Oman, the Yemens: Country Report*, No 2, p. 51; see also the *Country Representation: Republic of Yemen, 1990*, for the Second United Nations Conference on the Least Developed Countries (UNCLDC II/CP.18), Geneva: UNCTAD, where the section by South Yemen – prepared before unification – is curiously split into a main body along traditional socialist planning lines, and a section tacked on at the end introducing a total turn-around on issues of private enterprise and investment.
28 FAO, *Production Yearbook*, several issues.

29 PDRY Central Statistical Office, *Statistical Yearbook*, 1988.
30 Economist Intelligence Unit, (1989), *Bahrain, Qatar, Oman, the Yemens: Country Report*, No 3, p. 43; and No. 4, p. 42.
31 People's Democratic Republic of Yemen, *Kitab al-Ihsa'i al-Sanawi li-'Am 1988*; see also UNIDO, (1989), *People's Democratic Republic of Yemen: Enhancing industrial productive capacity* (Industrial Development Review Series), Geneva: UNIDO, pp. 26, 28.
32 UNIDO, (1989), *People's Democratic Republic of Yemen*, pp. 9, 63–67.
33 *Al-Majalla*, 4/1/89, pp. 36–37; *The Middle East*, April 1989; *South*, December 1989; Economist Intelligence Unit, (1988) *Bahrain, Qatar, Oman, the Yemens: Country Report*, No 4, p. 42; and (1989), No. 2, pp. 40–41.
34 *MEED*, 23/2/90; 23/3/90; Economist Intelligence Unit, (1990), *Bahrain, Qatar, Oman, the Yemens: Country Report*, No 2, P. 53.
35 Economist Intelligence Unit, (1990) *Bahrain, Qatar, Oman, the Yemens: Country Report*, No 3, p. 39.
36 Economist Intelligence Unit, (1990) *Bahrain, Qatar, Oman, the Yemens: Country Report*, No 4, p. 41.
37 See *MEED*, 30/8/91, quoting statements by Vice-President Ali Salim Al-Baidh; also *MEED*, 26/4/91; 12/7/91.
38 *MEED*, 3/5/91.
39 *MEED*, 29/3/91; 5/4/91; 9/8/91.
40 Economist Intelligence Unit, (1991), *Oman, Yemen: Country Report*, No. 1, p. 25.
41 *MEED*, 26/7/91.

BIBLIOGRAPHY

The bibliography contains all the books, articles and reports mentioned in the text, together with a selection of some of the most important writings on economic liberalization in the developing world and the Middle East (whether mentioned in the text or not). The bibliography is divided into the following sections:

General works

Liberalization theory/experience in general: books and reports

Liberalization theory/experience in general: articles and chapters

Developing countries generally: books and reports

Developing countries generally: articles and papers

The Middle East: books and reports

The Middle East: articles, papers and theses

General works

Anderson, P. 1974. *Passages from Antiquity to Feudalism*, London: New Left Books.

Aristotle, 1932. *The Politics*. London: Heinemann.

Diodorus Siculus, 1933. *Library of History*, 10 vols. C. H. Oldfather trans. Loeb. edn. London: Heinemann.

Drucker, P. 1979. The first technological revolution and its lessons. In Burke, J. and Marshall, C. (eds), *Technology and Change*. San Francisco, Ca.: Boyd and Fraser.

Eatwell, J., Milgate, M. and Newman, P. (eds) 1987. *The New Palgrave Dictionary of Economics*, London: Macmillan.

Marx, K. 1973. *Grundrisse*, Martin Nicolaus, trans. Harmondsworth: Penguin.

Marx, K. 1974. *The Ethnological Notebooks*, Lawrence Krader (ed). Assen: Van Gorcum.

Morgan, L. H. 1877. *Ancient Society, or Researches into the Lives of Human Progress from Savagery through Barbarism to Civilisation*. Chicago: Charles H. Kerr and Co.

Rumaihi, M. 1986. *Beyond Oil*. London: Al Saqi Books.

Schumpeter, J. 1942. *Capitalism, Socialism and Democracy*. New York: Harper and Brothers.

Springborg, P. 1990. *Royal Persons: Patriarchal Monarchy and the Feminine Principle*. London: Unwin Hyman.

Springborg, P. 1992. *Western Republicanism and the Oriental Prince*. Cambridge: Polity.

Weber, M. 1962. *The Protestant Ethic and the Spirit of Capitalism*. London: Allen and Unwin.

Liberalization theory/experience in general: books and reports

Baumol, W. J., Panzar, J. and Willig, R. D. 1982. *Contestable Markets and the Theory of Industry Structure*. New York: Harcourt Brace Jovanovich.

Burnham, J. 1941. *The Managerial Revolution: What is Happening in the World*. New York: John Day.

Hanke, S. H. 1987. *Prospects for Privatisation*. Washington D.C.: Academy of Political Science.

Hara, Y. 1991. An historical analysis of the structure of the Japanese-style market economy. (In Japanese.) In *Keizai Kenkyu*, Vol. 42, No. 2.

Hemming, R. and Mansoor, A. M. 1988. *Privatisation and Public Enterprise*. Occasional Paper 56, Washington D.C.: International Monetary Fund.

Institute of Economic Affairs. 1978. *The Economics of Politics*. London: Institute of Economic Affairs.

International Energy Association. 1985. *Electricity in IEA Countries*. Paris: International Energy Association.

International Monetary Fund. 1986. *Fund-Supported Programs, Fiscal Policy and Income Distribution*. Fiscal Affairs Department Occasional Paper 46, Washington D.C.: International Monetary Fund.

Johnson, C. 1988. *Privatisation and Ownership*. London: Pinter.

O'Donnell, G., Schmitter, P. and Whitehead, L. 1986. *Transitions from Authoritarian Rule, Prospects for Democracy*. Baltimore, Md: Johns Hopkins University.

Peacock, A. 1979. *The Economic Analysis of Government and Related Themes*. Oxford: Martin Robertson.

Pirie, M. 1985. *Dismantling the State: The Theory and Practice of Privatisation*. Dallas, Tex.: National Center for Policy Analysis.

Ramanadham, V. V. (ed.) 1989. *Privatisation in Developing Countries*. London: Routledge.

Swann, D. 1988. *The Retreat of the State*. New York: Harvester-Wheatsheaf.

Veljanovski, C. (ed.) 1989. *Privatisation and Competition*. IEA Hobart Paperback 28.

Vickers, J. and Yarrow, G. 1988. *Privatisation – An Economic Analysis*. Cambridge, Mass: MIT Press.

Liberalization theory/experience in general: articles and chapters

Beesely, M. and Littlechild, S. 1983. Privatisation: principles, problems and priorities. *Lloyds Bank Review*, July.

Brittan, S. 1986. Privatisation: a comment on Kay and Thompson. In *Economic Journal*, Vol. 96, No. 381, March.

Dahrendorf, R. 1987. Liberalism. In *The New Palgrave Dictionary of Economics*. London: Macmillan Press Ltd.

Haggard, S. and Kaufman, R. 1989. The politics of stabilisation and structural adjustment. In Sachs, J. D. (ed.), *Developing Country Debt and Economic Performance Volume One: The International Financial System*. Chicago, Ill.: University of Chicago Press.

Haile-Mariam, Y. and Mengistu, B. 1988. Public enterprises and the privatisation thesis in the third world. In *Third World Quarterly*, Vol. 10, No. 4.

Handoussa, H. 1987. Privatisation: throwing the baby out with the bathwater. In *Business Monthly – Journal of the American Chamber of Commerce in Egypt*. Vol. 3, No. 11, December.

Heilbroner, R. 1987. Capitalism. In Eatwell, Milgate and Newman (eds).

Hemming, R. and Mansoor, A. M. 1988. *Privatisation and Public Enterprise*. Occasional Paper 56, International Monetary Fund, Washington D.C.

Kay, J. A. and Thompson, D. J. 1986. Privatisation: a policy in search of a rationale. In *Economic Journal*, No. 96, pp. 18–32.

Klein, R. 1984. Privatisation and the Welfare State. In *Lloyds Bank Review*, January.

Littlechild, S., Price, C., Robinson, C. and Sykes, A. 1988. *Energy Privatisation*. Surrey Energy Economics Discussion Paper, No. 39, June. Guildford: Surrey Energy Economics Centre.

McConnell and Muscarella 1985. Corporate capital expenditure decisions and the market value of the firm. In *Journal of Financial Economics*, September.

Odaka, T. 1988. *Analysis of Labour Markets*. (In Japanese.) Tokyo: Iwanami.

Penrose, E. 1990. 'Dumping', 'unfair' competition and multinational corporations. *Japan and the World Economy*, No. 2.

Tullock, G. 1987. Rent-seeking. In Eatwell, Milgate and Newman (eds).

Developing countries generally: books and reports

Andersson, T. 1991. *Multinational Investment in Developing Countries*. London: Routledge.

Asian Development Bank, 1985. *Privatisation: Policies, Methods and Procedures*. Manila: Asian Development Bank.

Balassa, B. and MacCarty, D. 1983. *Adjustment Policies in Developing Countries*, Washington, D.C.: The World Bank.

Berg, E. 1982. *Changing the Public–Private Mix: a Survey of Some Recent Experience in LDCs*, DM/83/10. Washington, D.C.: International Monetary Fund.

Berg, E. and Shirley, M. 1987. *Divestitures in Developing Countries*, Washington, D.C.: The World Bank.

Bird, R. M. and Oldman, O. 1975. *Readings on Taxation in Developing Countries*, 3rd edn. Baltimore: Johns Hopkins Press.

Candoy-Sekse, R. 1989. *Techniques of Privatisation of State-Owned Enter-*

prises: Inventory of Country Experience and Reference Materials. Washington, D.C.: The World Bank.

Chokski, A. M. and Papageorgiu, D. (eds) (1986). *Economic Liberalisation in Developing Countries.* Oxford: Basil Blackwell.

Cook, P. and Kirkpatrick, C. (eds) 1988. *Privatisation in Less Developed Countries.* London: Harvester Wheatsheaf.

Diamond, L., Linz, J. J. and Lipsett, S. M. 1989. *Democracy in Developing Countries: Asia.* Boulder, Colo.: Lynne Reiner.

Eshag, E. 1983. *Fiscal and Monetary Policies and Problems in Developing Countries.* Cambridge: Cambridge University Press.

Glade, W. (ed.) 1986. *State Shrinkage: Comparative Inquiry into Privatisation,* Austin, Tex.: University of Texas Press.

Hanke, S. (ed.) 1987. *Privatisation and Development.* San Francisco, Calif.: Institute for Contemporary Studies.

International Monetary Fund 1986. *Fund-Supported Programs, Fiscal Policy and Income Distribution.* Occasional Paper 46, Washington, D.C.: IMF.

Killick, T. 1984. *The Quest for Economic Stabilisation, the IMF and the Third World.* Aldershot: Gower.

Latin America Bureau 1983. *The Poverty Brokers: the IMF and Latin America.* London: Latin America Bureau.

McVey, R. (ed.) 1992, *Southeast Asian Capitalists,* New York: Cornell University Press.

Nankani, H. 1988. *Techniques of Privatisation of State-Owned Enterprises: Selected Country Studies.* Washington, D.C. The World Bank.

Newbery, D. and Stern, S. 1987. *The Theory of Taxation for Developing Countries.* Oxford: Oxford University Press (for the World Bank).

Overseas Development Institute 1986. *Privatisation: the developing country experience.* Briefing Paper, London: Overseas Development Institute.

Overseas Development Institute 1988. *The Rich and the Poor: Changes in the Incomes of Developing Countries since 1960.* Briefing Paper, London: Overseas Development Institute.

Ramanadham, V. V. (ed.) 1989. *Privatisation in Developing Countries.* London: Routledge.

Roth, G. 1987. *The Private Provision of Public Services in Developing Countries.* Washington, D.C.: The World Bank.

Teplitz-Sembitzky, W. 1990. *Regulation, Deregulation, or Regulation – What is Needed in the LDC Power Sector?* Washington D.C.: Industry and Energy Department, World Bank.

Trimberger, E. 1978. *Revolutions from Above: Military Bureaucrats and Development in Japan, Turkey, Egypt and Peru.* New Brunswick.

UN Centre on Transnational Corporations (1990). *The New Code Environment,* UNCTC Current studies, Series A, No. 16. New York: United Nations.

World Bank 1985. *Ghana: Towards Structural Adjustment.* Vol. 1, Washington, D.C.: The World Bank.

World Bank 1986. *Financing Adjustment with Growth in Sub-Saharan Africa,* Washington, D.C.: The World Bank.

World Bank 1990. *World Development Report 1990*. Washington, D.C.: The World Bank.

World Bank 1991. *World Development Report 1991*. Oxford: Oxford University Press.

Developing countries generally: articles and papers

Addison, T. and Demery, L. 1986. Liberalisation strategies and income distribution in developing countries. Mimeo, London: Overseas Development Institute.

Aylen, J. 1987. Privatisation in developing countries. *Lloyds Bank Review*, No. 63, pp. 15–30.

Aylem, M. 1988. Privatisation in developing countries. In Johnson, C. (ed.) , *Privatisation and Ownership*, London: Pinter.

Babai, D. 1988. The World Bank and the IMF: rolling back the state or backing its role. In Vernon, R. (ed.), *The Promise of Privatisation: a Challenge for US Policy*. New York: Council on Foreign Relations.

Bedrani, S. 1989. Les enjeux actuels des restructurations dans l'agriculture. In *Economie et Humanisme*, No. 309, pp. 23–9.

Cassen, R. 1991. Policy reform and conditionality. *Development Research Insights*, Spring, pp. 1–2.

Colclough, C. and Green, R. 1988. Do stabilisation policies stabilise?. *IDS Bulletin*, Vol. 19, No. 1.

Diniz, E. 1986. The political transition in Brazil: a reappraisal of the dynamics of the political opening. *Comparative International Development*, No. 21, pp. 63– 73.

Dooley, M. and Mathieson, D. 1987. Financial liberalisation and stability in developing countries. IMF Working Paper, WP/97/19, Washington, D.C.: International Monetary Fund.

Edwards, S. 1987. Sequencing economic liberalisation in developing countries. *Finance and Development* , Vol. 24, No. 1, pp. 26–30.

Haile-Mariam, Y. and Mengistu, B. 1988. Public enterprises and the privatisation thesis in the third world. *Third World Quarterly*. No. 4, pp. 1565–87.

Harris, N. 1988. New bourgeoisies?. *Journal of Development Studies*, Vol. 2, No. 2, pp.237–49.

Killick, T. 1981. Twenty-five years in development: the rise and impending decline in market solutions. *Development Policy Review*, Vol. 4, No. 2, pp. 49–116.

Killick, T. and Commander, S. 1988. State divestitures as a policy instrument in developing countries. *World Development*, Vol. 16, No. 2, pp. 1465–79.

Lal, D. 1987. The political economy of economic liberalisation. *The World Bank Economic Review*, Vol. 1, No. 2, pp. 273–99.

Latham-Koenig, A. 1989. Privatisation in developing countries. Butler, E. and Pirie, M. (eds), *The Manual on Privatisation*, London: Adam Smith Institute, pp. 144–7.

Nankani, H. 1990. Lessons of privatisation in developing countries. *Finance and Development*, March 1990, pp. 43–5.

Nelson, J. 1984. The political economy of stabilisation: commitment, capacity and public response. *World Development*. Vol. 12, no. 10, pp. 983–1006.

Toye, J. 1986. Promoting the private sector: should the World Bank do more or less? *Recovery in the Developing World*, Washington, D.C.: The World Bank.

Walton, J. and Ragin, C. 1990. Global and national sources of political protest: third world responses to the debt crisis. *American Sociological Review* V, Vol. 55, No. 6.

Winpenny, J. 1984. The divestiture of public enterprises in developing countries. *Development Policy Review*, No. 5, pp. 399–406.

The Middle East: books and reports

Abdel-Khalek, G. and Ignor, R. (eds) 1982. *The Political Economy of Income Distribution in Egypt*. New York: Holmes and Meier.

Algar, H. 1980. *Constitution of the Islamic Republic of Iran*. Berkeley: Mizan Press.

Amirahmadi, H. 1990. *Revolution and Economic Transition: The Iranian Experience*. New York: State University of New York.

Amuzegar, J. 1977. *Iran: An Economic Profile*. Washington D.C.: The Middle East Institute.

Arudki, Y. 1972. *al-Iqtisad al-Suri al-Hadith* (The Modern Syrian Economy). Vol. 1, Damascus.

Asad, T. and Owen R. (eds) 1983. *Sociology of Developing Societies – The Middle East*. London: Macmillan.

Atiqpour, M. 1979. *Naqsh Bazar va Bazariha dar Enqelab Iran* (The Role of the Bazaar and Bazaaris in the Iranian Revolution). Tehran: Naqsh-e Jahan Press.

Badr, H. 1983. *Joint Prospects and Gulf Cooperation: Performance and Prospects*. Qatar: GOIC. Undated but based upon a paper presented at the International Seminar on Economic Outlook for the Middle East, Athens, Greece in April 1983.

Baillet, J. 1912, 1913. *Le Regime Pharaonique dans ses Rapports avec l'Evolution de la Morale en Egypte*, 2 vols. Paris: Blois.

Beblawi, H. and Luciani, G. (eds) 1987. *The Rentier State*. London: Croom Helm.

Bermant, C. and Weitzman, M. 1979. *Ebla*. London: Weidenfeld and Nicolson.

Boratav, K. 1987. *Turkey: Stabilisation and Adjustment Policies and Programmes*. Helsinki: World Institute for Development Economics, United Nations University.

Bowman, A. K. 1971. *The Town Councils of Roman Egypt*. Toronto: A. M. Hakkert.

Brown, R. 1990. *Sudan's Debt Crisis: the Interplay between International and Domestic Responses, 1978–88*, The Hague: Institute of Social Studies.

Brumberg, D. 1989. *Democratic Bargains and the Politics of Economic Stabilisation: The Case of Egypt in Comparative Perspective*. Paper delivered to the annual conference of the Middle East Studies Association, Toronto.

Business International 1988. *Critical Issues for the American Investor in the Yemen Arab Republic*. Geneva.

Central Bank of Algeria 1982. *Code des Investissements*. Algiers: Central Bank.

Clawson, P. 1989. *Unaffordable Ambitions: Syria's Military Buildup and Economic Crisis*. Washington D.C.: The Washington Institute for Near East Policy.

Commander, S. 1987. *The State and Agricultural Development in Egypt since 1973*. London: Ithaca Press.

Cooper, M. 1982. *The Transformation of Egypt*. London: Croom Helm.

Cumont, F. 1956. *The Oriental Religions in Roman Paganism*. New York: Dover.

Daines, V. and Seddon, D. 1991. *Survival Struggles, Protest and Resistance: Women's Responses to 'Austerity' and 'Structural Adjustment'*. Gender Analysis in Development Studies, University of East Anglia.

Diakonoff, I. 1974. *Structure of Society and State in Early Dynastic Sumer*. Los Angeles: Undena Press.

Driver, G. R. and Miles, J. C., (eds) 1952, 1955. *The Babylonian Laws*. Oxford: Clarendon Press.

Drysdale, A. and Hinnebusch, R. 1991. *Syria and the Middle East Peace Process*. New York: Council on Foreign Relations.

Ehteshami, A. 1987. *Succession Within and Without the Context of the Islamic Republic of Iran*. Paper presented at the BRISMES Annual Conference, University of Exeter, 12–14 July.

Ehteshami, A. 1990. *Political Upheaval and Socio-economic Continuity: The Case of Iran*. RUSEL Working Paper No. 6. Exeter: University of Exeter.

Ehteshami, A. and Nonneman, G. 1991. *War and Peace in the Gulf: Domestic Politics and Regional Relations into the 1990s*. Reading: Ithaca.

El-Naggar, S. 1987. *Adjustment Policies and Development Strategies in the Arab World*. Washington, D.C.: International Monetary Fund.

El-Naggar, S. (ed.) 1990. *Investment Policies in the Arab Countries*. Washington, D.C.: International Monetary Fund.

El-Naggar, S. 1989. *Privatisation and Structural Adjustment in the Arab Countries*. Washington, D.C.: International Monetary Fund.

Goitein, S. 1967, 1978, 1981, 1983. *A Mediterranean Society: The Jewish Communities of the Arab World as Portrayed in the Documents of the Cairo Geniza*, 4 vols. Berkeley, Calif.: University of California Press.

Griffiths, J. 1960. *The Conflict of Horus and Seth: From Egyptian and Classical Sources*. Liverpool: Liverpool University Press.

Handoussa, H. 1990a. *The Burden of Public Service Employment and Remuneration: A Case Study of Egypt*. Monograph commissioned by the International Labour office. Geneva: ILO.

Hansen, B. 1988. *The Political Economy of Poverty, Equity and Growth: Egypt and Turkey*. Berkeley, Calif.: unpublished ms.

Herodotus 1972. *The Histories* (Aubrey de Selincourt, trans., revised with notes by A. R. Burn). Harmondsworth: Penguin.

Hershlag, Z.Y. 1968. *Turkey: The Challenge of Growth*. Leiden: E. Brill.

Hilan, R. 1969. *Culture et Developpement en Syrie et dans les pays retardes*. Paris: Editions Anthropos.

Hilan, R. 1973. *Suriya bayna al-Takhalluf wa al-Tanmiya* (Syria between backwardness and development). Damascus: Hilan.

Hinnebusch, R. 1989. *Peasant and Bureaucracy in Ba'thist Syria: The Political Economy of Rural Development*. Boulder, Colo.: Westview Press, pp. 31–60.

Hinnebusch, R. 1990. *Authoritarian Power and State Formation in Ba'thist Syria: Army, Party and Peasant*. Boulder, Colo.: Westview Press.

Hopkins, N. 1987. *Agrarian Transformation in Egypt*. Boulder, Colo.: Westview Press.

Ibn Khaldun 1958. *The Muqaddimah: An Introduction to History* (trans. from the Arabic by Rosenthal, F.). London: Routledge and Kegan Paul.

IBRD (International Bank for Reconstruction and Development) 1955. *The Economic Development of Syria*. Baltimore, Md: Johns Hopkins University Press.

Iran Shows the Way. 1976, leaflet, Tehran, NP.

Islamic Republic of Iran: 1980. *Constitution of the Islamic Republic of Iran* (Translated by Hamid Algar). Berkeley, CA.: Mizan Press.

Jabbur, G. 1987. *al-Fikr al-siyasi al-mu'asir fi Suriya* (Contemporary Political Thought in Syria). London: Riad al-Rayyes.

Jacobsen, T. 1976. *The Treasures of Darkness: A History of Mesopotamian Religion*. New Haven, Conn.: Yale University Press.

Keneko, N. 1990. *The Network of Islamicity*. Tokyo: Institute of Middle Eastern Studies.

Kerr, M. and Yassin, E. S. (eds) 1982. *Rich and Poor states in the Middle East*. Boulder, Colo.: Westview Press.

Kramer, S. N. 1963. *The Sumerians*. Chicago, Ill.: University of Chicago Press.

Kuroda, T. 1988. *Islamic Economy* (in Japanese). Tokyo: Sansusha.

Looney, R. 1973. *The Economic Development of Iran – A Recent Survey with projections to 1981*. New York: Praeger Pubs.

Mabro, R. 1974. *The Egyptian Economy: 1952–1972*. Oxford: Oxford University Press.

McLachlan, K. S. 1990. *Kuwait in the 1990s: A Society Under Siege*. Economist Intelligence Unit Special Report, No. 2035.

Maine, H. 1861. *Ancient Law*. London: Routledge.

Mann, M. 1986. *The Sources of Social Power*. Vol. 1, *A History of Power from the Beginning to A.D. 1760*. Cambridge: Cambridge University Press.

Masters, B. 1988. *The Origins of Western Economic Dominance in the Middle East: Mercantilism and the Islamic Economy in Aleppo, 1600–1750*. New York: New York University Press.

Mathias, G. and Salama, P. 1983. *L'Etat Surdeveloppe: Des Metropoles au Tiers Monde*. Paris: Maspero.

Matthiae, P. 1980. *Elba: an Empire Rediscovered*. London: Hodder and Stoughton.

Moore, C. H. 1980. *Images of Development: Egyptian Engineers in Search of Industry*. Cambridge, Mass.: MIT Press.

Morony, M. G. 1984. *Iraq after the Muslim Conquest*. Princeton, NJ: Princeton University Press.

Nas, T. and Odekon, M. (eds) 1988. *Liberalisation and the Turkish Economy.* New York.

O'Brien, P. K. 1966. *The Revolution in Egypt's Economic System.* Oxford: Oxford University Press.

Paul Barker Associates 1988. *Yemen Bank Study.* Section II, Mimeo.

People's Democratic Republic of Yemen 1988. *Statistical Yearbook.* Central Statistical Office.

People's Democratic Republic of Yemen 1988. *Kitab al-ihsa'i al-sanawi li'am 1988.*

Republic of Tunisia (1990). *Recent Experience in Structural Adjustment and Main Economic Indicators.* Tunis: Government Printing Press.

Republic of Yemen 1990. *Country Representation: Republic of Yemen.* United Nations Conference on the Least Developed Countries (UNCLD) CII/CP.18, Geneva.

Richards, A. and Waterbury, J. 1990. *A Political Economy of the Middle East: State, Class and Economic Development.* Boulder, Colo.: Westview.

Roe, A., Roy, J. and Sengupta, J. 1989. *Economic Adjustment in Algeria, Egypt, Jordan, Morocco, Pakistan, Tunisia and Turkey.* EDI Policy Report No. 15, Washington, D.C.: World Bank.

Rostovtzeff, M. 1932. *Caravan Cities.* Oxford: Clarendon Press.

Seale, P. 1988. *Asad: The Struggle for the Middle East.* London: I.B. Tauris. Berkeley, Calif.: University of California Press.

Senses, F. and Yamada, T. 1990. *Stabilisation and Structural Adjustment Program in Turkey.* Tokyo: Institute of Developing Economies.

Springborg, R. 1982. *Family, Power and Politics in Egypt: Sayed Bey Marei – his Clan, Clients and Cohorts.* Philadelphia, Pa: University of Pennsylvania Press.

Springborg, R. 1989. *Mubarak's Egypt: Fragmentation of the Political Order.* Boulder, Colo.: Westview.

Sultanate of Oman, Development Council 1986. *The Third Five-Year Development Plan, 1986–90.*

Sultanate of Oman, Development Council 1991. *The Fourth Five-Year Development Plan, 1991–95.*

Syrian Arab Republic 1984. *Statistical Abstract, 1984.* Damascus: Central Bureau of Statistics.

Syrian Arab Republic 1989. *Statistical Abstract, 1989.* Damascus: Central Bureau of Statistics.

Tarabayn, A. 1986. *Ta'ir al-Mashriq al-Arabi al-Mu'asir.* Damascus: University of Damascus.

UNIDO 1989. *Yemen Arab Republic: Diversifying the Industrial Base.* Industrial Development Review Series, Geneva.

UNIDO 1989. *People's Democratic Republic of Yemen: Enhancing Industrial Productive Capacity.* Industrial Development Review Series, Geneva.

United States Embassy, Sana'a 1988. *Foreign Economic Trends Report.*

United States Embassy, Sana'a 1988. *Yemen Arab Republic: Investment Climate Statement.*

Walton, J. and Seddon, D. 1992. *Free Markets and Food Riots: The Politics of Global Adjustment.* Oxford: Blackwell.

Waterbury, J. 1983. *The Egypt of Nasser and Sadat: the Political Economy of Two Regimes*. Princeton, NJ: Princeton University Press.

Weinbaum, M. 1982. *Food, Development and Politics in the Middle East*. Boulder, Colo.: Westview Press.

Wolf, P. 1987. *Stabilisation Policy and Structural Adjustment in Turkey: the Role of the IMF and the World Bank in an Externally-Supported Adjustment Process*. Berlin: German Development Institute.

World Bank 1980. *Syrian Arab Republic Development Prospects and Politics*, 4 vols. Washington, D.C.

World Bank 1988. *World Development Report*. Washington, D.C.

World Bank 1990. *World Development Report*. Washington, D.C.

Zaalouk, M. 1989. *Power, Class and Foreign Capital in Egypt: the Rise of the New Bourgeoisie*. London: Zed Books.

Zartman, I. W. 1990. *Tunisia: the Political Economy of Reform*. London: Lynne Rienner Publishers.

Ziadeh, N. 1970. *Urban Life in Syria Under the Early Mamluks*. Westport, CT.: Greenwood Press.

The Middle East: articles, papers and theses

Abdel-Khalek, G. 1981. Looking outside or turning northwest? On the meaning and external dimension of Egypt's infitah, 1971–80. *Social Problems*. Vol. 28, No. 4, pp. 394–409.

Abdel-Khalek, G. 1982. The open door economic policy in Egypt: its contribution to investment and its equity implications. In Kerr, M. H. and Yassin, E. S. (eds), *Rich and Poor States in the Middle East: Egypt and the New Arab Order*, pp. 259–84. Boulder, Colo.: Westview Press.

Abdel-Rahman, I. and Abu Ali, M. 1989. Role of the public and private sectors with special reference to privatisation: the case of Egypt. In El-Naggar, S. (1989).

Ajami, F. 1982. The open door economy: its roots and welfare consequences. In Abdel-Khalek, G. and Tignor, R. (eds), *The Political Economy of Income Distribution in Egypt*. pp. 469–516. New York: Holmes and Meier.

Al-Hindi, W. 1987. Re-centralisation, exemption and privatisation of state-owned enterprises in Saudi Arabia. Unpublished PhD thesis, Florida State University.

Al-Mu'allimi, A. 1988. 'Afaq al-Tuhawwal ila al-Qita' al-Khas fi al-Mamlakah al-arabiah al-Su'udiyah (Horizons of transfer to the private sector in the kingdom of Saudi Arabia). Paper delivered to the Conference on the Private Sector's Role in Development, Riyadh, 20/12/88.

Al-Nafaieh, D. 1990. Privatisation for development: an analysis of potential private sector participation in Saudi Arabia. Unpublished PhD thesis, University of Pittsburgh.

Amin, G. 1982. External factors in the reorientation of Egypt's economic policy. In Kerr, M. H. and Yassin, E. S. (eds), *Rich and Poor States in the Middle East: Egypt and the New Arab Order*, pp. 285–315. Boulder, Colorado: Westview Press.

Amin, G. 1987. Adjustment and development: the case of Egypt. In El-Naggar (1987), pp. 92–116.

Amin, G. A. 1983. Economic and Cultural Dependence. In Asad T. and Owen R. (eds). *The Middle East*. London: Macmillan.

Anani, J. 1987. Adjustment and development: the case of Jordan. In El-Naggar (1987), pp. 124–48.

Anani, J. and Khalaf, R. 1989. Privatisation in Jordan. In El-Naggar (1989), pp. 210–225.

Anderson, L. 1987. The state in the Middle East and North Africa. *Comparative Politics*, No. 20, pp. 1–18.

Anderson, L. 1991. Political pacts, liberalism and democracy: the Tunisian National Pact of 1988. In *Government and Opposition*, Vol. 26, No. 2.

Anthes, R. 1954. Note concerning the great corporation of Heliopolis. In *Journal of Near Eastern Studies*, No. 13, pp. 191–2.

Arab British Chamber of Commerce 1989. General article on privatization, year 12, No. 2, April.

Ashraf, A. and Banuazizi, A. 1985. The state, cases and modes of mobilisation in the Iranian revolution. *State, Culture and Society*, Vol. 1, No. 3, pp. 3–30.

Ayallon, A. and Shahed, H. (eds) 1988. Israel. In *Contemporary Middle East Survey*, Westview Press, Vol. 12, p. 570.

Ayubi, N. 1982. Implementation capability and political feasibility of the open door policy in Egypt. In Kerr, M. H. and Yassin, E. S. (eds), *Rich and Poor States in the Middle East: Egypt and the New Arab Order*. Boulder, Colo.: Westview Press.

Ayubi, N. 1990. 'Etatism versus privatisation: the case of the public sector in Egypt. *International Review of Administrative Sciences*, Vol. 56, pp. 89–103.

Badr, H. 1983. Joint projects and Gulf cooperation: performance and prospects. Qatar: GOIC. Undated but based upon a paper presented at the International Seminar on Economic Outlook for the Middle East, Athens, Greece, April.

Bietak, M. 1979. Urban archaeology and the 'town' problem. In Weeks, K. (ed.), *Egyptology and the Social Sciences*. Cairo: American University in Cairo Press.

Bouaouaja, M. 1989. Privatisation in Tunisia: objectives and limits. In El-Naggar (1989), pp. 234–46.

Brown, R. 1987. The rationale and the effects of the IMF stabilisation programme in Sudan. In Campbell, B. (ed.), *Political Dimensions of Third World Debt*, pp. 51–91. London: Macmillan.

Burgat, F. and Leca, J. 1990. La mobilisation islamiste et les elections algeriennes du 12 Juin 1990. In *Maghreb-Machrek*, No. 129.

Chaudhry, K. 1990. The price of wealth: business and state in labor remittance and oil economies. Unpublished PhD thesis, Harvard University.

Chaudhry, K. 1991. On the way to market: economic liberalisation and Iraq's invasion of Kuwait. *Middle East Report*, No. 170, pp. 14–23.

Cockroft, J. D. 1980. On the ideological and class character of Iran's anti-imperialist revolution. In Stauth, G. (ed.), *Iran: Capitalism and Revolution*. Germany: Verlag Breitenbach.

Cooper, M. 1983. State capitalism, class structure and social transformation in the Third World: the case of Egypt. In *International Journal of Middle East Studies*, Vol. 15, No. 4.

Cooper, M. 1983b. Egyptian state capitalism in crisis: economic policies and political interests. In Asad, T. and Owen, R. (eds.), *Sociology of Developing Societies: the Middle East*, pp. 77–94. London: Macmillan.

Dessouki, A. E. H. 1982. The politics of income distribution in Egypt. In Abdel-Khalek, G. and Tignor, R. (eds), *The Political Economy of Income Distribution in Egypt*. New York: Holmes and Meier.

Diakonoff, I. 1956. Main features of the economy in the monarchies of ancient western Asia. Third International Conference of Economic History, Munich. Paris: Mouton.

El-Ghandour, A. (1990). Comments. In El-Naggar (ed), pp. 181–87.

El-Za'im, I. 1967. Le probleme agraire Syrien: etapes et bilan de la reform. *Developpement et Civilisations*, No. 31, pp. 68–78.

Escher, A. 1990. 'Private business and trade in the region of Yabroud, Syria. Paper given at Middle East Studies Association Conference.

Field, M. 1990a. Continuing investment seen as vital to attract investment to Jordan. *Financial Times*, 23/1/91.

Field, M. 1990b. Cairo lacks either the strength or the legitimacy to administer the medicine. *Financial Times*, 25/1/91.

Field, M. 1990c. The changes are in place, but Tunisia's bureaucratic past lives on. *Financial Times*, 30/1/90.

Gilles, F. 1990a. Morocco's royal paraphernalia line the road to a modern economy. *Financial Times*, 19/1/90.

Gilles, F. 1990b. Algeria attempts a bold U-turn on the road to economic reform. *Financial Times*, 1/2/90.

Gilles, F. 1990c. Drought-stricken Tunisia slow to dismantle ailing state sector. *Financial Times*, 19/4/90.

Gillespie, K. and Stoever, W. 1988. Investment promotion policies in Sadat's Egypt: lessons for less-developed countries. *Journal of Arab Affairs*, No. 7, pp. 19–48.

Hamdouche, B. 1987. Adjustment and development: the case of Morocco. in El-Naggar (1987), pp. 156–87.

Handoussa, H. 1990b. Egypt's investment strategy, policies and performance since the Infitah. In El-Naggar (1990) pp. 143–80.

Hansen, B. 1972. Economic development of Syria. in Cooper, C. A. and Alexander, S. (eds), *Economic Development and Population Growth in the Middle East*. pp. 333–66. New York: American Elsevier.

Hasan, P. 1987. Structural adjustment in selected Arab countries: need, challenge and approaches. in El-Naggar (1987), pp. 49–67.

Heydemann, S. 1990. Liberalisation from above and the limits of private sector autonomy in Syria: the role of business associations. Paper given at Middle East Studies Association Conference.

Hill, E. 1989. Egypt's new capitalism after fifteen years of al-Infitah. Paper delivered to the annual conference of the Middle East Studies Association, Toronto.

Hofmann, M. 1986. The informal sector in an intermediate city: a case in Egypt. *Economic Development and Cultural Change*, No. 34, pp. 262–77.

Hopfinger, H. 1990. Capitalist agro-business in a socialist country: Syria's new share-holding companies as an example. Paper presented to the conference of the British Society for Middle Eastern Studies, July 1990.

International Monetary Fund 1991. 'Tunisia's economic reforms advance: IMF approves fourth year of support under extended arrangement. *IMF Survey*, Vol. 20, No. 16, 12 August 1991.

Issawi, C. 1969. Economic change and urbanisation in the Middle East. In Lapidus, I. M. (ed.), *Middle Eastern Cities*. Berkeley, Calif.: University of California Press.

Jacobsen, T. 1970. Toward the image of Tammuz. In Moran, W. L. (ed.), *Toward the Image of Tammuz and Other Essays on Mesopotamian History and Culture*. Cambridge, Mass.: Harvard University Press.

Joffé, G. 1990. Privatisation and decentralisation in the Arab world. *Journal of the Japan Institute of Middle Eastern Economies*, No. 8, pp. 56–70.

Joffé, G. 1990a. Privatisation: the Moroccan experience. *Arab–British Chamber Economic Reports*, No. 90, pp. 25–37.

Joffé, G. 1990b. Developments in Iraq since the cease-fire. In Davies, C. (ed.), *After the War: Iraq, Iran and the Gulf*. Chichester: Carden.

Kemp, B. 1983. Old Kingdom, New Kingdom and second intermediate period c. 2686–1552 BC. In Trigger, B. and Kemp, B. (eds), *Ancient Egypt: A Social History*. Cambridge: Cambridge University Press.

Khalaf, R. 1989. Privatisation in Jordan. In Ramanadham (1989), pp. 236–49.

Khatrawi, M. 1989. Privatisation and the regional public joint ventures in the Gulf Cooperation Council region. In El-Naggar (1989), pp. 189–206.

King, D. A. 1978. Islamic mathematics and astonomy. In *Journal for the History of Astronomy*. No. 9, pp. 212–18.

King, D. A. 1980. The exact sciences in medieval Islam: some remarks on the present state of research. In *Middle East Studies Association of North America, Bulletin*, Vol. 14, No. 1, pp. 10–26.

Kirkpatrick, C. and Onis, Z. 1988. Structural adjustment lending and policy reform in Turkey, 1980–86. Paper presented to the Development Studies Association of the United Kingdom conference, Birmingham, September 1988.

Kirkpatrick, C. and Onis, Z. 1991. Turkey. In Mosley, P., Harrigan, J. and Toye, J. (eds), *Aid and Power: the World Bank and Policy-based Lending*, Vol. 2, Case Studies, London: Routledge.

Kuroda, M. 1991. On the specific nature of economic activities in the Middle East. (In Japanese.) *Bulletin of the Institute of Middle Eastern Studies*, International University of Japan, Vol. 5.

Lawson, F. 1982. Social Basis for the Hamah Revolt. In *MERIP Reports*, Vol. 12, No. 9, pp. 24–8.

Lawson, F. (1988). Political-economic trends in Ba'thi Syria: a reinterpretation. *Orient* (Opladen), Vol. 29. No. 4, December. pp. 579–94.

Lawson, F. 1990. Liberalisation economique en Syrie et en Iraq. *Maghreb-Machrek*, No. 128.

Leeds, R. 1988. Turkey: rhetoric and reality. In Vernon, R. (ed.), *The Promise of Privatisation: a Challenge for US Policy*. New York: Council on Foreign Relations.

Lloyd, A. B. 1983 The late period, 664–323 BC. In Trigger, B. J. and Kemp, B. (eds), *Ancient Egypt: A Social History*. Cambridge: Cambridge University Press.

Longueness, E. 1979. The class nature of the state in Syria. *MERIP Reports*, Vol. 9, No. 4, pp. 3–11.

Luciani, G. 1990. Allocation versus production states: a theoretical framework. In Luciani, G. (ed.), *The Arab State*, pp. 65–84. Berkeley, Calif.: University of California Press.

Mansfield, E. 1980. Syria: Gulf War adds to supply problems. In *Petroleum Economist*, vol. 47, No. 11, pp. 467–8.

Margulies, R. and Yildizaglu, F. 1988. Austerity packages and beyond: Turkey since 1980. *Capital and Class*, No. 36, pp. 141–62.

Meyer, G. 1987. Economic development in Syria since 1970. In Allen, J. A. (ed.), *Politics and the Economy in Syria*. London: School of Oriental and African Studies.

Michalet, C. 1987. De l'échange internationale à l'économie mondiale: une nouvelle problematique (Japanese translation by J. Tanabe). In *Keizai Hyoron*, Vol. NNN.

Moore, C. 1986. Money and power: the dilemma of the Egyptian infitah. *Middle East Journal*, Vol. 40, No. 4.

Najmabadi, A. 1987. Depoliticisation of a rentier state: the case of Pahlavi Iran. In Beblawi, H. and Luciani, G. (eds), *The Rentier State*. London: Croom Helm.

Niblock, T. 1989. The state of the art in British Middle Eastern Studies. In Israel, T. (ed), *Middle Eastern Studies: International Perspectives on the State of the Art*. New York: Praeger.

Onis, Z. 1991. The evolution of privatisation in Turkey: the institutional context of public-enterprise reform. *International Journal of Middle Eastern Studies*. Vol. 23, No. 2, pp. 163–76.

Oppenheim, A. L. 1969. Mesopotamia – land of many cities. In Lapidis, I. M. (ed.), *Middle Eastern Cities: a Symposium on Ancient, Islamic and Contemporary Middle Eastern Urbanism*. Berkeley, Calif.: University of California Press.

Ozbudun, E. 1989. Turkey: crisis, interruptions, reequilibrations. In Diamond *et al.*, *Democracy in Developing Countries*. Boulder, Colo.: Lynne Reiner.

Perthes, V. 1990. The Syrian private industrial and commercial sectors and the state. Paper given to Middle East Studies Association conference.

Perthes, V. 1991. The bourgeoisie and the Ba'th: a look at Syria's upper class. *Middle East Report*, No. 170, pp. 31–7.

Pestman, P. W. 1983. Some aspects of Egyptian law in Graeco-Roman Egypt. In van't Dack, E. *et al.* (eds), *Egypt and the Hellenistic World*. Leuven: Lovanii.

Picard, E. 1979. Classes militaires et pouvoir ba'thiste en Syrie. *Orient*. Vol. 20, pp. 49–62.

Rafeq, A. K. 1983. The impact of Europe on a traditional economy. In *Economie et Sociétés dans l'Empire Ottoman*. Paris: Editions du CNRS.

Raymond, A. 1957. Une liste des corporations de metiers au Caire en 1801. *Arabica*, No. 4, pp. 150–63.

Richards, A. 1989. Agricultural employment, wages and government policy in Egypt during and after the oil boom. Paper prepared for the ILO, Cairo.

Sadowski, Y. 1985. Cadres, guns and money: The Eighth Regional Congress of the Syrian Ba'th. *MERIP Reports*, Vol. 15, No. 6, July–August.

Sadowski, Y. 1990. Political vegetables? businessmen and bureaucrats in the development of Egyptian agriculture. Unpublished ms. Washington, D.C.: The Brookings Institution.

Sadowski, Y. 1991. Arab economies after the Gulf War. *Middle East Report*, No. 170, pp. 4–10.

Seddon, D. 1989a. The politics of 'adjustment' in Morocco. In Campbell, B. and Loxley, J. (eds), *Structural Adjustment in Africa*. London: Macmillan.

Seddon, D. 1989b. Riot and rebellion in North Africa: political responses to economic crisis in Tunisia, Morocco and Sudan. In Berberoglu, B. (ed.), *Power and Stability in the Middle East*. London: Zed Press.

Seddon, D. 1989c. Zaio transformed: two decades of change in northeast Morocco. In Lawless, R. (ed.), *The Middle Eastern Village: Changing Economic and Social Relations*. London: Croom Helm.

Seddon, D. 1991. Politics and the Gulf crisis: popular responses in the Maghreb. In Bresheeth, H. and Yuval-Davis, N. (eds), *The Gulf Crisis and the New World Order*. London: Zed Press.

Shaalan, S. 1987. Adjustment challenges and strategies facing Arab countries in light of recent experience and new initiatives. In El-Naggar (1987) pp. 24–43.

Shihata, I. F. I. 1990. Promotion of Arab and foreign investment. In El-Naggar (1990), *Investment Policies in the Arab Countries*, pp. 127–42. Washington, D.C.: International Monetary Fund.

Springborg, P. 1986. Politics, primordialism and orientalism: Marx, Aristotle and the myth of the gemeinschaft. *American Political Science Review*, Vol. 80, No. 1. pp. 185–211.

Springborg, P. 1987a. The contractual state: reflections on orientalism and despotism. In *History of Political Thought*, Vol. 8, No. 3, pp. 395–433.

Springborg, P. 1987b. Early history of the state: West and East. *Politics*. Vol. 22, No. 2. pp. 105–13.

Springborg, R. 1975. Patterns of association in the Egyptian political elite. In Lenczowski (ed), *Political Elites in the Middle East*. Washington, D.C.: American Enterprise Institute.

Springborg, R. 1990a. The primacy of the political: Rahe and the myth of the polis. *Political Studies*, Vol. 38, No. 1, pp. 83–104.

Springborg, R. 1991. State-society relations in Egypt: the debate over owner-tenant relations. *Middle East Journal*, No. 45, pp. 232–49.

Stern, S. M. 1970. The constitution of the Islamic city. In Hourani, A. H. and Stern, S. M. (eds), *The Islamic City*. Oxford: Oxford University Press.

Stevens, P. 1989. Privatisation in the Middle East and North Africa. *Arab Affairs*, Vol. 1, No. 10, pp. 58–75.

Sullivan, D. 1990. The political economy of reform in Egypt. *International Journal of Middle Eastern Studies*, Vol. 22, No. 3, pp. 317–34.

Sutton, K. 1978. Conflict between the growth of Greater Algiers and Algeria's regional development policies. In *Cahiers de URBAMA* No. 3, pp. 5–39.

Sutton, K. 1982. Agrarian reform in Algeria – progress in the face of disappointment, dilution and diversion. In Jones, S. and Murmis, M. (eds), *Rural Poverty and Agrarian Reform*. New Delhi: Allied Publishers.

Sutton, K. 1990. Agricultural policy in Algeria in the 1980s: progress towards liberalisation. Paper presented to the conference of the British Society for Middle Eastern Studies, July 1990.

Trigger, B. J. 1983. The rise of Egyptian civilisation. in Trigger, B. J. and Kemp. B. (eds), *Ancient Egypt: a Social History*. Cambridge: Cambridge University Press.

United States Embassy, Damascus 1989. Foreign economic trends: Syria. October.

Vanderwalle, D. 1991. Qadhafi's 'Perestroika': economic and political liberalisation in Libya. *Middle East Journal*, Vol. 45, No. 2, pp. 216–31.

Waterbury, J. 1991. Twilight of the state bourgeoisie? *International Journal of Middle East Studies*, No. 23, pp. 1–17.

Weigel, D. 1990. Foreign direct investment: the role of joint ventures and investment authorities. In El-Naggar (1990), *Investment Policies in the Arab Countries*. pp. 70–88. Washington, D.C.: International Monetary Fund.

Weinbaum, M. 1986. Dependent development and US economic aid to Egypt. *International Journal of Middle East Studies*. Vol. 18, No. 2.

Wilson, J. 1960. Egypt through the New Kingdom: civilisation without cities. In Kraeling, C. H. and Adams, McC. (eds), *City Invincible*, pp. 124–36. Chicago, Ill.: University of Chicago Press.

Zartman, W. 1984. L'élite algerienne sous le President Chadhli Benjedid. In *Maghreb-Machrek*, no. 106.

CONTRIBUTORS

Anoushiravan Ehteshami is Director of the Middle East Politics Programme, University of Exeter.

Raymond Hinnebusch is Professor of Politics at the College of St Catherine, Minnesota.

George Joffé writes for the Economist Intelligence Unit. He is Research Associate at the Near and Middle East Centre, School of Oriental and African Studies, and Honorary Research Fellow at the University of Exeter.

Miyoko Kuroda is Research Fellow in Middle Eastern Studies at the International University of Japan.

John Marks is Northern Africa correspondent for the *Middle East Economic Digest*.

Emma Murphy is British Academy Research Fellow in the Department of Politics, University of Exeter.

Tim Niblock is Director of the Graduate School in Political and Administrative Studies, and Senior Lecturer in Middle East Politics, University of Exeter.

Gerd Nonneman is Research Fellow in Middle East Politics, University of Exeter.

Edith Penrose is Professor Emeritus in Economics at the School of Oriental and African Studies, University of London.

David Pool is Lecturer in Middle East Politics in the Department of Government, University of Manchester.

David Seddon is Reader in Development Studies, University of East Anglia.

Patricia Springborg is Reader in Government at the University of Sydney.

Robert Springborg is Professor of Politics at Macquarie University, Sydney.

Dr Paul Stevens is Senior Lecturer in Economics, University of Surrey.

Index